In Defense of History

Marxism and the Postmodern Agenda

Edited by

Ellen Meiksins Wood

John Bellamy Foster

In Defense of History: Marxism and the Postmodern Agenda
Edited by Ellen Meiksins Wood and John Bellamy Foster

First Published in India 2006
Reprinted 2021
Reprinted 2026

ISBN 978-81-87879-76-3

Published in agreement with Monthly Review Press, New York for publication and sale only in South Asia.

Published by
AAKAR BOOKS
28 E Pocket IV, Mayur Vihar Phase I
Delhi 110 091, India
www.aakarbooks.com

Printed at
D.K. Fine Art Press, Delhi

CONTENTS

1 : Introduction

2 : Postmodernism and Intellectuals

3 : Postmodernism and Movements

4 : Afterword

1: INTRODUCTION

What is the "postmodern" agenda?

ELLEN MEIKSINS WOOD

The many deaths of modernity

During World War I, Oswald Spengler wrote his famous and distasteful book, *The Decline of the West,* proclaiming that Western Civilization and its dominant values were coming to an end. The bonds and traditions that had held society together were decomposing, the solidarities of life disintegrating, together with the unity of thought and culture. Like every other civilization that had gone through its natural cycle, he argued, the West had inevitably passed from its autumn of (an already destructive) "illumination" or "enlightenment" to a winter of individualism and cultural nihilism.

About four decades later, C. Wright Mills announced that "We are at the ending of what is called The Modern Age." This age "is being succeeded by a post-modern period," in which all the historic expectations that have characterized "Western culture" are no longer relevant. The Enlightenment faith in the united progress of reason and freedom, together with the two principal ideologies grounded in that faith—liberalism and socialism—"have virtually collapsed as adequate explanations of the world and of ourselves." J.S. Mill and Karl Marx were equally outdated.[1]

Between these two announcements of epochal decline, one published in 1918, the other in 1959, there are, of course, great ideological differences—the antidemocratic sentiments of Spengler as against the radicalism of Mills, Spengler's hostility (or at least ambivalence) toward the Enlightenment, as against Mills's continuing, if somewhat hopeless, adherence to Enlightenment values. But there is also a catastrophic intervening history of depression, war, and genocide, followed by the promise of material prosperity, the one exceeding humanity's worst fears to date, the other its most visionary hopes.

When Spengler wrote *The Decline of the West,* Europe was certainly in turmoil, in a time of war and revolution, not to mention the apparent threat to ruling classes, even in non-revolutionary situations, coming from the spread of mass democracy. Mills's vantage point was rather different. Since 1918, the world had passed through horrors far greater than Spengler could have imagined; but Mills was writing in the quiet 1950s, on a rising tide of capitalist prosperity (the "affluent society"), in a climate of political apathy. And he was teaching a generation of university students who, though still living in the shadow of the cold war and the nuclear threat, enjoyed uniquely bright material prospects.

In fact, this "Golden Age" of capitalism (as Eric Hobsbawm[2] has called it) was just then convincing other academics of Mills's generation (most of them apparently blind to what Michael Harrington called "the other America," not to mention U.S. imperialism) that the problems of Western society had been more or less solved; that the conditions of social harmony were more or less in place; that, in fact, the Enlightenment vision of progress had been more or less realized, or at the very least that nothing much better was likely, necessary, or even desirable. This is what Mills's colleague Daniel Bell (who, in a later edition of his famous book, was to attack Mills viciously as a traitor over Cuba) called the "end of ideology."

So the death of Enlightenment optimism was not, for Mills, the outcome of some unambiguous catastrophe. On the contrary, his pessimism was born of success as much as failure. Many of the Enlightenment's principal objectives, he suggested, had indeed been realized: the "rationalization" of social and political organization; scientific and technological progress that would have been inconceivable to the most optimistic Enlightenment dreamer; the spread of universal education in advanced Western societies; and so on.

Yet these advances, Mills maintained, had done little to increase the "substantive rationality" of human beings. If anything, instead of enhancing human freedom, "rationalization," bureaucracy, and modern technology had restricted it. They had even been the source of many unexpected evils. The frightening consequence of this lack of correspondence between "rationality" and freedom had been the advent of alienated human beings, or "cheerful robots," who adapted themselves to conditions—giant organizations and overpowering forces—over which they had, and felt they had, no control, people who could no longer be assumed to have an urge for freedom or a will to reason.

Some of these themes had long been a part of Western social theory—in the sociology of Max Weber or Karl Mannheim, for instance, not to mention Marxist theories of alienation. And ambivalence toward the Enlightenment, together with pessimism about progress, has been a common theme of twentieth-century culture, on the left and the right, for both good and bad reasons. But in Mills's day, there was another dimension, and this too had less to do with failure than (apparent) success: the flourishing of "welfare" and "consumer" capitalism in the long postwar boom.

The conviction that the boom was here to stay and that it represented capitalist normality became a major determining factor in the development of left social theory. Many social critics on the left—Marcuse is a prime example—felt sure that this new kind of capitalism had cast an irrevocable spell on the "masses," and the working class in particular. Mills, who urged the left to abandon the "labor metaphysic," was certainly not alone in thinking that the working class was no longer available as an oppositional force. There were even people who thought of themselves as Marxists yet shared something like this view. It was to become a dominant theme in the "revolutions" of the 1960s, in student radicalism, and in forms of Marxist theory that gave an increasing prominence to students and intellectuals as the main agents of resistance, and to "cultural revolution" in place of working class struggle.[3]

A decade after the sixties "revolutions" the boom was effectively over; but today, in a period of capitalist stagnation, its intellectual heritage lives on. Among its legacies is yet another "postmodernity." This time, there exists a large body of intellectuals who are not content just to diagnose the current epoch as a period of postmodernity but who self-consciously identify themselves as "postmodern*ists*." Although they acknowledge various influences—from earlier philosophers like Nietzsche to more recent thinkers like Lacan, Lyotard, Foucault, and Derrida—today's postmodernism belongs above all to the sixties generation and their students. This postmodernism, then, is the product of a consciousness formed in the so-called golden age of capitalism, however much it may insist on the new ("post-Fordist," "disorganized," "flexible") shape of capitalism in the 1990s.

Some postmodernists, in fact, seem scarcely to have noticed the end of the boom, so intent are they on the triumphs of capitalism and the joys of consumerism. But even those more sensitive to current realities have their intellectual roots in that "golden" moment, with a belief in the triumph of capitalism that long predates the fall of Communism. So while some on the right have proclaimed the "end of history" or the final triumph of capitalism, we are being told yet again by some left intellectuals that an epoch has ended, that we are living in a "postmodern" epoch, that the "Enlightenment project" is dead, that all the old verities and ideologies have lost their relevance, that old principles of rationality no longer apply, and so on.

As we shall see in a moment, it is far from clear that the new postmodernism allows for any kind of historical analysis. But if for today's postmodernist intellectuals "postmodernity" does represent a historical epoch, this time it seems that the real watershed occurred some time in the late 1960s or early 1970s. Yet, though much historical water has passed under the bridge between the early epochal milestones and the most recent ones, what is striking about the current diagnosis of postmodernity is that it has so much in common with older pronouncements of death, both radical and reactionary versions. What is striking, in other words, is the continuity, or at least the repetition, in this story of discontinuity. If we have come to another historic ending, what has ended, apparently, is not so much another, different epoch but the same one all over again.

This dialectic of continuity and discontinuity should come as no surprise. After all, the apparent epochal ruptures of the twentieth century have been bound together in a single historical unity by the logic—and the internal contradictions—of capitalism, the dynamic but crisis-ridden system that dies a thousand deaths.

Historic change without history?

And yet, there are some significant differences between today's postmodernism and the earlier analyses of epochal decline. Until now, the end of "modernity" (or the "decline of the West") has always been treated as a historical condition, available to historical knowledge, itself susceptible to historical change and just maybe even to political action. There do exist Marxist intellectuals today, like David Harvey and Fredric Jameson, who talk about "postmodernity" as a historical condition, a phase of contemporary capitalism, a social and cultural form with historical origins and material foundations, subject to change and political agency.[4] We may disagree with their historical judgments, but we can at least engage them in debates about history. "Postmodernism," however, is something else—and that is the subject of this book.

Here, first, is a sketch of the most important themes of the "postmodernist" left (I shall use that term broadly to cover a variety of intellectual and political trends which have emerged in recent years, including "post-

Marxism" and "poststructuralism"). Postmodernists are preoccupied with language, culture, and "discourse." For some, this seems to mean quite literally that human beings and their social relations are constituted by language, and nothing more, or at the very least that language is all we can know about the world and that we have access to no other reality. In its extreme "deconstructionist" version, postmodernism has not only adopted those forms of linguistic theory according to which our patterns of thought are limited and shaped by the underlying structure of the language that we speak. Nor does it simply mean that society and culture are structured in ways *analogous* to language, with underlying rules and patterns that govern social relations in much the same way that the rules of grammar, or their "deep structure," govern language. Society is not simply *like* language. It *is* language; and since we are all entrapped in our language, no external standard of truth, no external referent for knowledge, is available to us outside the specific "discourses" that we inhabit.

Other postmodernists, while still insisting on the importance of "discourse," may not give language, in its simple meaning as words and speech, this kind of primacy. But at the very least, they will insist on the "social construction" of knowledge. On the face of it, this insistence on the social construction of knowledge may seem fairly unobjectionable and even conventional, not least for Marxists who have always recognized that no human knowledge comes to us unmediated, that all knowledge is appropriated through the medium of language and social practice. But postmodernists seem to have in mind something more extreme than this reasonable proposition. The most vivid illustration of postmodernist epistemology is their conception of scientific knowledge. Sometimes they go so far as to claim that Western science—founded on the conviction that nature is governed by certain universal, immutable, mathematical laws—is just an expression of the imperialistic and oppressive principles on which Western society is based. But short of that extreme claim, postmodernists—either deliberately or out of simple confusion and intellectual sloppiness—have a habit of conflating the forms of knowledge with its objects: it is as if they are saying not only that, for instance, the science of physics is a historical construct, which has varied over time and in different social contexts, but that the laws of nature themselves are "socially constructed" and historically variable.

Postmodernists will often deny that they are epistemic relativists. They will insist that they know there is a "real" world out there. But the irony that, in the very act of defending themselves, they are likely to prove the case against them and to demonstrate the very conflation (or confusion) of which I'm accusing them here—proceeding, for example, as if not only the science of physics but the physical reality represented by, say, the laws of thermodynamics is itself a historically variable social construct. They surely do not believe this to be literally true; but something like this is the practical consequence of the epistemological assumption that human knowledge is enclosed within particular languages, cultures, and interests, and that science should not and cannot aspire to apprehend or approximate some common external reality. If the standard of scientific "truth" resides not in the natural world itself but in the particular norms of specific communities, then the laws of nature might as well be nothing more than what any particular community says they are at any given time.[5]

Not all intellectuals who think of themselves as "postmodernists" would knowingly subscribe to this kind of extreme epistemic relativism, even solipsism—though it seems an inevitable consequence of their epistemological assumptions. But at the very least, postmodernism implies an emphatic rejection of "totalizing" knowledge and of "universalistic" values—including Western conceptions of "rationality," general ideas of equality, whether liberal or socialist, and the Marxist conception of general human emancipation. Instead, postmodernists emphasize "difference": particular identities such as gender, race, ethnicity, sexuality; their various, particular, and separate oppressions and struggles; and particular "knowledges," including even sciences particular to ethnic groups.

These basic principles imply that we must reject the left's traditional "economistic" concerns and forms of knowledge like political economy. We must, in fact, repudiate any "grand narratives," such as Western ideas of progress, including Marxist theories of history. All of these themes are typically lumped together in a denunciation of "reductionism," "foundationalism," or "essentialism"—of which Marxism is supposed to be a particularly virulent strain, on the grounds that it allegedly reduces the varied complexity of human experience to a monolithic view of the world, "privileging" the mode of production as a historical determinant, class as against other "identities," and "economic" or "material" determinants as against the "discursive construction" of reality. This denunciation of "essentialism" tends to cover not just truly monolithic and simplistic explanations of the world (like Stalinist varieties of Marxism) but any kind of causal explanation.

The meaning of postmodernist jargon should become clearer in the course of the articles that follow here; but for the moment, it should be obvious that the main thread running through all these postmodern principles is an emphasis on the fragmented nature of the world and of human knowledge. The political implications of all this are fairly clear: the human self is so fluid and fragmented (the "decentered subject"), and our identities are so variable, uncertain, and fragile, that there can be no basis for solidarity and collective action founded on a common social "identity" (such as class), a common experience, and common interests.

Even in its least extreme manifestations, postmodernism insists on the impossibility of any emancipatory politics based on some kind of "totalizing" knowledge or vision. Even an anticapitalist politics is too "totalizing" or "universalist." Capitalism as a totalizing system can hardly be said to exist at all in postmodern discourse, so that even the critique of capitalism is precluded. In fact, "politics" in any traditional sense of the word, having to do with the overarching power of classes or states and opposition to them, is effectively ruled out, giving way to the fractured struggles of "identity politics" or even the "personal as political." Although there are more universal projects that do hold some attractions for the postmodern left, such as environmental politics, it is difficult to see how they—or, indeed, any political action—can be consistent with postmodernism's most fundamental principles: a deep epistemological scepticism and a profound political defeatism.

How, then, does this postmodernism compare to earlier theories about the end of the "modern" era? What is immediately striking is that postmodernism, which seems to combine so many features of older diagnoses of epochal decline, is remarkably unconscious of its own history. In their conviction that what they say represents a radical rupture with the past, today's postmodernist intellectuals seem sublimely oblivious to everything that has been said so many times before. Even the epistemological scepticism, the assault on universal truths and values, the questioning of self-identity, which are so much a part of the current intellectual fashions, have a history as old as philosophy. More particularly, the postmodern sense of epochal novelty depends on ignoring, or denying, one overwhelming historical reality, the "totalizing" unity of capitalism which has bound together all the epochal ruptures of the twentieth century.

This brings us to the most distinctive characteristic of the new postmodernists: despite their insistence on epochal differences and specificities, despite their claims to have exposed the historicity of all values and knowledges (or precisely because of their insistence on "difference" and the fragmented nature of reality and human knowledge), they are remarkably insensitive to history. This insensitivity is revealed not least in a deafness to the reactionary echoes of their attacks on "Enlightenment" values and their fundamental irrationalism.

Here, then, is one major difference between the current enunciations of epochal change and all the others. Earlier theories were based—by definition—on some particular conception of history, and were predicated on the importance of historical analysis. C. Wright Mills, for example, insisted that the crisis of reason and freedom which marked the onset of the postmodern age represented "structural problems, and to state them requires that we work in the classic terms of human biography and epochal history. Only in such terms can the connections of structure and milieux that affect these values today be traced and causal analysis be conducted." Mills also took it for granted, in classic Enlightenment fashion, that the whole point of such historical analysis was to mark out the space of human freedom and agency, to formulate our choices and "enlarge the scope of human decisions in the making of history." And for all his pessimism, he assumed that the limits of historical possibility were, in his time, "very broad indeed."[6]

This statement is in nearly every particular antithetical to current postmodernist theories, which effectively deny the very existence of structure or structural connections and the very possibility of "causal analysis." Structures and causes have been replaced by fragments and contingencies. There is no such thing as a social system (e.g. the capitalist system) with its own systemic unity and "laws of motion." There are only many different kinds of power, oppression, identity, and "discourse." Not only do we have to reject the old "grand narratives," like Enlightenment concepts of progress, we have to give up any idea of intelligible historical process and causality, and with it, evidently, any idea of "making history." There are no structured processes accessible to human knowledge (or, it must be supposed, to human action). There are only anarchic, disconnected, and inexplicable differences. For the first time, we have what appears to be a contradiction in terms: a theory of epochal change based on a denial of history.

There is one other especially curious thing about the current postmodernism, one particularly notable paradox. On the one hand, the denial of history on which it is based is associated with a kind of political pessimism. Since there are no systems and no history susceptible to causal analysis, we cannot get to the root of the many powers that oppress us; and we certainly cannot aspire to some kind of united opposition, some kind of general human emancipation, or even a general contestation of capitalism, of the kind that socialists used to believe in. The most we can hope for is a lot of particular and separate resistances.

On the other hand, this political pessimism appears to have its origins in a rather optimistic view of capitalist prosperity and possibility. For today's postmodernism (typically embraced, as we have seen, by survivors of the "sixties generation" and their students), with its view of the world still rooted in the "golden age" of capitalism, the dominant feature of the capitalist system is "consumerism," the multiplicity of consumption patterns, and the proliferation of "life-styles." Even the postmodernist emphasis on language and "discourse" may be traceable to an obsession with consumer capitalism and to the conviction, already prominent in the sixties, that the old political agencies (the labor movement in particular) have been permanently "hegemonized" by capitalist consumerism. Postmodernism has simply taken to the ultimate, and often absurd, extreme the familiar attempt to replace these hegemonized agencies with new ones, by situating intellectual practice at the center of the social universe and promoting intellectuals—or, more particularly, academics—to the vanguard of historical agency.

Here too postmodernist intellectuals reveal their fundamental ahistoricism. The structural crises of capitalism since the "golden" moment of the postwar boom seem to have passed them right by, or at least to have made no significant theoretical impression. For some, this means that the opportunities for opposition to capitalism are severely limited. Others seem to be saying that, if we can't really change or even understand the system (or even think about it as a system at all), and if we don't, and can't, have a vantage point from which to criticize the system, let alone oppose it, we might as well lie back and enjoy it—or better still, go shopping.

Exponents of these intellectual trends certainly know that all is not well; but there is very little in these fashions that helps, for example, to make sense of today's increasing poverty and homelessness, the growing class of working poor, new forms of insecure and part-time labor, and so on. Both sides of the twentieth century's ambiguous history—both its horrors and its wonders—have no doubt played a part in forming the postmodernist consciousness; but the horrors that have undermined the old idea of progress are less important in defining the distinctive nature of today's postmodernism than are the wonders of modern technology and the riches of consumer capitalism. Postmodernism sometimes looks like the ambiguities of capitalism as seen from the vantage point of those who enjoy its benefits rather more than they suffer its costs.

In the final analysis, "postmodernity" for postmodernist intellectuals seems to be not a historical moment but the human condition itself, from which there is no escape. If for Mills the central problem of his age was that cheerful robots could no longer be relied on to possess an urge for freedom or a will to reason, the new postmodernists themselves display the very attitudes lamented by Mills. They even regard those threatened Enlightenment values as the root of modern evils and have openly rejected them as intrinsically oppressive. To put it another way, postmodernism is no longer the diagnosis. It has become the disease.

Cheerful robots or socialist critics?

In its defeatist submission to apparently uncontrollable forces combined with a surrender to, and sometimes even a celebration of, consumerism, the postmodernist current seems to represent an intellectual manifestation of Mills's robots. But where Mills appears to have held the elitist view that workers were more likely to be robots, leaving it for students and intellectuals to rise above the robotic condition, now it is those very intellectuals who have become, so to speak, the cheerful robot's theoretical consciousness.

It would be easy after having said all this just to dismiss the current fashions. But for all their contradictions, their lack of historical sensitivity, their apparently unconscious repetition of old themes, and their defeatism, they are also responding to something real, to real conditions in the contemporary world in the current conditions of capitalism, with which people on the socialist left must come to terms.

None of us would want to deny the importance of some postmodernist themes. For instance, the history of the twentieth century could hardly inspire confidence in traditional notions of progress, and those of us who profess to believe in some kind of "progressive" politics have to come to terms with all that has happened to undermine Enlightenment optimism. And who would want to deny the importance of "identities" other than class, of struggles against sexual and racial oppression, or the complexities of human experience in such a mobile and changeable world, with such fragile and shifting solidarities? At the same time, who can be oblivious to the resurgence of "identities" like nationalism as powerful, and often destructive, historical forces?

Don't we have to come to terms with the restructuring of capitalism, now both more global and more "segmented" than ever before? For that matter, who is unaware of the structural changes that have transformed the nature of the working class itself? And what serious socialist has ever been unconscious of the racial or sexual divisions within the working class? Who would want to subscribe to the kind of ideological and cultural imperialism that suppresses the multiplicity of human values and cultures or disdains the particular "knowledges" of non-privileged groups, with their own wealth of experience and skills? And how can we possibly deny the importance of language and cultural politics in a world so dominated by symbols, images, and "mass communication," not to mention the "information superhighway"? Who would deny these things in a world of global capitalism so dependent on the manipulation of symbols and images in a culture of advertisement, where the "media" mediate our own most personal experiences, sometimes to the point where what we see on television seems more real than our own lives, and where the terms of political debate are set—and narrowly constricted—by the dictates of capital in the most direct way, as knowledge and communication are increasingly in the hands of corporate giants?

We don't have to accept postmodernist assumptions in order to see all these things. On the contrary, these developments cry out for a materialist explanation. For that matter, there have been few cultural phenomena in human history whose material foundations are more glaringly obvious than those of postmodernism itself. There is, in fact, no better confirmation of historical materialism than the connection between postmodernist culture and a consumerist and mobile global capitalism. Nor does a materialist approach mean that we have to devalue or denigrate the cultural dimensions of human experience. A materialist understanding is, instead, an essential step in liberating culture from the stranglehold of commodification.

Postmodernists reject Enlightenment universalism on the grounds that it denies the diversity of human experience, cultures, values, and identities; but this rejection of universalism on behalf of an emancipatory pluralism is contradictory and self-defeating. A healthy respect for difference and diversity, and for the plurality of struggles against various oppressions, does not oblige us to jettison all the universalistic values to which Marxism at its best has always been attached, or to abandon the idea of a universal human emancipation. On the contrary, even the mildest forms of "pluralism" have been unsustainable without appeals to certain universalistic values like the classic liberal principle of "toleration." The radical pluralism espoused by postmodernists—based as it is on denying any fundamental commonality, or even the possibility of mutual access and understanding, among plural identities—has fatally undercut its own foundations. As Aijaz Ahmad puts it later in this volume: "if in the constitution of your identity, I have no rights of cognition, participation, criticism, then on what basis may you ask for my solidarity with you except on the basis of some piety, some voluntaristic good will that I can withdraw at any moment?" In the end, it is hard to imagine how any of the diverse struggles that supposedly constitute the left postmodernist agenda can be sustained without some appeal to those dreaded "modernist" and Enlightenment values of democracy, equality, social justice, and so on.

For that matter, it is difficult to understand how any kind of action is possible on the epistemological assumptions that postmodernists profess. Not only are their views on knowledge politically disabling, one cannot help wondering how they can conduct the normal business of everyday life without suspending their postmodernist disbelief. Either that, or postmodernist theories are guilty of more than a little bad faith.

One of the ironies of postmodernism is that, while embracing—or at least surrendering to—capitalism, it rejects the "Enlightenment project," holding it responsible for crimes that would more justly be laid at the door of capitalism. This is, by the way, something that C. Wright Mills too might usefully have considered when outlining the failures of reason and freedom. Of course it would be foolish to maintain that capitalism has been responsible for all our modern ills or even to deny the material benefits that have often accompanied it. But it would be just as foolish to deny the destructive effects associated with capitalist imperatives of self-expansion, "productivism," profit-maximization, and competition. It is hard to see how these effects intrinsically belong to the Enlightenment. At the very least, we have to ask whether an emancipatory universalism amounts to the same thing as capitalist expansionism or imperialism, and whether the fruits of "Western" science and technology must by definition serve the needs of capitalist exploitation, accumulation, and the destruction of nature that inevitably accompanies them.[7]

At any rate, we are living in a historical moment that more than any other demands a universalistic project. This is a historical moment dominated by capitalism, the most universal system the world has ever known—both in the sense that it is global and in the sense that it penetrates every aspect of social life and the natural environment. In dealing with capitalism, the postmodernist insistence that reality is fragmentary and therefore accessible only to fragmentary "knowledges" is especially perverse and disabling. The social reality of capitalism is "totalizing" in unprecedented ways and degrees. Its logic of commodification, accumulation, profit-maximization, and competition permeates the whole social order; and an understanding of this "totalizing" system requires just the kind of "totalizing knowledge" that Marxism offers and postmodernists reject.

Opposition to the capitalist system also requires us to call upon interests and resources that unify, instead of fragmenting, the anticapitalist struggle. In the first instance, these are the interests and resources of *class,* the single most universal force capable of uniting diverse emancipatory struggles; but in the final analysis, we are talking about the interests and resources of our common humanity, in the conviction that, for all our manifold differences, there are certain fundamentally and irreducibly common conditions of human well-being and self-fulfillment which capitalism cannot satisfy and socialism can.

For people on the left, and especially for a younger generation of intellectuals and students, the greatest appeal of postmodernism is its apparent openness, as against the alleged "closures" of a "totalizing" system like Marxism. But this claim to openness is largely spurious. The problem is not just that postmodernism represents an ineffectual kind of pluralism which has undermined its own foundations. Nor is it simply an uncritical but harmless eclecticism. There is something more serious at stake. The "openness" of postmodernism's fragmentary knowledges and its emphasis on "difference" are purchased at the price of much more fundamental closures.

Postmodernism is, in its negative way, a ruthlessly "totalizing" system, which forecloses a vast range of critical thought and emancipatory politics—and its closures are final and decisive. Its epistemological assumptions make it unavailable to criticism, as immune to critique as the most rigid kind of dogma (how do you criticize a body of ideas that *a priori* rules out the very practice of "rational" argument?). And they preclude—not just by dogmatically rejecting but also by rendering impossible—a systematic understanding of our historical moment, a wholesale critique of capitalism, and just about any effective political action.

If postmodernism does tell us something, in a distorted way, about the conditions of contemporary capitalism, the real trick is to figure out exactly what those conditions are, why they are, and where we go from here. The trick, in other words, is to suggest historical explanations for those conditions instead of just submitting to them and indulging in ideological adaptations. The trick is to identify the real problems to which the current intellectual fashions offer false—or no—solutions, and in so doing to challenge the limits they impose on action and resistance. The trick is to respond to the conditions of the world today not as cheerful (or even miserable) robots but as critics.

This collection of essays is not intended simply as a critique of postmodernism, though it is certainly that too. Others have provided more detailed accounts and refutations of postmodernist views on epistemology, language, identity, and so on, than we can do here. Our intention is rather to suggest some of the ways in which historical materialism can shed light on the issues that most preoccupy postmodernists, though obviously, in such a small space, we can only scratch the surface. In organizing the special issue of *Monthly Review* on which this volume is based, John Foster and I sent a letter to potential contributors explaining what we had in mind, so let me conclude this introduction with some extracts from that letter. It starts with a quotation from an earlier article of mine on E.P. Thompson:[8]

> The critique of capitalism is out of fashion—and here there is a curious convergence, a kind of unholy alliance, between capitalist triumphalism and socialist pessimism. The triumph of the right is mirrored on the left by a sharp contraction of socialist aspirations. Left intellectuals, if they are not actually embracing capitalism as the best of all possible worlds, have little hope for anything more than a bit more space within the interstices of capitalism; and they look forward, at best, to only the most local and particular resistances. And there is another curious effect of all this. Capitalism is becoming so universal, so much taken for granted, that

> it is becoming invisible. Now clearly we have plenty to be pessimistic about. Recent and current events have given us plenty of cause. But there is something curious about the way many of us are reacting to all this. If capitalism has indeed triumphed, you might think that what we need now more than ever is a critique of capitalism. Why is this the right moment to embrace modes of thought which seem to deny the very possibility not only of surpassing capitalism but even of critically understanding it?...
>
> I really do think we are in an unprecedented situation now, something we have not seen in the whole history of capitalism. What we are experiencing now is not just a deficit of action, or the absence of the necessary instrumentalities and organization of struggle (though those are certainly thin on the ground). It is not only that we do not know how to *act* against capitalism but that we are forgetting even how to *think* against it.

Our letter then went on to spell out our intentions:

> This is the context in which we are planning the special issue. We start from the premise that historical work like E.P. Thompson's, and Marxist political economy at its best, are essential to the left's critical project.... The point, though, is this: we can't now take it for granted that other left intellectuals share our view; and, speaking as teachers, we are both all too conscious that many, if not most, of our students—even those who think of themselves as on the left—are unlikely to agree, either about our understanding of capitalism or about our epistemological and historical presuppositions. And these disagreements are expressed in a very different intellectual, not to mention political, agenda.... What we are proposing, then, is a collection of articles that will offer some suggestions about how historical materialism can deal with that other agenda in more fruitful, forceful, and liberating ways than the current intellectual and political fashions are able to do. We are not suggesting that people like us should abandon our own terrain. On the contrary, part of the object is to demonstrate that our terrain is where it's at—for example, that the old bread-and-butter issues of the left (like "politics" in the old sense, having to do with state and class power) are still at the center of things, and still important to other emancipatory projects, not just to traditional forms of class politics. But we can grab the attention of our students and other people like them if we confront them on their own favorite turf.

That, then, is what we have set out to do, in a very limited way, in the belief that this is just the right time to revitalize Marxist critique. The world is increasingly populated not by cheerful robots but by some very angry human beings. As things stand, there are very few intellectual resources available to understand that anger, and hardly any political ones (at least on the left) to organize it. Today's postmodernism, for all its apparently defeatist pessimism, is still rooted in the "Golden Age of Capitalism." It's time to leave that legacy behind and face today's realities.

Notes

1. C. Wright Mills, *The Sociological Imagination* (Oxford: Oxford University Press, 1959), pp. 165-67.
2. In Hobsbawm's *Age of Extremes: The Short Twentieth Century, 1914—1991* (New York: Pantheon, 1995), the "golden age" (roughly 1947 to 1973) is sandwiched between the "age of catastrophe" and "the landslide."
3. I discuss some of these developments in "A Chronology of the New Left, or: Who's Old-Fashioned Now?" *Socialist Register 1995.*
4. See, for example, Fredric Jameson's "Five Theses on Actually Existing Marxism" in this volume; and David Harvey, *The Condition of Postmodernity* (Oxford: Basil Blackwell, 1990). I discuss such theories of postmodernity as a historical condition in "Modernity, Postmodernity, or Capitalism?" *Monthly Review* 48, no. 3 (July/August 1996).
5. See, for example, Stanley Fish's irate response ("Professor Sokal's Bad Joke," *New York Times*, 21 May 1996) to Alan Sokal's hoax. Against the charge of epistemic relativism, Fish acknowledges the "reality" of the physical world by comparing its laws to the rules of baseball: both scientific laws and the rules of baseball are "real," though they are both "socially constructed," albeit for different purposes. So what does this mean? The rules of baseball are socially constructed rules governing a socially constructed reality, a human practice, the game of baseball. Fish's argument makes it difficult to avoid the conclusion that a similar relation exists between the science of physics and the natural reality it seeks to describe.
6. Mills, *The Sociological Imagination,* pp. 173-74.
7. This also raises large questions about the historical relation between capitalism and the Enlightenment, which there is no room to discuss here. In "Modernity, Postmodernity, or Capitalism?" I try to sketch out some distinctions between the historical conditions that gave rise to the Enlightenment and those that gave rise to the process of capitalist development.
8. "E.P. Thompson: Historian and Socialist," *Monthly Review* 45, no. 8 (January 1994).

2: POSTMODERNISM AND INTELLECTUALS

Where do postmodernists come from?

TERRY EAGLETON

Imagine a radical movement that had suffered an emphatic defeat. So emphatic, in fact, that it seemed unlikely to resurface for the length of a lifetime, if at all. As time wore on, the beliefs of this movement might begin to seem less false or ineffectual than simply irrelevant. For its opponents, it would be less a matter of hotly contesting these doctrines than of contemplating them with something of the mild antiquarian interest one might have previously reserved for Ptolemaic cosmology or the scholasticism of Thomas Aquinas. Radicals might come to find themselves less overwhelmed or out-argued than simply washed up, speaking a language so quaintly out of tune with their era that, as with the language of Platonism or courtly love, nobody even bothered any longer to ask whether it was true. What would be the likely response of the left to such a dire condition?

Many, no doubt, would drift either cynically or sincerely to the right, regretting their earlier views as infantile idealism. Others might keep the faith purely out of habit, anxiety, or nostalgia, clinging to an imaginary identity and risking the neurosis that that may bring. A small clutch of left triumphalists, incurably hopeful, would no doubt carry on detecting the stirrings of the revolution in the faintest flicker of militancy. In others, the radical impulse would persist, but would be forced to migrate elsewhere. One can imagine that the ruling assumption of this period would be that the system was, at least for the moment, unbreachable; and a great many of the left's conclusions could be seen to flow from this glum supposition. One might expect, for example, that there would be an upsurge of interest in the margins and crevices of the system—in those ambiguous, indeterminate places where its power seemed less secure. If the system could not be breached, one might at least look to those forces which might momentarily transgress, subvert, or give it the slip. There would be, one might predict, much celebration of the marginal—but this would be partly making a virtue out of necessity, since the left would itself have been rudely displaced from the mainstream, and might thus come, conveniently enough, to suspect all talk of centrality as suspect. At its crudest, this cult of marginality would come down to a simpleminded assumption that minorities were positive and majorities oppressive. Just how minorities like fascist groups, Ulster Unionists, or the international bourgeoisie fitted into this picture would not be entirely clear. Nor is it obvious how such a position could cope with a previously marginal movement—the ANC, for example—becoming politically dominant, given its formalist prejudice that dominance was undesirable as such. The historical basis for this way of thinking would be the fact that political movements that were at once mass, central, and creative were by and large no longer in business. Indeed, the idea of a movement that was at once central and subversive would now appear something of a contradiction in terms. It would therefore seem natural to demonize the mass, dominant, and consensual, and romanticize whatever happened to deviate from them. It would be, above all, the attitude of those younger dissidents who had nothing much, politically speaking, to remember, who had no actual memory or experience of mass radical politics, but a good deal of experience of drearily oppressive majorities.

If the system really did seem to have canceled all opposition to itself, then it would not be hard to generalize from this to the vaguely anarchistic belief that *system* is oppressive as such. Since there were almost no examples of attractive political systems around, the claim would seem distinctly plausible. The only genuine criticism could be one launched from outside the system altogether; and one would expect, therefore, a certain fetishizing of "otherness" in such a period. There would be enormous interest in anything that seemed alien, deviant, exotic, unincorporable, all the way from aardvarks to Alpha Centauri, a passion for whatever gave us a tantalizing glimpse of something beyond the logic of the system altogether. But this romantic ultra-leftism would coexist, curiously enough, with a brittle pessimism—for the fact is that if the system is all-powerful, then there can be by definition nothing beyond it, any more than there can be anything beyond the infinite curvature of cosmic space. If there *were* something outside the system, then it would be entirely unknowable and thus incapable of saving us; but if we could draw it into the orbit of the system, so that it could gain some effective foothold there, its otherness would be instantly contaminated and its subversive power would thus dwindle to nothing. Whatever negates the system in theory would thus be logically incapable of doing so in practice. Anything we can *understand* can by definition not be radical, since it must be within the system itself; but anything which escapes the system could be heard by us as no more than a mysterious murmur.

Such thinking has abandoned the whole notion of a system which is internally contradictory—which has that installed at its heart which can potentially undo it. Instead, it thinks in the rigid oppositions of "inside" and "outside," where to be on the inside is to be complicit and to be on the outside is to be impotent. The typical style of thought of such a period, then, might be described as *libertarian pessimism*—libertarian, because one would not have given up on the dream of something quite other than what we have; pessimism, because one would be much too bleakly conscious of the omnipotence of law and power to believe that such a dream could ever be realized. If one still believed in subversion, but not in the existence of any flesh-and-blood agents of it, then it might be possible to imagine that the system in some way subverted itself, deconstructed its own logic, which would then allow you to combine a certain radicalism with a certain skepticism.

If the system is everywhere, then it would seem, like the Almighty himself, to be visible at no particular point; and it would therefore become possible to believe, paradoxically enough, that whatever was out there was not in fact a system at all. It is only a short step from claiming that the system is too complex to be represented to declaring that it does not exist. In the period we are imagining, then, some would no doubt be found clamoring against what they saw as the tyranny of a real social totality, whereas others would be busy deconstructing the whole idea of totality and claiming that it existed only in our minds. It would not be hard to see this as, at least in part, a compensation in theory for the fact that the social totality was proving difficult to crack in practice. If no very ambitious form of political action seems for the moment possible, if so-called micropolitics seem the order of the day, it is always tempting to convert this necessity into a virtue—to console oneself with the thought that one's political limitations have a kind of objective ground in reality, in the fact that social "totality" is in any case just an illusion. ("Metaphysical" illusion makes your position sound rather more imposing.) It does not matter if there is no political agent at hand to transform the whole, because there is in fact no whole to be transformed. It is as though, having mislaid the breadknife, one declares the loaf to be already sliced. But totality might also seem something of an illusion because there would be no very obvious political agent for whom society might present itself as a totality. There are those who need to grasp how it stands with them in order to be free, and who find that they can do this only by grasping something of the overall structure with which their own immediate situation intersects. Local and universal are not, here, simple opposites or theoretical options, as they might be for those intellectuals who prefer to think big and those more modest academics who like to keep it concrete. But if some of those traditional political agents are in trouble, then so will be the concept of social totality, since it is those agents' *need* of it that gives it its force.

Grasping a complex totality involves some rigorous analysis; so it is not surprising that such strenuously systematic thought should be out of fashion, dismissed as phallic, scientistic, or what have you, in the sort of period we are imagining. When there is nothing in particular in it for you to find out how you stand—if you are a professor in Ithaca or Irvine, for example—you can afford to be ambiguous, elusive, deliciously indeterminate. You are also quite likely, in such circumstances, to wax idealist—though in some suitably newfangled rather than tediously old-fashioned sense. For one primary way in which we know the world is, of course, through practice; and if any very ambitious practice is denied us, it will not be long before we catch ourselves wondering whether there is anything out there at all. One would expect, then, that in such an era a belief in reality as something that resists us ("History is what hurts," as Fredric Jameson has put it) will give way to a belief in the "constructed" nature of the world. This, in turn, would no doubt go hand in hand with a full-blooded "culturalism" which underestimated what men and women had in common as material human creatures, and suspected all talk of nature as an insidious mystification. It would tend not to realize that such culturalism is just as reductive as, say, economism or biologism. Cognitive and realist accounts of human consciousness would yield ground to various kinds of pragmatism and relativism, partly because there didn't any longer seem much politically at stake in knowing how it stood with you. Everything would become an interpretation, including that statement itself. And what would also gradually implode, along with reasonably certain knowledge, would be the idea of a human subject "centered" and unified enough to take significant action. For such significant action would now seem in short supply; and the result, once more, would be to make a virtue out of necessity by singing the praises of the diffuse, decentered, schizoid human subject—a subject who might well not be "together" enough to topple a bottle off a wall, let alone bring down the state, but who could nevertheless be presented as hair-raisingly avant-garde in contrast to the smugly centered subjects of an older, more classical phase of capitalism. To put it another way: the subject as producer (coherent, disciplined, self-determining) would have yielded ground to the subject as consumer (mobile, ephemeral, constituted by insatiable desire).

If the "left" orthodoxies of such a period were pragmatist, relativist, pluralistic, deconstructive, then one might well see such thought-forms as dangerously radical. For does not capitalism need sure foundations, stable identities, absolute authority, metaphysical certainties, in order to survive? And wouldn't the kind of thought we are imagining put the skids under all this? The answer, feebly enough, is both yes and no. It is true that capitalism, so far anyway, has felt the need to underpin its authority with unimpeachable moral foundations. Look, for example, at the remarkable tenacity of religious belief in North America. On the other hand, look at the British, who are a notably godless bunch. No British politician could cause anything other than acute embarrassment by invoking the Supreme Being in public, and the British talk much less about metaphysical abstractions like Britain than those in the United States do about something called the United States. It is not clear, in other words, exactly how much metaphysical talk the advanced capitalist system really requires; and it is certainly true that its relentlessly secularizing, rationalizing operations threaten to undercut its own metaphysical claims. It is clear, however, that without pragmatism and plurality the system could not survive at all. Difference, "hybridity," heterogeneity, restless mobility are native to the capitalist mode of production, and thus by no means inherently radical phenomena. So if these ways of thinking put the skids under the system at one level, they reproduce its logic at another.

If an oppressive system seems to regulate everything, then one will naturally look around for some enclave of which this is less true—some place where a degree of freedom or randomness or pleasure still precariously survives. Perhaps you might call this desire, or discourse, or the body, or the unconscious. One might predict in this period a quickening of interest in psychoanalysis—for psychoanalysis is not only the thinking person's sensationalism, blending intellectual rigor with the most lurid materials, but it exudes a general exciting air of radicalism without being particularly so *politically*. If the more abstract questions of state, mode of production, and civil society seem for the moment too hard to resolve, then one might shift one's political attention to something more intimate and immediate, more living and fleshly, like the body. Conference papers entitled "Putting the Anus Back into Coriolanus" would attract eager crowds who had never heard of the bourgeoisie but who knew all about buggery.

This state of affairs would no doubt be particularly marked in those societies which in any case lacked strong socialist traditions; indeed, one could imagine much of the style of thought in question, for all its suspiciousness of the universal, as no more than a spurious universalizing of such specific political conditions. Such a concern with bodiliness and sexuality would represent, one imagines, an enormous political deepening and enrichment, at the same time as it would signify a thoroughgoing displacement. And no doubt just the same could be said if one were to witness an increasing obsession with language and culture—topics where the intellectual is in any case more likely to feel at home than in the realm of material production.

One might expect that some, true to the pessimism of the period, would stress how discourses are policed, regulated, heavy with power, while others would proclaim in more libertarian spirit how the thrills and spills of the signifier can give the slip to the system. Either way, one would no doubt witness an immense linguistic inflation, as what appeared no longer conceivable in political reality was still just about possible in the areas of discourse or signs or textuality. The freedom of text or language would come to compensate for the unfreedom of the system as a whole. There would still be a kind of utopian vision, but its name now would be increasingly poetry. And it would even be possible to imagine, in an "extremist" variant of this style of thought, that the future was here and now—that utopia had already arrived in the shape of the pleasurable intensities, multiple selfhoods, and exhilarating exchanges of the marketplace and the shopping mall. History would then most certainly have come to an end—an end already implicit in the blocking of radical political action. For if no such collective action seemed generally possible, then history would indeed appear as random and directionless, and to claim that there was no longer any "grand narrative" would be, among other things, a way of saying that we no longer knew how to construct one effectively in these conditions. For this kind of thought, history would have ended because freedom would finally have been achieved; for Marxism, the achievement of freedom would be the *beginning* of history and the end of all we have known to date: those boring prehistorical grand narratives which are really just the same old recycled story of scarcity, suffering, and struggle.

Even the densest reader may by now have guessed that the condition I am describing is not entirely hypothetical. Why should we be invited to imagine such a situation when it is staring us in the face? Is anything to be gained by this tiresome rhetorical ploy? Only, I think, a kind of thought experiment by which, putting actual history in brackets for the moment, we can come to recognize that almost every central feature of postmodern theory can be deduced, read off as it were, from the assumption of a major political defeat. It is as though, confronted with the fact of postmodern culture, we could work our way backward from it until we arrived at the defeat in question. (Whether it has been, in reality, as absolute and definitive a defeat as the existence of postmodernism seems to imply is not at issue here.) This whole speculative enterprise has, of course, the advantage of hindsight, and should not be taken entirely seriously; nobody could actually read off deconstruction or political correctness or *Pulp Fiction* from the winding down of working class militancy or of national liberation movements. But if postmodernism is not an *inevitable* outcome of such a political history, it is, for all that, a logical one—just as Act V of *King Lear* is not dictated by the four preceding acts, but is not just an accident either.

But isn't this just the kind of historically reductionist explanation that postmodernism itself finds most distasteful? No, because there is no suggestion here that postmodernism is *only* the consequence of a political failure. It is hard to see how Madonna or mock-Gothic buildings or the fiction of Umberto Eco are the offspring of such a repulse, though some ingenious cultural commentator will probably try it on. Postmodernism has many sources—modernism proper, so-called postindustrialism, the emergence of vital new political forces, the recrudescence of the cultural avant-garde, the penetration of cultural life by the commodity form, the dwindling of an "autonomous" space for art, the exhaustion of certain classical bourgeois ideologies, and so on. But whatever else it is, it is the child of a political rebuff. Its raising of issues of gender and ethnicity have no doubt permanently breached the ideological enclosure of the white male Western left, about whom the most that can be said is that at least we're not dead, and at the same time taken for granted a rampantly culturalist discourse which belongs precisely to that corner of the globe. These valuable preoccupations have also often enough shown a signal indifference to that power which is the invisible color of daily life, which determines our existence—sometimes literally so—in almost every quarter, which decides in large measure the destiny of nations and the internecine conflicts between them. It is as though every other form of oppressive power can be readily debated, but not the one which so often sets the long-term agenda for them or is at the very least implicated with them at their core. The power of capital is now so wearily familiar that even large sectors of the left have succeeded in naturalizing it, taking it for granted as an immutable structure. One would need, for an apt analogy, to imagine a defeated right wing eagerly discussing the monarchy, the family, and the death of courtesy, while maintaining a stiff silence on what after all most viscerally engages them, the rights of property, since these had been so thoroughly expropriated that it seemed merely academicist to wish them back.

Postmodernist culture has produced a rich, bold, exhilarating body of work across the whole span of the arts, and has generated more than its fair share of execrable kitsch. It has pulled the rug out from beneath a number of complacent certainties, pried open some paranoid totalities, tainted some jealously guarded purities, bent some oppressive norms, and shaken some rather solid-looking foundations. It has also tended to surrender to a politically paralyzing skepticism, a flashy populism, a full-blooded moral relativism, and a brand of sophism for which, since all conventions are arbitrary anyway, we might as well conform to those of the Free World. In pulling the rug out from under the certainties of its political opponents, this postmodern culture has often enough pulled it out from under itself too, leaving itself with no more reason why we should resist fascism than the feebly pragmatic plea that fascism is not the way we do things in Sussex or Sacramento. It has brought low the intimidating austerity of high culture with its playful, parodic spirit, and in thus imitating the commodity form has succeeded in reinforcing the crippling austerities of the marketplace. It has released the power of the local, the vernacular, the regional, at the same time as it has contributed to making the globe a more drearily uniform place. Its nervousness in the face of concepts like *truth* has alarmed the bishops and charmed the business executives. It consistently denies the possibility of describing how the world is, and just as consistently finds itself doing so. It is full of universal moral prescriptions—plurality is preferable to singularity, difference to identity, otherness to sameness—and denounces all such universalism as oppressive. It dreams of a human being set free from law and constraint, gliding ambiguously from one "subject-position" to another, and sees the human subject as no more than the determined effect of cultural forces. It believes in style and pleasure, and commonly churns out texts that might have been composed by, as well as on, a computer.

All of this, however, belongs to a dialectical assessment of postmodernism—and postmodernism itself insists that dialectical thought can be consigned to the metaphysical junkheap. It is here, perhaps, that it differs most deeply from Marxism. Marxists are supposed to be "doctrinaire" thinkers, yet recognize that there can be no authentic socialism without the rich heritage of enlightened bourgeois liberalism. Postmodernists are self-declared devotees of pluralism, mutability, open-endedness, yet are constantly to be caught demonizing humanism, liberalism, the Enlightenment, the centered subject, and the rest. But bourgeois Enlightenment is like social class: in order to get rid of it, you must first work your way through it. It is on this point more than any other that Marxism and postmodernism are perhaps most profoundly at odds.

Postmodernism has a quick eye for irony; but there is one irony above all that seems to have escaped it. Just at the time when it was denouncing the idea of revolution as "metaphysical," scorning the notion of a "collective subject," and insisting on the dangers of totality, revolution broke out where everyone had least expected it, as a collective subject of some kind struck against the "total system" of the postcapitalist bureaucracies. The current results of that transformation are not, of course, ones that a socialist can contemplate with any equanimity; but the dramatic upheavals in Eastern Europe give the lie to many of the fashionable assumptions of the postmodern West. In a powerfully estranging gesture, they expose postmodernism as the ideology of a peculiarly jaded, defeatist wing of the liberal-capitalist intelligentsia, which has mistaken its own very local difficulties for a universal human condition in exactly the manner of the universalist ideologies it denounces. But, though postmodernism may be thus usefully "estranged" by what has happened to the east of it, it was certainly not caused by that collapse. Postmodernism is less a reaction to the defeat of Communism (which it anyway long predated), than—at least in its more reactionary versions—a response to the "success" of capitalism. So here is another irony. In the crisis-ridden 1990s, it seems more than a little odd to treat capitalist success as if it were a general and immutable law of nature. If that is not just the kind of unhistorical absolutizing that postmodernists so fiercely reject in others, it is hard to see what is.

Language, history, and class struggle

DAVID McNALLY

Language and the new idealism

> *Language* is the immediate actuality of thought. Just as philosophers have given thought an independent existence, so they were bound to make language into an independent realm.
>
> —MARX and ENGELS, *The German Ideology*

We are witnessing today a new idealism, infecting large sections of the intellectual left, which has turned language not merely into an independent realm, but into an all-pervasive realm, a sphere so omnipresent, so dominant, as virtually to extinguish human agency. Everything is discourse, you see; and discourse is everything. Because human beings are linguistic creatures, because the world in which we act is a world we know and describe through language, it allegedly follows that there is nothing outside language. Our language, or "discourse," or "text"—the jargon varies but not the message—defines and limits what we know, what we can imagine, what we can do.

There is a political theory here too. Oppression is said to be rooted ultimately in the way in which we and others are defined linguistically, the way in which we are positioned by words in relation to other words, or by codes which are said to be "structured like a language." Our very being, our identities and "subjectivities," are constituted through language. As one trendy literary theorist puts it in David Lodge's novel *Nice Work*, it is not merely that you are what you speak; no, according to the new idealism, "you are what speaks you." Language is thus the final "prison-house." Our confinement there is beyond resistance; it is impossible to escape from that which makes us what we are.

This new idealism corresponds to a profound collapse of political horizons. It is the pseudoradicalism of a period of retreat for the left, a verbal radicalism of the word without deed, or, rather, of the word *as* deed. In response to actual structures and practices of oppression and exploitation, it offers the rhetorical gesture, the ironic turn of phrase. It comes as little surprise, then, when one of the chief philosophers of the new idealism, Jacques Derrida, tells us that he "would hesitate to use such terms as 'liberation.' "[1] Imprisoned within language, we may play with words; but we can never hope to liberate ourselves from immutable structures of oppression rooted in language itself.

The new idealism and the politics it entails are not simply harmless curiosities; they are an abdication of political responsibility, especially at a time of ferocious capitalist restructuring, of widening gaps between rich and poor, of ruling class offensives against social programs. They are also an obstacle to the rebuilding of mass movements of protest and resistance. It is not the purpose of this article, however, to conduct another critique of linguistic idealism whether it goes by the name of poststructuralism, postmodernism, or post-Marxism. Instead, I want to shift to a different terrain of debate by showing that Marxism can do more than attack the idealist nature of these intellectual currents. I want to demonstrate that Marxism has the resources for an account of language and its position within the constellation of human practice that is richer and more profound than these idealist views, and that this account can understand language as, among other things, one site of social interaction which is decisively shaped by relations of work and conflict, i.e., as shaped by class struggle.

Social labor and the "language of real life"

Marx and Engels did not develop a theory of language. Yet the little that they did say on the subject bears highlighting at a time when confusion is widespread with respect to some of the basic tenets of historical materialism.

It is worth reminding ourselves, to begin with, that the materialist conception of history set out in early works such as *The German Ideology* does not deny the role of consciousness in human life. Rather, the materialist conception seeks to counter the *detachment* of consciousness, thought, the realm of ideas, from labor, social production, practical human activity as a whole. Marx and Engels do not condemn idealism for taking thought and language seriously but, rather, as the passage which opens this article indicates, for giving these an "independent existence." Human beings, they insist, produce ideas as part of the production of the totality of their conditions of life. The production of ideas and concepts, therefore, "is directly interwoven with the material activity and the material intercourse" that takes place among people. Indeed this, they suggest, is "the language of real life."

A defining feature of human life is social labor, the way in which we organize the interconnected productive activities of individuals in order to reproduce ourselves materially. Just as human work presupposes consciousness, so it requires communication among individuals, a capacity to share and exchange ideas in order to coordinate social labor. And language is the medium of such communication, the very stuff of human consciousness. Language is the form of specifically human consciousness, the consciousness of uniquely social beings. It follows that "language is as old as consciousness, language *is* practical, real consciousness that exists for other men as well."[2] Sketchy though this account may be, it is indispensable for any outlook which wants to take language seriously without detaching it from the totality of practical human activity. Yet Marx and Engels provide no more than a framework for understanding language. Fortunately, later writers in the Marxist tradition have developed and extended this account in ways that leave us with a much enriched materialist theory of language.

Signs, speech, and class struggle

Among the most important of these efforts is the pioneering work of V.N. Voloshinov, *Marxism and the Philosophy of Language* (1929). Voloshinov's work was developed during a period of vigorous debate about literature, art, language, and culture in the aftermath of the October Revolution of 1917. That debate was shut down as Stalin consolidated his dictatorship. Voloshinov himself disappeared during the purges of the 1930s. In recent years, however, the writings of Voloshinov and Mikhail Bakhtin, the intellectual figure who most influenced his work, have enjoyed something of a renaissance.[3]

Three initial propositions are fundamental to Voloshinov's views on language. First, all signs—from words to traffic signals—are material, they are embodied in some physical form or other. Second, signs are social in nature; they exist on the boundaries between individuals and have no meaning outside of communicative interaction. Third, because signs are social, any comprehensive approach to language must focus on speech, on that medium through which most linguistic interaction occurs. Outside of speech, language is lifeless, it is a collection of means of communicating without the act of communication itself, a form without substance. The life of language, its very dynamism, thus resides in speech, in verbal interaction among people.

But social interaction is not simply discursive. Speech is not a realm with an "independent existence"; it is one aspect of a multifaceted nexus of social relations. It follows that signs are immersed in the relations that prevail among human beings. In particular, relations of hierarchy among individuals have a tremendous influence on language and speech. "The forms of signs," Voloshinov writes, "are conditioned above all by the social organization of the participants involved" (p. 21). Speech is thus conditioned by hierarchy and domination—and by resistance to these. Different groups attempt to *accent* words in ways that express their experience of social interaction and their social aspirations. This applies especially, but by no means exclusively, to people in distinct class relationships. As a result, "sign becomes an arena of the class struggle" (p. 23).

It should be emphasized that this argument differs substantially from poststructuralist accounts that may in some respects look similar. Michel Foucault, for example, is noted for his view of language as a terrain of power and domination embodied in particular social institutions such as hospitals, asylums and prisons; and, especially in some of his later writings, Foucault appears to allow for the possibility of resistance to practices of domination. Foucault's emphasis on power was an attempt to counter the political emptiness of theories that reduce social relations to their linguistic forms. In a vigorous riposte to Derrida, he charged deconstruction with locating everything in texts "so as not to put discursive practices back into the field of transformations in which they are carried out."[4] This position has considerable strengths. Yet, while disavowing enclosure within texts, Foucault himself fails to break out of discourse as a field closed in upon itself. Indeed, his whole concept of "power-knowledge" tends towards the position that power relations are constructed in and through practices of "knowing" humans. And these practices—of classifying, measuring, and surveying people—originate in the realm of discourse, where people are assigned to different categories of thought and description. It follows that "the development of humanity is a series of interpretations." Thus, for all his insights into social institutions and their practices of domination, Foucault reverts to his own version of discursive determinism; he is led by the logic of his position to conclude that inevitably "one remains within the dimension of discourse."[5]

A further observation is perhaps necessary in this regard with respect to Jacques Lacan and his poststructuralist reading of psychoanalysis. Often, Lacan's emphasis on the unconscious mind and its determinants is seen as representing a refusal of linguistic determinism. Yet, things are not so straightforward since Lacan offers up a linguistic interpretation of the unconscious. In so doing, he breaks sharply from the materialist impulse that in many respects represents Freud's most radical and subversive side: his theory of bodily drives or instincts which seek pleasure. True, Freud saw these instincts as socially mediated, as pliable and capable of a variety of forms of expression. Nevertheless, Freud's insistence that the human mind is a site in which bodily drives express themselves and come into conflict with social rules and conventions, stands removed from those traditions which see the realm of mind, language, and thought as an essentially self-sufficient one. For Freud, the unconscious is, among other things, a site where repressed bodily desires continue to express themselves. Much if not all of this is lost in Lacan's claim that "the unconscious is structured like a language."[6] For what Lacan has done is largely to dematerialize Freud's theory, to loosen its ties to the human body, and to reconstruct it on linguistic lines. When he describes human nature as "woven by effects in which is to be found the structure of language," he is recasting Freud's theory on the model of linguistics. As a result, language is severed from the human body and the socio-material practices in which people engage. Whatever Lacan's intent, he puts us back in the prison-house where language speaks "through man."[7]

Let us return now to Voloshinov to see how his insistence on language as a site of social conflict avoids enclosing us in the linguistic realm. If the "sign" is an arena of class struggle, this does not mean that words (or signs generally) have entirely different meanings for members of different social classes. Voloshinov resists a simple-minded relativism. At the same time, he attacks those who reify words and meanings, those who abstract them from the living field of social interaction and conflict. Words, he insists, have reasonably stable and abstract meanings of the sort that we find in a dictionary. But speech involves both meanings and themes. Themes have to do with the accents and emphases that members of specific social groups try to give to words in order to transmit their experiences. Indeed, in different contexts, individuals participate in distinct *"speech genres"* which have their own accents, norms, vocabularies, dialects, and so on. Thus, a secretary in a large office will employ a quite different genre when speaking with a supervisor than she will with a group of workmates at lunch, or at a union meeting after work. The first genre may be characterized by apparent deference and subordination. The second might involve relatively egalitarian speech with humorous attacks on bosses and supervisors. Finally, the third context would tend to involve a more codified oppositional discourse characterized by solidarity ("sisters and brothers") and resistance to employers.

This approach to language and speech sees people as engaged in different kinds of relations and activities in which distinct genres provide them with a range of resources for coming to understand and articulate their experiences. There is no one master discourse which permeates all contexts, although those who exercise power may try to impose a single discourse upon their subordinates. Because they interact, however, the oppressed and the exploited develop genres of their own which accent aspects of social experience, oppositional attitudes, and the like that official discourses attempt to deny. Signs are thus, according to Voloshinov, *multiaccentual;* they can be accented in a variety of ways that express the experiences of different social groups. But official discourses, the rhetorical systems of ruling classes, attempt to deny the multiaccentuality of the sign. Ruling classes aspire to depict a single worldview through discourse; as a result they try to assert a unified set of meanings and themes as the only possible way of describing things. "The ruling class," writes Voloshinov, "strives to impart a supraclass, eternal character to the ideological sign" (p. 23). It attempts, in other words, to reify signs, to treat them as static and unchanging, as capable of a singular, unitary, eternal meaning.

But try as they might, the ruling class cannot completely shut down attempts to accent signs in ways that fall outside the official discourse. Voloshinov is not entirely clear as to why this is so. But the answer seems straightforward. All systems of human labor are social to one degree or another. History has known no system of production by solitary individuals. Direct producers, be they peasants, plantation slaves, or wage-laborers, cooperate and collaborate in the labor process and in their interactions outside of work. And in these contexts they communicate in ways that elude the direct control and supervision of their exploiters. Alternative discourses develop, in other words, because official discourses do not capture the whole of the life experiences of the oppressed. The latter have a range of social interactions wholly or partly free from the direct interference of their rulers. And in these "spaces" they develop discourses or genres which express feelings, sentiments, ideas, views, and aspirations which go unacknowledged by the official discourse.

Rather than being monolithic, signs are full of contradictory accents. Most of the time, however, this is not readily apparent. "In the ordinary conditions of life," argues Voloshinov, "the contradiction embedded in every ideological sign cannot emerge fully" (p. 23). But in times of social crisis or revolutionary upheaval when the legitimacy of ruling classes is under attack, these contradictions burst to the fore as dominant discourses are challenged by rebellious peoples claiming more and more public space for alternative and oppositional discourses. This is one of the reasons that popular upheavals have the character of "festivals of the oppressed," to borrow Lenin's phrase; at times when structures of control and censorship are breaking down, practices and discourses of resistance and opposition find a tremendously enhanced field of expression. Yet, the images of a world-turned-upside-down that burst out during a carnival of revolt are not instantaneous creations; they grow out of the genres that oppressed and exploited groups have created throughout history to express their experiences and to unify, however unevenly, their practices of resistance.

Voloshinov's theory of language is thus above all historical; as such it is a powerful corrective to the static and ahistorical notions prevalent within the new idealism. It is striking that idealist treatments of language, even when they appear to be stressing the historicity of discourses—as Foucault is famous for doing—are profoundly ahistorical. History appears for them as a series of discursive *differences,* a disconnected succession of linguistic paradigms, not a dynamic process generated by interactions and conflicts among living people in concrete social relations. Voloshinov shifts us to the living field of communication, of verbal interaction among people steeped in the tensions and contradictions of social life. In so doing, he restores history, social interaction, and class conflict to the study of language. Nevertheless, his analysis remains at a quite general level and needs to be fleshed out more concretely. This is so in two key respects. First, with regard to the nature of the social practices out of which the oppressed and exploited develop their own speech genres. And, second, in terms of the implications of his analysis for political practice. In addressing the first issue, I want to show how a rich body of historical writings might help us understand the dialectic of resistance in practice and in discourse. Then, in taking up the second question, I want to turn to some key arguments about language, consciousness, and political organization developed by Antonio Gramsci in his *Prison Notebooks*.

Exploitation and cultures of resistance

Voloshinov's concept of the multiaccentual sign has been misread by some as implying that meanings are so unstable as to be utterly random and infinitely multipliable. Such a reading moves towards an idealist detachment of language and speech from the complex of relations people enter into in the production and reproduction of the conditions of life. I have already hinted at the flaw in such a view: its failure to recognize that unofficial or alternative discourses grow out of actual social experiences, especially those related to production. In order to more powerfully defend Voloshinov's position in this regard, we can find significant resources in social history. For, as a whole number of major historical studies have shown, oppositional discourses tend especially to grow out of *practices of resistance* to the appropriation of surplus product by an exploiting class and its representatives.

One of the most interesting things about the images of resistance that run through popular tales, songs, rituals, sayings, and the like is the way they invert the experience of exploitation. At the heart of exploitation, after all, is the sense of theft, that one has been robbed. Inverting that relationship, robbing the robber, be it one's master, lord, or boss, is a constant theme of popular culture.

This is certainly true of the trickster tales created by plantation slaves in the U.S. South. "One of the trickster's greatest pleasures," notes one historian, "was eating food he had stolen from his powerful enemies."[8] These stories, using animals in place of masters and slaves, were told and retold, legitimating a culture of defiance in which theft from one's master was not simply condoned but praised. Moreover, these stories were no mere fantasies; they were part of actual practices of pilfering which slave communities sought to protect.

One finds similar phenomena among displaced peasants, poor cottagers and yeoman farmers in early eighteenth-century England. As E.P. Thompson showed in his marvelous works like *Whigs and Hunters* and *Customs in Common,* people engaged in various transgressive practices, such as poaching (the "stealing" of deer, rabbits, fish, and more from recently enclosed common lands), to challenge new definitions of property and restrictions on their customary rights; and these transgressions were sustained by a rich popular culture which delegitimatized the practices of the rich while encouraging outright defiance of the law. This popular culture had its own language, rhetoric, and symbols, and has left a documentary record in the form of wall notices, songs, threatening letters, and so on.[9]

With Thompson in mind, we might also note that forms of class expression and resistance are not simply economic in nature, nor are they confined to struggles at the point of production. Beginning with *The Making of the English Working Class* (1963), Thompson sought to depict class as a dynamic, living experience that weaves its way through the fabric of social life. Class experience manifests itself in language and literature; at work, in the pub, and in the home; in song and sexual relations; in overt forms of organization and in secret rituals. When he shows us people struggling in class ways, Thompson takes us to sites where work, gender relations, sexuality, and diverse modes of resistance intersect. Rather than exclude these, a notion of class struggle as lived experience requires that we tease out how work, exploitation, and resistance to exploitation shape other dimensions of social life just as they are shaped by them in turn. Yet, because we are productive creatures, because work is central to the way in which we make ourselves and are made, social relations and conflicts centered on work will figure decisively in our lives. And running through all of this in class society is the experience of being robbed and of trying to subvert or reverse this robbery.

While the structure of such practices is different from those of plantation slaves or eighteenth-century laborers, we can observe the same thing in the case of modern factory workers. I take two examples: the first from Hungary in the 1970s; the second from Flint, Michigan a few years later.[10] Describing factory life in Hungary in his book *A Worker in a Worker's State,* author Miklos Haraszti takes us into a world of "us" and "them," a world in which time devoted to work for oneself is the ultimate form of resistance. That resistance is captured in the workers' own language:

> They, Them, Theirs: I don't believe that anyone who has ever worked in a factory, or even had a relatively superficial discussion with workers, can be in any doubt about what these words mean ... *them* means the same thing: the management, those who give the orders and take the decisions, the men and their agents who are in charge—who remain inaccessible even when they cross our field of vision (p. 71).

The workers Haraszti describes are on piece rates. They find time, while meeting their quotas, to produce items for themselves, things which will be smuggled out of the plant and taken home. They have invented a word for these works of free activity: "homers." It is these which bring the greatest joy into their working day. "This humble little homer, made secretly and only through great sacrifices, with no ulterior motive, is the only form possible of free and creative work" (p. 142). "By making homers we win back power over the machine and our freedom from the machine" (p. 143). But while largely made individually, homers require a culture of cooperation: certain kinds of cutting and shaping can only be done by co-workers on their machines, and smuggling homers out often requires the involvement of others. "Making homers ... demands cooperation, voluntary cooperation." Indeed, "most friendships begin with the making of a joint homer" (pp. 143, 144).

Cooperation, friendship, solidarity, free creative activity: all these are entailed in the making of homers. This is no rarefied discourse of opposition; the making of homers involves practices of resistance. Homers are the material embodiment of oppositional values and attitudes; they project the vision of social cooperation and workers' control of production. Homers, as Haraszti notes, "are the model for all protest movements" (p. 143).

A final set of examples comes from Ben Hamper's wonderful book, *Rivethead*. Chronicling the experiences of assembly line workers at GM's truck and bus plant in Flint, Hamper too shows us the key role of struggles over time. The time turned over to GM is experienced as time torn away from life. One of the subversive practices that Hamper describes is that of "doubling up" in which two workers agree to do their own job and that of their workmate for half the shift. The rest of the time can be devoted to sleeping, reading, writing, or even sneaking out of the plant to do what one chooses. It is clear reading Hamper's account that he and his co-workers glory in their ability to "steal back" some of the time the company robs from them.

Describing how he reestablished a doubling-up operation with a new co-worker after being moved to the Rivet Line, Hamper writes:

> It was like 1978 all over again. Four hours' work, eight hours' pay. Once again there was that certain exhilaration knowing that your job was being nursed along in able hands while you howled at the screen in Mark's Lounge after Lou Whitaker had blasted a hangin' curve into the right field upper deck. Such things seemed to make more sense than manual labor.

He continues: "Above all, I liked the idea of outsmarting all those management pricks with their clean fingernails and filthy bonuses" (p. 191).

Hamper too shows us a rich culture of resistance. He does not idealize; division and backwardness are there in his account. But so is cooperation—to beat the clock, defeat an authoritarian foreman or supervisor, to reclaim a small part of their common humanity, even if simply by injecting humor into the monotony of life on the assembly line.

The examples I have chosen, which could be multiplied many times over, trace a certain logic of resistance. They show producers attempting to reverse the experience of exploitation, trying to steal something for themselves from those who appropriate the product of their labor, their freedom, their life-activity itself, and typically inventing language to convey and conduct their subversive practices. Discourses of resistance are thus anything but random or arbitrary. Many of the most powerful and enduring are responses—often highly creative ones—to structures of labor and exploitation. There is "play" here, to use a term favored by deconstructionists; there is irony, humor, carnivalesque inversion. But there is also struggle, damned serious struggle, over livelihoods, over life and limb. And over liberty.

Gramsci on Language and Hegemony

Yet, if the oppressed are not completely dominated by official discourses, if they create rich practices and discourses of resistance to their rulers, how are we to explain the persistence of domination and exploitation? Here, the considerations of the Italian revolutionary Antonio Gramsci on language and hegemony can be of considerable assistance.

Gramsci sought to develop a perspective which recognized the hegemony of ruling ideas, the ideas of the ruling class, *and* the extent to which such hegemony is never total, but instead always exists in an uneasy relationship with ideas and attitudes that are "counter-hegemonic," that stand in opposition to the dominant values and ideas.

"All men are 'philosophers,'" argues Gramsci in defiance of intellectual elitism.[11] This is so because, by virtue of using language, which involves "a totality of determined notions and concepts," every individual employs a conception of society, of the world in which he or she lives. Most of the time, such a worldview is not systematically elaborated according to its basic principles. But by virtue of speech we are immersed in a world of concepts which presupposes some overall view of things.

But such worldviews are rarely consistent; they typically involve a contradictory amalgam of ideas. Thus, most working class people have absorbed a variety of ideas and attitudes that derive from the dominant ideology. At the same time, their day to day life-activity involves them, as we have seen, in practices which contradict at least some aspects of the dominant worldview. Thus, when looking at a member of the producing classes, it is often the case that

> his theoretical consciousness can indeed be historically in opposition to his activity. One might almost say that he has two theoretical consciousnesses (or one contradictory consciousness): one that is implicit in his activity and which in reality unites him with all his fellow-workers in the practical transformation of the real world; and one, superficially explicit or verbal, which he has inherited from the past and uncritically absorbs (p. 333).

The contradictory character of working class consciousness is a highly dynamic phenomenon. To begin with, there is no homogeneous consciousness within the working class. Among a single group of workers, some will veer towards near-total acceptance of the ideas of bosses, supervisors, heads of state, and so on, while others will tends towards an almost thorough-going opposition to such figures. Between these two positions one will find the majority of workers. But their consciousness will not be fixed. Great events—mass strikes and demonstrations, union drives, and so on—coupled with the organized propagation of oppositional ideas can contribute to significant radicalizations; while defeats, setbacks, and the decline of oppositional discourse can have a deeply conservatizing effect.

But whatever the existing state of affairs at any one point in time, Gramsci is clear that the contradictory nature of working class consciousness cannot be eliminated. It is an intrinsic feature of capitalist society that the ruling class tries to win ideological consent to its rule (and that such efforts are usually successful to a significant extent), *and* that the life experiences of workers, their resistance to exploitation and domination, generate practices which do not fit with the dominant ideas and which, in fact, entail an implicit worldview that challenges these ideas. Indeed, one of the crucial functions of a revolutionary socialist party for Gramsci is that it try to draw out and systematize the worldview which is implicit in such practices of resistance. This view enables Gramsci to approach the question of revolutionary politics in terms of the contradictions which pervade the experience, activity, and language of oppressed members of society.

Revolutionary politics begins, he argues, with the common sense of the working class. This common sense contains all these, largely implicit, oppositional attitudes. And since socialism, as Marx insisted, is the self-emancipation of the working class, revolutionary ideas cannot be some foreign discourse injected into the working class movement. On the contrary, the connection between revolutionary ideas and the working class must be organic; it is the task of Marxists to show that socialism is the logical and consistent outgrowth of practices of working class resistance. The revolutionary party must thus be a living part of the working class movement; it must share their experiences and speak their language. At the same time, it must also be the force that generalizes experiences of opposition into an increasingly systematic program, the force which challenges the traditional and dominant ideas inherited by workers (patriotism, sexism, racism, etc.) by showing how they conflict with the interests and aspirations implicit in resistance to exploitation and oppression. Contrary to certain idealist renderings of Gramsci which have made the rounds in recent years, he is insistent that the building of such a mass counter-hegemonic movement does not take place on a strictly cultural plane or as some rarefied intellectual process of ideological dissent. Counter-hegemonies, he argues, are created through political struggle, movements in which economic resistance and ideological combat go hand in hand. For the oppressed, in other words, "critical understanding of self takes place therefore through a struggle of political 'hegemonies'" (p. 333). And "political parties," he insists, operate as the "historical laboratory" of counter-hegemonic worldviews; they are "the crucibles where the unification of theory and practice, understood as a real historical process, takes place" (p. 335).

Gramsci's discussion of language, hegemony, and political struggle thus assists us in translating Voloshinov's conception of speech genres onto the terrain of practical politics. For Gramsci's contradictory consciousness is simply one way of transposing Voloshinov's notion that members of the exploited classes participate in dominant speech genres (according to their subordinate position) and more egalitarian genres which embody a different relationship to others (one's equals), different values, different practices. Central to revolutionary socialist politics, Gramsci suggests, is the effort to unify these oppositional practices—which is a question of real struggles around concrete issues, and of efforts to elaborate and systematize the worldview implicit in those popular genres that entail solidarity, cooperation, and egalitarianism.

Language and Liberation

What conclusions can we draw from this brief excursus through some Marxist considerations on language? First, we have seen that Marxism insists upon the unity of life-experience. Language, like consciousness, is not a separate and detached realm of human existence; rather, it is an expressive dimension of that existence. As such, it is permeated by the conflicts, tensions, and contradictions of real life. The new idealism sees none of this. By treating language "as a system of abstract grammatical categories," in Bakhtin's words, rather than understanding it as "ideologically saturated," as "contradiction-ridden, tension-filled," idealism impoverishes our understanding of the relations between language, life, history, and society. The new idealism may claim to understand ideology, conflict, contradiction, and resistance, but it has in a sense gone one step further than the old idealism, not just abstracting language but in effect transforming society itself into a linguistic system.

The word, argues Bakhtin, "enters a dialogically agitated and tension-filled environment of alien words, value judgments and accents, weaves in and out of complex interrelationships, merges with some, recoils from others...." Words and utterances are never neutral; they are always situated, positioned in a context charged with tensions, struggles, conflicts. As "an abstract grammatical system" language may be considered unitary, a closed object of study. But this is to treat it "in isolation from the uninterrupted process of historical becoming that is characteristic of all living language."

Language is thus social *and* historical. Meanings exist for me only in my relations with others; and these others exist in concrete, structured social relationships. And these social relations themselves are dynamic; they involve struggles over domination and resistance, shifting balances of force and power. Meanings are thus historical as well; they are immersed in a process of "historical becoming" in which relationships are not fixed, and in which past and present interweave in our orientation towards the future.

Language does not present me with a single structure of grammatical relations and meanings. On the contrary, my involvement in language entails my immersion in a social and historical field of themes, accents and meanings which are always contested and never closed. The words I choose, the utterances I convey, involve a positioning within that field. There are always alternative ways of expressing and articulating my experiences, my positions, my aspirations. This is what it means when Bakhtin writes that "consciousness finds itself inevitably facing the necessity of *having to choose a language*."[12]

I take a mundane example from a recent newspaper story on the strike by major league baseball players. "Replacement players—you are free to call them scabs or strikebreakers if you don't like euphemisms—have begun their first faltering workouts of spring training," writes a sports reporter.[13] The journalist is here presenting readers with a choice. We are offered alternatives: replacement players, scabs, strikebreakers. It is clear that the choice we make is not neutral; it is socially and politically charged. And in the Marxist tradition I have been discussing, this applies to all utterances, to speech (living language) in general.

Moreover, language presents us with resources for the construction of meanings which reach out towards the future, which point to possibilities that transcend our experience in the present. And many of the resources with which language presents us derive from past meanings that are not closed off to us, that live on in our language, our culture, our experience. For, like language, human beings exist in a state of "historical becoming." That is why language enables us to reach into the past while being oriented towards the future. Past experiences—gains, losses, victories, defeats, joys, sorrows—may speak to present predicaments; they may provide inspiration, lessons, resources of hope in the here-and-now. In reaching forward, I can simultaneously reach back—and language assists me in doing so. For language is the stuff of memory, personal and historical. Not only does it enable me to have an enduring sense of self over the years; it also helps me to use historical memory to position myself towards the future. I am able to call up Toussaint L'Ouverture and the slave army which fought the colonial powers, the Parisian Communards of 1871, the St. Petersburg Soviet of Workers' Deputies of 1917, the sit-down strikers at Flint in 1937, the Hungarian insurgents of 1956, the French students and workers of 1968....

To be "enclosed" in language is thus, for historical materialism, to be embodied in history, in "historical becoming." Rather than closing off alternative possibilities, our existence as historical beings means we are able to recall the past and envision a future that is different from the present. For language is not just a depository for the dominant ideas; it is also a dimension in which struggles against domination can be remembered and retained, in which resistance can be envisioned and organized.

To see language in this way means that, unlike the new idealists, one can theorize liberation as a meaningful idea. It means that, however bleak the circumstances, liberation is always possible precisely because our practical activity and our language carry with them themes, accents, aspirations that express different kinds of relations among people and the work they do. So long as there is hierarchy, domination, exploitation, so there will be practices of resistance and subversion that leave their traces in language. Language is not a prison-house, but a site of struggle. To be sure, struggle takes place and is ultimately resolved principally on the field of very real material structures—workplaces, prisons, armies, and so on. But wherever our struggles may be located, language will be found there, as one of the spheres in which social experience is lived. And those fighting for liberation from oppression and exploitation will invariably find within language words, meanings, themes for expressing, clarifying, and coordinating their struggle for a better world.

NOTES

1. Jacques Derrida, "Deconstruction and the other" in Richard Kearney (ed.), *Dialogues with Contemporary Continental Thinkers*, (Manchester: Manchester University Press, 1984), p. 121.
2. Karl Marx and Frederick Engels, *The German Ideology*, third edition (Moscow: Progress Publishers, 1976), pp. 43, 49.
3. I will not enter into the debate as to whether Bakhtin wrote some or all of *Marxism and the Philosophy of Language*. I attribute the book essentially to Voloshinov, while recognizing that Bakhtin's ideas were a crucial influence. Page numbers for all passages from Voloshinov's book will be given in the text. They refer to V.N. Voloshinov, *Marxism and the Philosophy of Language* (Cambridge: Harvard University Press, 1986).
4. Michel Foucault, "Mon corps, ce papier, ce feu," in *Histoire de la folie* (Paris, 1972).
5. Michel Foucault, "Nietzsche, Genealogy, History" in Donald F. Bouchard (ed.), *Language, Counter-Memory, Practice: Selected Essays and Interviews by Michel Foucault* (Ithaca: Cornell University Press, 1977), p. 152; Foucault, *The Archaeology of Knowledge*, Alan Sheridan, trans. (New York: Pantheon Books, 1972), p. 76.
6. Jacques Lacan, *The Four Fundamental Concepts of Psychoanalysis*, Alan Sheridan, trans. (Harmondsworth: Penguin Books, 1979), p. 20.
7. Jacques Lacan, *Écrits: A Selection*, Alan Sheridan, trans. (New York: W.W. Norton, 1977), p. 284. The best attempt to explore the radical implications of Freud's thought is Herbert Marcuse, *Eros and Civilization: A Philosophical Inquiry into Freud* (New York: Vintage Books, 1962).

8. Alex Lichtenstein, "That Disposition to Theft, with Which They Have Been Branded: Moral Economy Slave Management, and the Law," *Journal of Social History*, Spring 1988.
9. See E.P. Thompson, *Whigs and Hunters* (New York: Pantheon Books, 1975), and *Customs in Common* (London: Merlin Press, 1991).
10. See Miklos Haraszti, *A Worker in a Worker's State* (Harmondsworth: Penguin Books, 1977) and Ben Hamper, *Rivethead: Tales from the Assembly Line* (Warner Books, 1991). Page references to these books will be given in the text.
11. Antonio Gramsci, *Selections from the Prison Notebooks* (New York: International Publishers, 1971), p. 323. Page numbers for all further citations will be given in the text.
12. All quotes from Bakhtin are from his *The Dialogic Imagination*, Caryl Emerson and Michael Holquist, trans. (Austin: University of Texas Press, 1981), pp. 271, 272, 276, 288, 295.
13. Larry Millson, "Sham players begin the charade," *Globe and Mail* (Toronto), 20 February 1995.

The politics of cultural studies

FRANCIS MULHERN

Among the more striking intellectual phenomena of these putatively postmodern times is the rise, in the metropolitan academy, of the new discipline of cultural studies. I say "new" because cultural studies properly understood was never merely the organized study of "culture"; it was, from the start, a directed, self-consciously oppositional program of theoretical and empirical investigation. Today, an idea that first took institutional shape as an annex of Birmingham University's English department has developed to fill out the entire repertoire of academic activity: specialized degree and graduate programs; a new generation of teachers who, unlike their improvising mentors, are graduates trained in the discipline; professional associations, high-profile conferences, networks that cross continents. Corporate publishers devote whole catalogues to the written output of cultural studies, which by now includes not only the prolific research in the field, but also histories of the discipline itself, bulky course readers, and not a few bluffer's guides. At the same time as building its own impressive organization, cultural studies proposes, with increasing success, to remodel teaching and research in other areas of the academy, notably those of literary studies, history, sociology, and women's studies. The radical minority intervention of thirty years ago is now increasingly widely relayed as a new general formula for work across the entire range of what, for convenience, we may call the human sciences.

The feeling of incongruity—or of simple unreality—that this development must induce in a lucid observer is sharpened by the reflection that it has come about in historical conditions that, on the face of things, should have tended to frustrate it. The years in which cultural studies—a self-defined project of radical innovation and reconstruction—has flourished have been ones of severe financial austerity for the academic institutions that house the subject (especially but not only in Britain) and of setback and disorientation for the radical movements that have been its inspiration. The cultural studies boom is an impressive reality, but no one should rush to celebrate it as a simple tale of progress. While acknowledging, as is proper, the individual and collective achievements that cultural studies has made possible, we should pause for some necessary critical reflection on the general logic of the project as a mode of cultural analysis, and on what is called cultural politics.

I attempt this here in the form of five brief notes, beginning with a definition of cultural studies as a distinctive trend in cultural analysis, going on to dwell on some paradoxes of life and thought in the discipline, and closing with some general critical remarks on the relationship that is at stake in it, namely that between culture and politics.

1

The classic definition of what came to be cultural studies was proposed by Raymond Williams: it would investigate the creation of meaning in and as a formative part of "a whole way of life," the whole world of sense-making (descriptions, explanations, interpretations, valuations of all kinds) in societies understood as historical material human organizations. In the first place, then, cultural studies called for a drastic *expansion* of the field of analysis, beyond the boundaries maintained by the literary criticism from which it emerged: *all* social meanings are eligible for scrutiny. However, this does not suffice to define it. The older tradition of cultural criticism (or *kulturkritik,* the standard German term which I prefer to use here, in roman type from now on, on the grounds that the familiar English words are too familiar to hold the strict definition my argument calls for) gave special importance to the study of everyday meaning. Writers in this tradition, like the literary critics F.R. and Q.D. Leavis in England, or the philosopher José Ortega y Gasset in Spain, or the younger Thomas Mann in Germany, responded passionately to the new "mass" culture of democracy and commercialized literacy, but always in a spirit of high-minded, traditionalist revulsion. Unlike them, cultural studies proposes a *procedural equalization* of its data: in other words, while poetry and popcorn advertisements may not be of equal value in any plausible moral terms, both are potentially interesting as carriers of social meanings and in that precise sense should be approached with equal analytic seriousness. However, this distinction, like the first, is insufficient to characterize cultural studies, which is not merely a style of anthropology, devoted to the study of society as a set of symbolic processes. There is a third specification, the crucial one. Cultural studies did not merely extend the range and social sensibility of *kulturkritik*; it set out to challenge the whole system of values that supported the older tradition, a whole system of cultural *authority,* and to explore, if not quite establish, the forms of an *alternative* authority. This is the sense in which cultural studies is defended as "intrinsically political."

2

This idea of an expanded, level field of study is a matter of principle rather than of actual practice. No one, no professional collective, can pretend to study "everything," and the notion of a truly indifferent selection of materials is self-contradictory. There are basic choices to make; and, for all the variety of its possible realizations and the diversity of institutional circumstance, cultural studies has seemed rather constant in its sense of priorities. Its main field of analysis has been the same range of social phenomena that so alarmed and repelled traditional *kulturkritik*: the "mass" cultural forms and practices of advanced capitalism—cinema, television, popular journalism, advertising, shopping. And its leading polemical theme, which flatly opposes the stock conviction of *kulturkritik*, has been that such culture is not a mere opiate, successfully designed to induce passivity in a homogenized mass, but on the contrary that popular participation in it is active, deliberate, selective, and even subversive.

These linked alterations of field and perspective are crucial for any socialist theory of culture. If the dogmatic propositions of *kulturkritik* were in fact valid—and some Marxists, most notably Herbert Marcuse, have veered close to that view—then the classical understanding of socialism as the self-emancipation of the working class would amount to little more than a sectarian piety. When Antonio Gramsci affirmed that all human beings are intellectuals, even though only some are assigned the social function and status of "intellectual," it was in just that classical spirit. However, the decisive aspect of Gramsci's formula is its twofold character: it asserts not only the material possibility of liberation but also the established fact of domination. The leading tendency in cultural studies has struck a different emphasis. Insofar as cultural studies neglects to integrate "high" cultural forms and practices into its field of analysis, it compromises its own theoretical ambition, which is to analyze "*whole* ways of life," or, in other, more pointed terms, the existing social relations of culture in their totality. And insofar as it insists, one-sidedly, on the active and critical element in popular cultural usages, it tends to overlook the overwhelming historical realities of inequality and subordination that condition them. These tendencies jointly work against the development of properly *critical* theory and analysis; claiming to supersede *kulturkritik*, they actually offer something more like a compensatory reaction to it.

A minority in cultural studies has stood out against these tendencies, but without much success. "Populism" is one charge laid against the majority inclination, and with good reason. But populism, in all its varieties, sees itself as oppositional; there is a still graver charge that might be laid here. Given that most metropolitan popular culture today takes the form of commodified recreation or aestheticized subsistence activity, all organized as a market in "lifestyles," the spontaneous bent of cultural studies is actually *conformist*—at its worst, the theoretical self-consciousness of satellite television and shopping malls.

3

This is a worst-case account, granted. Against it must be set the evidence of remarkable energy and talent, and a remarkable record of work. But it prompts further reflection on the meaning of the received conviction that cultural studies is necessarily on the left or, as we are repeatedly told, in a phrase that is both emphatic and apparently empty, "intrinsically political."

There is no doubt that cultural studies has attempted to further emancipatory social aims—socialist, feminist, antiracist, anti-imperialist. Its intervention has been in those substantial, specified senses political. But it is romantic to go on thinking of cultural studies as an "intervention." It is now an instituted academic activity; and academic activity, whatever its intrinsic merits, is inevitably not the same thing as a political project. What happens when an oppositional tendency becomes a budget-holding discipline, offering credentials, careers, and research funds? More or less what any realistic observer would expect. No academic discipline may honorably or realistically apply political tests to its students and teachers. The day cannot be far off—indeed, it has probably arrived already—when the first real professionals of the discipline, trained in it and now pursuing it as a scholarly career, take their places in classrooms to give the introductory lecture on "subversion" or some other such routine syllabus heading. This is not just a sour hypothesis—if we seek a precedent, we need only recall the case of F.R. Leavis and his circle, whose militant, truculently anti-academic style of literary criticism was widely copied, becoming in the end quite conventional but retaining its oppositional mannerisms. It is useless to moralize; but leftist practitioners in cultural studies have need of far greater ironic self-consciousness than their new "political" discipline seems inclined to encourage.

4

This recall of Leavis prompts further thought about the relationship between *kulturkritik* and cultural studies—and this time in the dimension where they appear most deeply opposed, that of politics.

For all its differing national and disciplinary colorations, *kulturkritik* was a stable intellectual phenomenon. Its exponents normally claimed to speak from an authoritative center of values, which might be characterized as "human" or "universal" or "traditional," and for which the most favored summarizing term was *culture*. Their self-defined task was to defend the interests of culture in this sense against the advancing threats of modernity, which might be epitomized in intellectual specialization or industrial technology or commercialism or "the masses," and for which the classic summarizing term was *civilization*. *kulturkritik* was invariably elitist: it was an indisputable truth that culture must always be a minority affair, to be sustained in the face of general indifference and incomprehension. The particular political options of its advocates were variable, from right to left, but in all cases they were secondary, for the inborn desire of *kulturkritik* was to assert a kind of social authority that would transcend the "merely" political. In effect, the key distinction between culture, the realm of essential values, and civilization, the realm of social "machinery," made it impossible to conceive of politics as a meaningful social activity at all.

Cultural studies has striven to overthrow *kulturkritik*. It has proposed an alternative understanding of "civilization" and "the masses," discovering activity, choice, and significance where *kulturkritik* could see only stupefaction and automatism, and it has done so in the name of radical social goals. Yet there is something curious here. Cultural studies, of course, has repeatedly challenged liberal and conservative thinking, but it has, if anything, been more preoccupied with what it perceives as the shortcomings of the left. Now it is true that there are many to perceive, but cultural studies has focused on one above all others: its persistent suggestion—the signature-tune of the discipline in effect—is that the analysis of popular culture does not merely enhance political understanding, but in some sense invalidates and supersedes the inherited political traditions of the left. In other words, cultural studies seeks to subordinate the merely political (the old concepts "class," "state," "struggle," "revolution," and the like) to the higher authority of popular culture. And in doing this, it faithfully repeats the basic pattern of *kulturkritik*. It does indeed negate *kulturkritik*, but only as a mirror-image reverses its original, preserving the form intact. Here if anywhere lies the source of the paradoxes that make up the life of the interventionist discipline called cultural studies.

5

How, then, may we try to think through the relationship between cultural theory and politics? I have claimed that cultural studies reiterates a specific, strong understanding of the relationship, and, by implication, that this understanding is false, and liable to compromise the sincere political intentions of the left in the discipline. By way of conclusion, I would like to venture an alternative way of thinking about the "political" status of socialist cultural theory.

The relationship between culture and politics has been subject to two kinds of reductionism on the left. We can, without regret, discard one major option: the familiar political reductionism, for which the communist movement became notorious, which categorizes all cultural initiative in the terms of an already given programmatic scheme, and whose sense of human possibilities begins and ends with the political bottom line. But we now have an alternative reductionism, this time of a culturalist variety, promoted in the academy under the leadership of cultural studies and in the wider world as postmodern wisdom. This reductionism honors all manifestations of cultural difference as political, so encouraging particularism and a narcissistic dissolution of politics in the necessary stricter sense. If the first acknowledged culture only as a political instrument, the second has effectively dissolved the very possibility of politics, and indeed, I would argue, the possibility of culture itself as a field of political struggle.

A socialist cultural theory must recognize both the possibilities and the limitations of cultural practices. It must be able to acknowledge that such practices are both more and less than politics. Though culture is a contested terrain, a space for political struggle, it cannot be only a political theater; nor can it wholly encompass the political. The first principle of a socialist theory of culture would say that the typical state of the politics-culture relationship is *discrepancy*. This may not seem a very glamorous proposition, but it must be emphasized once we expand the field of "culture" to include the totality of social meanings or "a whole way of life." For while this expanded understanding may be vital for socialist cultural theory, it also creates its own conceptual problems.

If culture is the totality of social meanings, and if political activity is aimed at the totality of social relations within a given space (as a truly emancipatory politics must surely be), it may look at first as if culture and politics really are the same thing, as cultural studies is now prone to assume. We cannot say, in principle, that one kind of social content is political and another not; if culture covers the whole society, it seems that any cultural tendency can legitimately call itself "political."

But there is a fundamental misconception here. Both culture and politics can be understood as encompassing the totality of social relations, but they do so in distinctive ways. Politics differs from other social practices by virtue of its role in *determining* the character of social relations. Even when it operates entirely in the zone of meaning—as word and image, say—political practice is regulated by its specialized function. It is a *deliberative* practice, normally oriented to decisions; the controlling question is always, What is to be *done?* In peaceful democratic conditions, it is an *injunctive* practice, a struggle for effective consent. And in the last resort, it turns to resources that cannot be reduced to culture: the means of physical coercion.

Cultural practices, which we may understand rather less abstractly as those whose *principal* function is to produce meanings, are not of this kind. They share the same world of meaning; they are rich in political suggestion; but they lack, have no need of, those specialized characteristics: it is not the function of culture to determine the nature of social relations by means of deliberation, injunction, and coercion. The implications of this distinction were perceived by Gramsci: cultural judgment and political judgment are by nature distinct and, moreover, tend *not* to coincide.

Cultural practices may treat any and all differences as absolute (as Georg Lukács once remarked, there are no united fronts in the realm of art and ideas). Politics, in seeking to bring about or to forestall some particular state of affairs, to secure this or that general condition of existence, cannot treat difference in the same way. It must be able to bridge the kinds of difference that cultural practices may regard as absolute, to create solidarities in pursuit of specific ends. At the same time, and for the same reason, political interests may make it necessary to promote division within what looks like a field of cultural affinity. For instance, to achieve a political goal (state-funded nursery provision, for instance), it may be necessary to draw out class and sex-gender antagonisms within a community of religious belief. Viewed in the perspective of any given cultural interest, a political demand is always either too much or too little; and the political complaint against culture is always of the same kind. Each, with regard to the other, is *both* sectarian *and* ecumenical.

This is the fundamental distinction that cultural studies elides. There is no space here to explore the historical reasons for this, but something can be said about its consequences. From the beginning, cultural studies has tended to dissolve politics into culture. Even Raymond Williams, who remained politically engaged and active outside the field of culture proper, in retrospect conceded that he had inflated the possibilities of cultural politics, and never quite escaped that tendency in his theoretical work. Yet he and other early practitioners of socialist cultural studies did at least two important things: first, while refusing the reduction of culture to political instrumentality in the Stalinist manner, they acknowledged its importance as a terrain of struggle, especially in the era of consumer capitalism and "mass" media. Second, they insisted on the legitimacy of "popular" culture, against the elitist tendency to dismiss it as so much narcotic mystification. Popular culture in capitalist society never existed outside relations of domination, or beyond the imperatives of commodification; yet within those relations and imperatives, "the masses" were never only passive and subordinate. Popular culture was marked by both subordination and resistance.

Cultural studies today is not only furthering the dissolution of politics into culture but in the process is also squandering the legacy of its pioneers. It leaves no room for politics beyond cultural practice, or for political solidarities beyond the particularisms of cultural difference. Indeed, there is hardly room even for a politics of cultural contestation. There is no space, and in fact no need, for struggle if all popular culture, abstracted from "high" culture and from the historical realities of inequality and domination, is already active and critical, if television and shopping are already theaters of subversion. But if nothing lies beyond these cultural manifestations, then the subordination of "the masses," their submission to consumer capitalism, must be as thorough as the exponents of *kulturkritik* assumed it was. Here is the deepest paradox of cultural studies: that it ends by confirming and even celebrating this antidemocratic judgment.

Culture, nationalism, and the role of intellectuals

AIJAZ AHMAD

An interview conducted by Slovenian journalists Erika Repovz and Nikolai Jeffs, edited for this volume by Ellen Meiksins Wood.

Q: Cultural studies are currently in vogue in the Atlantic academy. Although many academics would claim that their cultural criticism is itself profoundly subversive, they regard as "vulgar" any cultural work that connects theory to political commitment outside the academy. So, for example, two of the most frequently cited precursors of cultural studies—Antonio Gramsci and Raymond Williams—are turned simply into cultural thinkers, though both were politically active intellectuals. How would you respond to this conception of cultural studies?

Ahmad: My own writings, actually even my prose style, should be testimony enough that I have no use for Stalinist kinds of distortions and simplifications of Marxism often called "vulgar." But that really is not what is at stake in today's culturalist charges of "vulgarity." Such charges are available, I think, against anyone who makes a direct and consistent connection between culture and class; between social oppression and economic exploitation; between cultural work in the academic institution and political accountability outside the institution; between a critique of capitalist culture and a commitment to socialist transformation in the sense of a revolutionary politics of the working classes. The avant-gardist consensus which dismisses all such work as "vulgar" became dominant in France after the defeat of 1968, the Gaullist restoration, the modernization of French capitalism during the 1970s, the continuation of all that in the time of Mitterrand. In the United States, such distancing of cultural studies from revolutionary Marxism and even labor traditions came in the last two decades, partly out of earlier and very powerful traditions of anticommunism, partly out of the importation of Parisian fashions, partly out of the decline of the 1960s left in the next decade. The bizarre acceptance of 1989 as a year of democratic revolution and liberation then authorized everyone to dismiss as "vulgar" everything that even spoke of the implacable reality of class conflict.

In this atmosphere, it is only natural that Gramsci's thought would be stripped of its revolutionary charge and that he would be presented in the United States as a cultural critic on the model of Matthew Arnold and Julien Benda. Edward Said goes so far as to trace a line of straight descent from Croce to Gramsci, which is like saying that Marx presents not a critique but a continuation of Hegel. And, mind you, *Croce!!!*—the Croce who campaigned actively for the fascists in the elections of 1924, the very elections that sealed Gramsci's fate forever. No one wants to say that Gramsci's thinking on "culture" simply cannot be separated from the fact that he was at the nerve-center of the largest proletarian uprising that Europe witnessed in the aftermath of the First World War or that it is not the category of "culture" but the issue of the strategic dilemmas of the Italian Communist movement that gives to the architecture of the *Prison Notebooks* its essential unity. If you were to say that there is some connection between celebrating Gramsci in glossy, avant-gardist journals and eliding the question of the central political commitment of his life, you would be called "vulgar," "moralistic," etc.

The case of Raymond Williams is not entirely comparable with that of Gramsci, but there is one thing about cultural studies that I find very striking. In England, the beginnings of cultural studies were inseparable from working class aspirations and, more generally, they were concerned with the way the disprivileged of society—the elderly poor, the women who gave their lives to domestic labor and low-wage work, the proletarian men, the children who can't even dream of private schools—get caught between pressures of upper class culture and the cultural worth of their own lives. The way Williams initially conceived of his project had a lot to do with his work in adult education and with his involvement in the socialist and peace movements. The Birmingham people (the Center for Contemporary Cultural Studies) initially came out of that sort of thinking, and it was only later that quite a few of them got sucked into the storm of French poststructuralism as it swept the British Isles. Much work that is now done in British cultural studies strikes me as being distributed between those earlier kinds of commitments and the later kinds of obscurity.

By the time cultural studies arrived in the United States, only a shadow of those origins remained, and that in the work of very few. The remarkable development there was that it came not out of the pressures from below but mostly from very established people. Black literature, for example, had become a serious academic discipline in the United States in the aftermath of the rebellions triggered off by the civil rights movement and black cultural nationalism. Cultural studies, by contrast, arrived as a cosmopolitan, continental pedagogy and style. In this situation, Williams was invoked often but very selectively. Of late, in fact, Williams has become an object of all sorts of derision.

Q: Much of your own cultural work has to do with literature and other cultural artifacts from what is typically called the third world. Yet you have expressed doubts both about the very idea of "third world culture" and about the subversive power of so-called third world cultural artifacts assimilated and naturalized by Western ideology. Why?

Ahmad: I don't quite accept the premise of your question. For one thing, I have doubts about the very notion of "Western ideology" no less than about the idea of third world culture. I don't actually think that there *is* such a thing as Western ideology. The so-called West, like the third world, is of course a very amorphous thing, but even individual nations cannot have just one ideology or a single culture. Each nation, I think, is comprised of clusters of ideological and cultural contestation. I have also said that countries of the third world have little direct access to each other's cultural productions. Indians, for example, don't import novels from Latin America. We read only those Latin American novels which get translated and published in English, in places like London and New York. In order to read such novels critically, an Indian would typically read the scholarship about Latin America that is produced in the same Atlantic zones. I don't mean that there is only *one* ideology that determines which Latin American novels will be translated or how they will be read. But I do mean that my knowledge of such novels is highly mediated, virtually determined by the complexes of knowledge assembled in Anglo-American universities and publishing houses.

As for the subversive power of such cultural artifacts, I don't at all believe that all, or even most, of the cultural artifacts that are assembled in the third world are necessarily subversive. Ask any woman, and she will tell you that a great many of such texts are quite normative and, in their own locales, profoundly conservative and anti-egalitarian. A novel by Tagore, for example, can be taught in the United States as coming from the third world, hence from the *margin* (as the newly fashionable term would have it), hence inherently subversive; inside India, however, Tagore is an immensely hegemonic figure and can hardly be treated as "subversive." On the other hand, yes, *some* cultural artifacts of the third world that arrive in the West do have subversive content which gets emptied out in the process of their assimilation into the pedagogical practices of the dominant culture. But this normalization takes place not because there is a Western ideology that normalizes third world texts in any special way (other than the usual play with exoticism), but because this academe seeks to domesticate *everything,* even Marx.

Q: Fredric Jameson has proposed an opposition between postmodernism and nationalism: postmodernism as the "cultural logic" of late capitalism in the first world; national allegory as the cultural logic of third world nationalist resistance. What are the implications of this opposition for cultural studies?

Ahmad: Frankly, I don't know. Some recent writings of Jameson that have come my way seem to suggest that he no longer holds that view, not at least in that binary way, and that he is now engaged in "mapping" the unfolding of postmodernist cultural logic on the global scale. Meanwhile, nationalism has fallen into terrible disrepute in the Anglo-American academe, but in such facile ways that I find myself in a very difficult situation. I have long been very suspicious of nationalism, because a great many nationalists strike me as at least very chauvinistic if not altogether fascistic. But a blanket contempt for all nationalisms tends to slide over the question of imperialism. I think that those who are fighting against imperialism cannot just forego their nationalism. They have to go through it, transform their nation-state in tangible ways, and then arrive at the other side. I might add here, as an aside, that the striking feature of all the nationalisms that have arisen in various regions of the former Yugoslavia is that they seem not to have an anti-imperialist content. Anticommunism is very useful in concealing this fact.

What does it all mean for cultural studies? I think that we have to break with the binary opposition you mentioned. We have to treat aesthetic postmodernism as a North American cultural style in the moment of its globalization, hence irretrievably linked to a certain hegemonic move which is imperialist at its very base. You may be able to use some of it for your own purposes, or you may not; but you should first know the nature of the beast. Nationalism, meanwhile, cannot be treated as simply the *other* of postmodernism. As I said, there are all kinds of nationalisms around, and a great many of them are a danger to human beings. Nor is it true that "nation" is the only way, the desirable way, in which we imagine our collectivity or that nationalism is what animates most oppositional cultural practices in the so-called third world. Before we affirm a particular nationalist cultural text, we should figure out what *kind* of nationalism it is affirming and what practices it is authorizing. In this sense, no privilege attaches to nationalism as a cultural form.

Beyond that, I think we have to return to the insistence that cultural studies is about how culture is lived materially by ordinary people in their specific circumstances—to the idea that culture is always specific, always constituted within fields of specific contention. We have to return, I think, to the idea of "common culture," in the sense of "the culture of the common people" and in the sense of making oppositional cultural practices that oppressed people across national boundaries may indeed come to have in common. And we have to return to the idea that the object of cultural studies should be not culture simply as "regimes of pleasure" (to use Foucault's phrase) but culture as those systems of communication that produce determinate meanings that transform actual lives, for better or worse. Culture in that sense is deeply implicated in practices of domination, so that constituting a cultural practice of resistance is much more difficult than is generally recognized.

Q: You say you are suspicious of many nationalisms. In what political circumstances can nationalism be progressive and at what point does it turn into a fascism?

Ahmad: That again depends on the *kind* of nationalism one is talking about, and on the situation in which it arises. Historically, nationalism has often played a progressive role in opposition to colonial conquest, not because those who are conquered always already constitute a nation or because nations have some preordained right to exclusive sovereignty, but mainly because resistance to foreign occupation tends to politicize populations that have hitherto remained outside the domains of modern politics and inevitably raises the question of the rights of the peoples thus politicized. In that sense, there is something profoundly democratic about anticolonial nationalisms. Some of these nationalisms also play a progressive role when they help create solidarity across narrow exclusivities of tribal or ethnic or religious or linguistically defined communities among the people who thus get organized into a modern nation.

You can probably see that I greatly favor the principle of multilingual, multidenominational, multiracial political solidarities, regardless of what happened in the former Yugoslavia or the Soviet Union. And I am deeply opposed to the quests for purified and homogeneous nations. I have come to this view certainly by *thinking* a great deal about nationalism, but the fact of *living* in India is probably a very large element in determining my outlook. Progressive people in India cherish the fact that we have a great many languages, religious denominations, literatures, traditions of music and dance, a great many distinct cultural traditions within a single polity. In a place like Slovenia, where you have just acquired a very compact nationhood, it may be difficult for you to even imagine that people like me are not much bothered by the fact that so many different languages are spoken in the country that none of us can even theoretically entertain the possibility of being able to speak directly to all the rest of our fellow Indians. There is something very comforting and deeply humane about a nation so very heterogeneous.

The difficulty of course is that the logic of most nationalisms goes not toward cultural diversity, inclusiveness, and heterogeneity but toward exclusivity, purification, or at least majoritarianism. It is in this other slant, so common in our time, that nationalism tends to become a close cousin of racism. The *dream* of socialism—what you might call the *utopian surplus* of socialism—was that we would move toward a human civilization that was at once egalitarian and universal, and one that would at once affirm the *right* of nations to self-determination but would also materially create multinational societies in which none would have any special privilege. We of course know the degradations that occurred in societies that had arisen initially out of that promise, but two things I think need to be kept in mind. One is that the record of capitalist societies is worse, whether we speak of the history of fascism in Europe or of racism in the United States. But, then, socialism at least *desires* civilizations of universal and multinational equality, whereas the market does not aim to create such civilizations even theoretically. My sense is that so many nationalisms of our time have become so revanchist and aggressive, even fascistic, precisely to the extent that the dream of an egalitarian, multicultural, universal civilization has been renounced.

As for the tie between nationalism and fascism, I think that all fascisms are built around a core ideology of ultranationalism but not all nationalisms necessarily tend toward fascism. I want to retain here the idea that nationalism has no essence of its own that determines its trajectory but that an essence is *given* to it, in particular situations, by the power bloc that takes hold of it. Which also means that to the extent that progressive forces of socialist democracy are defeated or otherwise decline, to that same extent nationalisms are likely to become retrogressive and fascistic. I have been writing a great deal on this very problem of fascism in our time and can't go into details here. Let me simply make the observation that fascisms are of course arising in a great many places in the world today, but the danger of resurgent fascisms is particularly great in countries where great antifascist struggles were waged in the course of the Second World War. It seems that those old scores are to be settled yet again. In large parts of the former Yugoslavia, fascism seems bent on reversing the verdict of half a century ago.

Q: What, then, about the relation between national culture and "world culture"? For example, if there is a "world literature" as Goethe or Marx understood it, can it be anything but the product of Western cultural domination? Is there any alternative to this (pseudo) world literature apart from national literatures and cultural nationalisms arising from them?

Ahmad: Contrary to prevailing fashions, I am a shameless advocate of the idea of universality. This is so despite the fact that colonialism has been intrinsic to the kind of universality that we have had so far and that the only universal civilization that exists today is the capitalist civilization. I think that human beings are perfectly capable of waking up to the barbarities of this civilization and making a far better universality—for which my word continues to be "socialism," but you are welcome to use some other word so long as you mean the same thing. As an idea, universality cannot be given up, because particular rights exist only to the extent that universal rights exist. No struggle against racism or any other kind of collective oppression is possible without some conception of universality. U.S. blacks want to have what I call a universal civilization, which would be blind to skin color and would correct the wrongs of the past. The fact that men have historically had infinitely more rights than women does not turn us against the concept of rights. The women's struggles which address the issue of structured oppression of women across national, religious, and ethnic boundaries, and which demand equal rights for women and men, are deeply universalist in their aspiration. Anti-imperialism itself will be merely xenophobic if it breaks with the idea of universality.

Within this perspective, then, I cannot give up the idea of an international art and a world literature, regardless of what you call "Western cultural domination." I actually don't think that the domination is Western, and I personally have no difficulty with learning a thing or two from someone French or British or even North American. The problem is imperialism. What you call Western domination is actually a capitalist universalization, in which the dominant ideologies and cultural artifacts are produced in the core countries and either exported to or copied in the rest of the world. Even at its best, nationalism alone cannot be the answer because capital can and does break down all national boundaries, especially in its cultural forms, and because most kinds of nationalism can easily accommodate themselves to this capitalist universalization. With the latest stage in telecommunications, North American cultural goods are arriving in homes around the globe, via satellites and TV antennae and information highways, bypassing the educational and cultural grids of nation-states. In the face of this capitalist universality, which is accepted by all the bourgeoisies of the world, no one is allowed simply to recoil into the folds of some pure national culture. You either build an anticapitalist—that is to say socialist—universality or you accept capitalist universality. For persevering individuals, of course, a great many exceptional practices are possible, but there is no third choice that people today can make in their collectivity.

The same applies to the matter of world literature and national literature. Historically, the idea of national literatures arose in Europe in tandem with the rise of the nation-state as such. This same idea has been generalized in the third world in the course of the rise of cultural nationalism in response to cultural imperialism, and then as one of the cultural modes through which the national-bourgeois state naturalizes itself. One need not subscribe to the idea, and certainly not to the procedures, of canonization that were first invented in Europe and through which national literatures are usually assembled. But the process is a real one, *both* as bourgeois project and as national assertion against imperialist hegemonies. I would say here what I was saying earlier about nationalism itself—that you can't bypass it, you have to go *through* it, find your way to the other side of it.

In this circumstance, both these categories, world literature and national literature, have their uses. Peoples of the third world need to know their regional literatures and their national literatures as a part of their own histories; and world literature is especially a useful category for curriculums in the advanced capitalist countries as an antidote against their own xenophobias. More generally, it is always a good thing to know more than your national cultures and literatures. However, at any given site of production and dissemination, world literature will always reflect the inequalities of the imperialist system so long as this system lasts.

One problem is how this world literature is to be actually taught and read. The idea of world literature in the traditional sense, à la Goethe, remains deeply canonical, even Arnoldian: all the best that has been thought and written is now to be culled not from this or that nation but from the world. If you think about it, this way of reading "great books" produced in the various continents in the world, assembled in a canonizing way, is perfectly reconcilable with the intensified integration of the upper classes of the world into something resembling a world bourgeoisie. It is very easy for world literature to represent this global integration and arrive at an easy, even very glossy capitalist universalization. In this area, we have to question the very idea of literature and we have to be very suspicious of all texts, certainly including the ones that arrive from the third world, insofar as they display the slightest potential for canonicity. We have to begin, in fact, with a great suspicion of the very fact that the category of world literature as a pedagogical object is arising in the core capitalist countries, whereas the poorer countries have no means of their own to constitute such objects.

But then there is also the problem of the levels of competence. In the colleges and universities of North America, for example, I have seen variations of world literature giving rise to a great deal of well-intentioned charlatanism. I personally know several people whose knowledge of South Asia was at best lamentable but who felt perfectly authorized to teach graduate courses filled with novels about South Asia, in universities where teachers with comparable levels of ignorance about North American social history would never be allowed to teach Melville or Henry James. There is an unthought presumption here that you are dealing with cultural artifacts of lesser density and therefore don't really need much expertise to explicate them, or that your good intentions are enough to make up for your ignorance. My fear, in other words, is that the idea of world literature is being pursued in this context more as a moral imperative and that the imperative is *lived,* more often than not, in a very facile manner. I don't mean that people who teach their national literatures—the teachers of Melville or James, let us say—are all erudite and enlightened people. But, generally speaking, certain norms of informed reading have been established. So far, we lack such norms with respect to world literature.

In short, then, world literature remains the horizon of universalist desire. But the ground reality is that there really is no alternative to picking up small chunks and doing them well, whatever those chunks get called. A good bit of what gets called "theory" in North American literary circles seems to have done much to promote not rigor in these matters but precisely the charlatanism I was talking about.

Q: It seems to us that academics in the United States and Britain are socially and politically isolated. For instance, there is no tradition of political relationships (as in France, where whole generations were involved in relations with the French Communist Party [PCF]). In Britain, those relations that have existed (the historians' group—Christopher Hill or E.P. Thompson within the Communist Party of Great Britain [CPGB]) have not been able to attract wider political affirmation despite the immense influence of their academic work. Do you think that this social isolation will become a permanent feature of Atlantic academic life? Will some kind of fruitful relation between theory and practice remain only in particular interest or "identity" groups, like blacks and gays, or will even these groups suffer detachment, as may already have happened with feminism?

Ahmad: The role that intellectuals come to play, from one country to the next, from one generation to the next, is a very intricate matter. It certainly involves the question of the agency and responsibility of particular individuals, especially since a place in academe actually gives to the intellectuals very considerable room to exercise their agency in society at large. But it is also a matter of how a given political field is constituted in a given place, at a given time. The United States has not had a powerful labor movement since the 1930s. In this situation, it becomes much easier for radical academics to believe that they are accountable to none outside academe. They can now blame the working class for its failures and need not take into account their own contribution to that failure. After all, working class movements have always relied on key support from intellectuals, and intellectuals, I think, need to be quite aware of what they have or have not done in solidarity with those who rely on them and who do not command similar resources of intellectual culture. Do you know that devastating poem by Brecht on the repressions in East Germany in 1953, where he ironically says that when a people loses the confidence of its leaders, those leaders have the right to elect another people? Many U.S. radicals sometimes strike me as looking for another people they might thus elect. But the detachment from mass politics that you speak of is true only at present, and especially among literary/cultural critics. It goes to the everlasting credit of the United States' 1968 that it organized history's largest peace movement that any country has ever witnessed against a war that its own government was waging. People from a wide spectrum of the U.S. left played the key role in organizing that movement, and it is a ghost that still haunts North America. U.S. radicals today are politically very isolated and careerism is quite rampant, but the very many who are doing very honest, very good work are doing so because they wish to hon that legacy. One of the most inspiring of them is of course Noam Chomsky, whose activism spans this whole phase since the mid-1960s; but there are also many, many others, less famous or not well known at all. They deserve our admiration because, as Che once famously put it, they are the ones living in the belly of the beast. That, you know, is not the best of habitats.

In Britain, the tradition of directly involved intellectuals is comparatively wider and more consistent, but this too is so because Britain has had a much more powerful tradition of working class politics. This has given many British intellectuals comparatively more solid anchorage, even though the Labourist stranglehold on the working class has been devastating, and a great many of those intellectuals have had to live very difficult public lives, terribly pressed by Stalinism on one side and Labourism on the other. A great many of them had to pay a very heavy price for it—and that includes those who left the CPGB as well as the ones who stayed. I would actually include Williams among those who paid that price; it shows even in the strain of his prose.

By contrast, you have cited the case of France and I would add the adjacent example of Italy. In both cases, Communist parties emerged out of the antifascist struggles as huge mass organizations with immense reserves of hegemony. It is difficult to remember now that in 1946 the PCF was the largest political party in France. It had already played a tremendous anti-fascist role in the 1930s, then in the resistance during the war. Wedged into all this was the issue of women's rights. French women gained the vote in 1944, on the morrow of liberation, and a host of patriarchal laws came crumbling down soon thereafter. Against all this was the right, which had never accepted 1789, which never really believed in the Republic, which welcomed U.S. dominance as it came with the Marshall Plan and the cold war, and which hated such books as Simone de Beauvoir's *Second Sex* when it appeared in 1949. Two generations of French intellectuals were responding to such facts, from inside the PCF and from the outside. But then, after the defeat of 1968, that particular relation between public intellectuals and mass working class politics has declined sharply in France as well.

What I am suggesting is that the role that intellectuals play has much to do with the practical choices they make for themselves, but we should remember also that intellectuals are also caught, individually and collectively, in movements of history much larger than themselves.

But then you have asked me also about future prospects for radical intellectuals in the United States, and you have said some provocative things about interest and identity groups, giving the example of blacks and gays and in a way feminism. Let me remark on the examples first. That everyone should have equal rights of course goes without saying. But there are also a number of ambiguities in relation to the political field. The gay rights movement, for example, cuts across the distinction between civil society and the state, the so-called private and the public. There are certain rectifications that only the state can undertake, and there is nothing structural about the U.S. state that prevents those rectifications. I don't at all wish to minimize the extent of prejudice against homosexuality when I say that in the political field, properly so called, there is really nothing that prevents the U.S. state from absorbing the pressures of the gay rights movements within its authorized ideologies of pragmatism and pluralism.

In that sense, the situation of women and blacks is quite different. Of course there are enormous prejudices against women and blacks, and of course these social prejudices are fully reflected in the behavior of the state. But I have something else in mind. The majority of blacks constitute a distinct underclass in the U.S. economy that has been reproduced over and over again since the time of slavery. The majority of women do the lowest paid work, in the United States and elsewhere; feminization of manual work in the core capitalist countries is part of the strategic offensive of capital against labor as such; and women's unpaid housework is a fundamental component in minimizing the aggregate wage bill, hence for ensuring a certain rate of profit. Despite all the celebrated successes of feminism in certain areas of academic and cultural life in the United States, there have been no gains in the incomes of poor women, not to speak of black youth. The issue of justice to that vast majority of women and blacks goes to the very heart of the *totality* of U.S. life and cannot be fully resolved without revolutionary transformations. Some white, upper-class feminisms may cultivate the detachment you mentioned, but most women can't afford that.

That every group has the right to fight for members of that group also goes without saying. But I want to raise a much more difficult question about democracy. A great problem for socialist theory and practice today is that of the relationship between difference and universality, group rights and indivisible universal rights, the right as woman and the right as citizen, and the right as worker, whether citizen or immigrant. The postmodernist answer is simple: universality is a chimera; identities are local, contingent, freely chosen; rights of identity are absolute, and self-representation is the only authentic form of representation. This absolutization of identity, this quick abrogation of universality, strikes me as politically very dangerous. For a start: if in the constitution of your identity, I have no rights of cognition, participation, criticism, then on what basis may you ask for my solidarity with you except on the basis of some piety, some voluntaristic good will that I may withdraw at any moment?

I can't explicate this problem here, so let me reduce the scope of what I'm saying. You see, at this historical juncture, when the issue of people's equal access to material goods has been posed by what I still call socialism, the capitalist state probably prefers to deal with a people that confronts it not in its unity but in its dispersal among communities and interest groups. Communities and interest groups typically raise the issue of social prejudice and *distribution* of the social surplus; the issue of the ownership of property as such can only be raised within the discourse of universal rights. Once we get distributed into distinct groups, our public rhetorics can then go on stressing how much we believe in everyone's equal rights, but in the actual dealings with the state each community and each interest group can become a distinct supplicant competing with all others for its own share of the social surplus. One way of putting this may be that the capitalist state can perhaps live more easily with multiple and competing claimants on the social surplus that it governs, making sure that they cancel out each other, than with a radicalized politics of universal rights where each is to be the equal of all others, not just juridically but in every conceivable dimension, most crucially the dimension of economic goods. What I am trying to say, I suppose, is that group egoism of discrete communities is perhaps not much of an improvement on the historical egoism of the bourgeois male individual, and that we need forms of politics that constitute human subjects both in their heterogeneity and their universality.

As for predicting the future—will group egoism of discrete identities now become the permanent characteristic of North American political life?—let me briefly say three things. One is that like much else that is North American, this North American mode of politics is itself getting globalized; indeed, some Italian Communists and socialist feminists were warning of this danger of the Americanization of European politics way back in the 1970s. The second thought that occurs to me, quite unconnected with the first, is that the experience of the past half century suggests that U.S. academic radicals respond much more to the global situation than to their own national situation. The upper layers of that intelligentsia performs, in other words, a cosmopolitan function much more readily than a national one. This of course corresponds to the fact that the United States is a very great global power despite its equally great national mediocrity. And it also reflects the very genuine dilemmas that come with the fact of being a citizen of the world's leading imperialist country; enormous energy goes into solidarity not with your fellow-citizens within the national confines but with your fellow-inhabitants of this globe in this U.S. century. In relation to the question you have asked, what all this means is that if there were to be an upsurge of mass movements elsewhere on the globe, this intellectual fraction in North America is likely to respond positively. You may call this a form of parasitism if you will, but even parasitisms of this kind have a very positive function in global politics. And we should all respect those who have given so much of their lives to international solidarities.

But the other thing I want to say is a bit more obscure. The difficulty with talking of the future is that in comparison with the very slow pace of historical change, spans of even the longest of individual lives are unfortunately very short. In my own lifetime, history has taken but three very short turns: the dissolution of most colonial rule as I was growing up, the seemingly revolutionary movements of "1968" in my youth, and the restorations of "1989" as I settle into middle age. I very much doubt that another historical turn of similar magnitude will come in my own lifetime. Given this painfully slow pace of historical change, it would be foolish of me to predict the future in the short run. This could also be said differently: since history moves so very slowly, it is inevitably the children who make history, not the parents.

Old positions/new necessities: history, class, and marxist metanarrative

BRYAN D. PALMER

What is history? Bunk, according to Henry Ford. A nightmare, thought Joyce. Falsehoods, snarled Nietzsche. The big hurt, replies Fredric Jameson. *Bo-r-ing,* say our children, who use the word *history* to convey what is dismissed, done with, and dead. Why defend this "thing" called history?

Much contemporary theory answers, often implicitly, but unmistakably, with the obvious injunction, "Don't!" Fashionable theory now posits an almost disembodied and fragmented contemporaneity as the site of history as *happening,* seemingly divorced from causality—a series of "perpetual presents." Interpretation appears to commence with labored efforts to liberate analysis from all forms of "*historical* thinking." A humble discipline, "dependent on the present, without any integrity of its own," history is poststructuralism's final social construction, always the product of subjectivity's moment.[1]

On one level this is not particularly new. But postmodernists/poststructuralists have wrapped their antagonism to history in a series of intellectually seductive tautologies which beg the fundamental questions of the historical process. Central to this outlook is a refusal of post-Enlightenment systems of rational thought, which are reduced to a form—narration—and a substance—accommodation of bourgeois rule—that relegates such "knowledge" to complicity with various oppressions.[2]

It is as though poststructuralism, in an immense social *reconstruction* of the deep historical past, would like to see the entire eighteenth-century Age of Revolution, which was, to be sure, a *bourgeois* project, jettisoned. In some staggering leap of idealism, it seeks to pole-vault over the class contents and transformations of thought associated with 1776, 1789, 1792, *and* the Industrial Revolution, leapfrogging the nineteenth century, the experience of colonial revolt, and the first workers' state (1917). Yet all of these occurred as historical process and have rich narrative structures of meaning in the politics and culture of modern times, from Blake and Beethoven to Marx and Munch to Veblen and Van Gogh. However incomplete the Enlightenment project, compromised as it was in its origins in the bourgeois proclamation of egalitarianism as a property-based legal right rather than a social condition of fulfillment, it was a revolutionary transcendence of the feudal order, which had been confined for centuries in caste-like conceptions of social station and the incarcerating thought of superstition, divinity, and absolutism.

It was the purpose of Marxism, as the maturing worldview of the emerging proletariat, to materialize and radicalize Enlightenment rationality, extending its potential not just to this or that privileged sector of society, but to all of humanity. Just as Mary Wollstonecraft took the possibilities inherent in the Enlightenment's Pandora's box of equality and extended her defense of the French Revolution and Thomas Paine's *Rights of Man* to a feminist articulation of the rights of woman, reaching well past patriarchy's powerful presence in bourgeois thought and practice, so too did Marx build on Enlightenment idealism to construct its oppositional challenge, historical materialism. Poststructuralism allows no such reading of distinctions and developments within Enlightenment thought, condemning all post-Enlightenment modes of discourse as hopelessly compromised with the project of subordination.

Particularly suspect in current theory is the Enlightenment "metanarrative," with its "explicit appeal to some grand narrative, such as the dialectics of Spirit, the hermeneutics of meaning, the emancipation of the rational or working subject, or the creation of wealth."[3] This obsolete discourse, a supposed product of the modernist crisis of metaphysical philosophy, merely masks the disintegrations of such narratives, and their dispersal into the unstable clouds of postmodernity's lofty discursiveness.[4] Postmodernists/poststructuralists thus disavow, in their formalist and ultimatist rejections, divergences of considerable, oppositional importance. They throw out Kant and Hegel as well as Marx, all of whom rely on metanarratives of one sort or another, little consideration being given to the fundamental differences separating such systems of thought. All states are simply states, and hence oppressive, an anarchist might argue (Down with the Bolsheviks!); all wars are to be condemned, asserts the pacifist (We take no sides in Vietnam!); all metanarratives are suspect and compromised, there being no master categories of explanatory authority, proclaims the poststructuralist (Away with all interpretive pests!).

In the comment that follows I concentrate on the Marxist "metanarrative," an unfulfilled project of radicalizing Enlightenment rationality that much contemporary theory refuses in its repudiation of historical materialism. Marxist metanarrative is rejected, ironically, at precisely the historical moment that it is critically necessary, its insistence on reading history in *class* terms, as a succession of identifiable structures and agencies propelled by material interests, being fundamental to the interpretation of the movement from past to present, especially in the context of contemporary life, where humanity is more and more connected in the global dimensions of exploitation and oppression.[5]

It is worth reiterating the obvious, since the obvious is precisely what poststructuralism/postmodernism often obfuscates, or even denies. Marxist and historical materialist criticism of contemporary theory and its insistence on the politics and historically central practices of class do not rest only on a series of denials. The significance of the knowledge/power coupling, for instance, which is associated with Foucault, is hardly alien to the Marxist method. Marxism has always been attentive to the relationship of ideas, dominance, and social transformation. Representation, imagery, discourses, and texts can hardly be said to be understated in the theory and practice of historical materialism, which has consistently grappled, sometimes for better, sometimes for worse, with the *problematized* meaning of the base-superstructure metaphor, most evident in the rich body of writing associated with British Marxist historians such as Christopher Hill, Edward Thompson, Rodney Hilton, and V.G. Kiernan, and the tradition of historicized literary criticism associated with Raymond Williams and Terry Eagleton.[6] Finally, to claim that Marxism is a metanarrative of explanatory importance, resting unambiguously on the causality of productive forces and the determinative boundaries set by fundamentally economic relations, such as class, does not necessitate refusing the significance of other points of self-identification, such as race and gender.

What separates Marxism's metanarrative from postmodernist incredulity of all master categories is not, however, this or that particular. Rather, there is a critical parting of the analytic seas in the two traditions' approaches to historical context as a material force, within which all struggles for emancipation and all acts of subordination take place. Poststructuralism/postmodernism sees history as an authorial creation, a conjuring up of the past to serve the discursive content of the present. Thus the past can only be textually created out of the imperatives of the ongoing instance. In its insistence that history be contextualized in the material world of possibilities of the past, rather than cut adrift to float freely in the cross-currents of our own time, Marxism's metanarrative attempts to recreate the past by attending to its obscured social relations *and* situating those corners of suppressed history within the larger ensemble of possibilities that were something more than the ideological fiction of the established archival record, attentive as it generally is to the instinctual preservationism of power. Moreover, Marxism's metanarrative tries to be true—believing that such a process can be located, just as it can be obscured or distorted—to the actors of the past, whatever side of the class divide their feet touch down upon.

Thus, a major historiographical difference separates the essentially Marxist understanding of class formation, struggle, and consciousness evident in E.P. Thompson's *The Making of the English Working Class* (1963) and Gareth Stedman Jones's poststructurally inclined reading of Chartism in *The Languages of Class* (1983). Thompson, whose political practice and theory ran headlong into Stalinist *and* mainstream social democratic containments, explores the opaque nooks and crannies of English popular radicalism, uncovering an underground insurrectionary tradition that flew in the face of constituted authority in the opening decades of the nineteenth century, as well as standing in stark revolutionary contrast to the stolid constitutionalism of later generations of working-class reformers and their Fabian historians. This is a long way from Stedman Jones, whose politics of the 1980s had been formed within the conservatizing and hostile drift of the Labour Party away from the working class. He reads Chartism's successes against the politics of mass upheaval in the 1830s and 1840s, seeing in the movement's ideas and actions not the class mobilizations of the time but the hangover of an eighteenth-century politics that somehow distanced itself from the class actualities of the historical context. There is no doubt that Thompson's *Making* is driven by a commitment to the revolutionary aspirations of the working class, past and present, but that does not undermine his text's authority precisely because it is, for all of its dissident commitments, engaged with the complexities of the material world of the early nineteenth century. Stedman Jones, in contrast, searches for ways to distance himself from the specificities of Chartism's times. The supreme irony is that the "present" of Stedman Jones's text is nothing more than an ideological adaptation to Thatcher's Britain, a displacement of the past that paints a major history of working-class mobilization into a derivative corner of denigration and denial. Thompson's "present," in striking contrast, is a moment of revolution thwarted, a "heroic" challenge that, whatever its failures, remains significant to both the history of the working class and the class content of contemporary left politics.[7]

It is when postmodernist/poststructuralist readings of history are scrutinized to see *how* metanarrative is suppressed, resulting inevitably in a particular structuring of past, present, and future, that the costs and content of abandoning metanarrative are most evident. When the French Revolution is interpreted, not as a contest between aristocracy and bourgeoisie, mediated by the involvement of the *sans-culottes,* but as the unfolding symbolic will of a population galvanized as much by imagery as political principle, the condescending *class* dismissiveness of contemporary historiographic fashion is strikingly evident.[8] An ironic consequence of postcolonial deconstructive writing, with its understandable refusal of the Orientalist metanarrative, and its unfortunate textualization of imperialist plunder and indigenous resistance, is the further silencing of those marginalized "others," whose differences are celebrated, but whose umbilical link to *class* formation on a global sale is twisted in the obscured isolations of cultures and countries.[9] In the words of David Harvey:

> Postmodernism has us accepting the reifications and partitionings, actually celebrating the activity of masking and cover-up, all the fetishisms of locality, place, or social grouping, while denying the kind of meta-theory which can grasp the political-economic processes (money flows, international divisions of labour, financial markets, and the like) that are becoming ever more universalizing in their depth, intensity and reach over daily life.[10]

Postmodernistic antagonism to metanarrative thus carries with it a particular price tag, one in which the significance of class is almost universally marked down.

That this process is embedded less in theory and more in the material politics of the late twentieth century, with their "retreat from class,"[11] a withdrawal hastened by new offensives on the part of capital and the state, and conditioned by "actually existing socialism's" Stalinist deformations and ultimate collapse, is evident in one historian's confident statement. Patrick Joyce claims that British history, once explained in terms of class struggle, must now be regarded differently:

> There is a powerful sense in which class may be said to have "fallen." Instead of being a master category of historical explanation, it has become one term among many, sharing rough equality with these others (which is what I meant by the "fall" of class). The reasons for this are not hard to

> find. In Britain, economic decline and restructuring have led to the disintegration of the old manual sector of employment, and of what was, mistakenly, seen to be a "traditional" working class. The rise of the right from the 1970s, and the decline of the left, together with that of the trade unions, pointed in a similar direction to that of economic change, towards a loosening of the hold class and work-based categories had, not only on the academic mind, but also on a wider public. Changes going on in Britain were mirrored elsewhere, but the greatest change of all was the disintegration of world communism, and with it the retreat of intellectual Marxism.[12]

To "deconstruct" such a statement is to expose the transparent crudeness of its content, which bears a disappointing likeness to *Time* magazine. Even if trends in the 1990s were unambiguously of the sort pointed to by Joyce, it is most emphatically *not* the case that the analytic meanings of this period of supposed change could be transferred wholesale to a past society quite unlike it—what possible relevance can the fall of a degenerated and deformed set of workers' *states* (the Soviet Union, Poland, Hungary, etc.) have on our exploration of the tangible class composition of *early nineteenth-century society?* Is it not rather unwholesome for supposed intellectuals to be bartering their interpretive integrity in the crass coin of political fashion, their supposedly pristine ideas dripping with the thoroughly partisan politics of a particular historical period?

Joyce's words, ironically, confirm rather than undermine historical materialism. As Joyce alludes to the "fall" of class as a product of global restructuring, trade union and left defeat, the implosion of the Soviet Union and Eastern Europe, and the rise of the right, what are we to see but the actual confirmation of "intellectual Marxism?" Did not Marx write that, "The ideas of the ruling class are in every epoch the ruling ideas," and suggest that at moments of "enthusiastic striving for innovation"—which is certainly a characteristic of the postmodern—such ideas might well result in a "more deeply rooted domination of the old routine?"[13] Historical materialism would suggest that there is a profound difference between the trajectory of political economy in one epoch, and its attendant ideologies, and the actual social relations of production and contestation in another historical period. Joyce collapses the two.

In doing so he does disservice, again, to both past and present. For while his simplified catalogue-like listing of the onward march of left defeat has some resonance in terms of contemporary political economic development,

Joyce conveniently understates the presence of other dimensions. His accounting is one-sided and distortingly one-dimensional.

Yes, to be sure, the Stalinist economies and their ruling castes have, outside of Cuba and (less so) China, taken a headlong plunge into the privatization despotisms of the 1990s, which Marxists from the Trotskyist tradition have been predicting since the publication of *The Revolution Betrayed* (1937). Against those who saw in the bureaucratic grip of Stalinism a fundamental, if flawed, blockade against the restoration of market relations, Trotsky wrote: "In reality a backslide to capitalism is wholly possible."[14] Class *politics* were dealt a severe blow in the capitalist counterrevolutions and Stalinist implosions of the post-1989 years. Nevertheless, there is no indication that this has lessened the importance of class as an agent of social transformation and human possibility (a master category of metanarrative). Indeed, it will be the revival of class mobilizations that will retrieve for socialized humanity what was lost over the course of the 1990s in Russia and elsewhere, or there will be no gains forced from the already all-too-apparent losses of recent capitalist restorationism. Almost a decade of tyrannical Yeltsin-like Great Russianism and the barbarism of small "nation" chauvinisms should have made it apparent where the politics of *national* identity lead.

Class, as both a category of potential and becoming and an agency of activism, has thus reasserted its fundamental importance. More and more of humanity now faces the ravages of capitalism's highly totalizing, essentializing, and homogenizing impulses, and these are currently unleashed with a tragic vengeance as even the once degenerate and deformed workers' states look to the ideological abstractions of the world market for sustenance rather than relying on proletarian powers. Mass strikes now routinely challenge capital and its states, from France to Canada, from Korea to Brazil. Once-Soviet workers, who saw socialism sour in the stale breath of generations of Stalinism, are voting Communist again, whatever the problematic connotations, in the 1990s. At the end of 1995, polls in the advanced capitalist economies of the West almost universally locate society's major discontents in the material failings of a social order that has visibly widened the gap between "haves" and "have-nots," undermining the mythical middle class and depressing the living conditions of those working poor fortunate enough to retain some hold on their jobs. There are no answers separate from those of class struggle, however much this metanarrative of materially structured resistance intersects with special oppressions. Class has not so much fallen as it has returned.

It had never, of course, gone anywhere. *Identified* as simply one of many plural subjectivities, class has actually been obscured from analytic and political view by poststructuralism's analytic edifice, erected at just the moment that the left is in dire need of the clarity and direction that class, as a category and an agency, a structure and a politics, can provide. The legacy of Marxism in general, and of historical materialism in particular, is to challenge and oppose this obfuscation, providing an alternative to such material misreadings, building an oppositional worldview that can play some role in reversing the class struggle defeats and weakening of the international workers' movement that has taken place as capital and the state have been in the ascendant over the course of the last thirty years. Those thinkers who have failed to see the transitory nature of postmodernism/poststructuralism, many of them academic fair-weather friends of Marxism, and have instead invested so much in recent proclamations of their discursively constructed identity politics, may well be among the last to acknowledge the blunt revival of class in the face of contemporary capitalism's totalizing materiality. They will no doubt find some variant of "difference" to cling to, the better to avoid the necessity of engaging subjectivity and its oppressive objectification under capitalism, where class, in its singular capacity to assimilate other categories of being and congeal varieties of power, rules and is ruled, a metanarrative of exploitation within which all identities ultimately find their level of subordination/domination. This is indeed an old way of looking at the world. But postmodernism/poststructuralism notwithstanding, all that is old is not always without value. As one "Old Man" of Marxism, a lifelong defender of radicalized Enlightenment values, once proclaimed, in a maxim particularly suited to the linked fortunes of materialism's past, present, and future: "Those who cannot defend old positions will never conquer new ones."[15]

Notes

1. Fredric Jameson, "Postmodernism and Consumer Society," in *The Anti-Aesthetic: Essays on Postmodern Culture*, Hal Foster, ed. (Port Townsend, WA: Bay Press, 1983), p. 125; Jameson, *Postmodernism: Or, the Cultural Logic of Late Capitalism* (Durham, NC: Duke University Press, 1991), pp. 217, 64-65; Pauline Marie Rosenau, *Postmodernism and the Social Sciences: Insights, Inroads, Intrusions* (Princeton, NJ: Princeton University Press, 1992), p. 64.

2. See Jean-François Lyotard, *The Postmodern Condition: A Report on Knowledge* (Minneapolis: University of Minnesota Press, 1984), esp. p. 30.
3. Lyotard, *Postmodern Condition*, p. xxiii.
4. For a Marxist rejection of this position see Joseph Fracchia, "Marx's *Aufhebung* of Philosophy and the Foundations of a Materialist Science of History," *History and Theory* 30 (1991): 153-179.
5. For an introduction to issues raised in the above paragraphs see Alex Callinicos, *Making History: Agency, Structure, and Change in Social Theory* (Ithaca, NY: Cornell University Press, 1988); Callinicos, *Theories and Narratives: Reflections on the Philosophy of History* (Cambridge: Polity Press, 1995); Ellen Meiksins Wood, *The Pristine Culture of Capitalism: A Historical Essay on Old Regimes and Modern States* (London: Verso, 1991), p. 93; Wood, "Identity Crisis," *In These Times*, 13 June 1994, pp. 28-29.
6. As a brief introduction see Harvey J. Kaye, *The British Marxist Historians* (Oxford: Basil Blackwell, 1984); Raymond Williams, "Base and Superstructure in Marxist Cultural Theory," in *Problems in Materialism and Culture* (London: Verso, 1980), pp. 31-49; Fred Inglis, *Raymond Williams* (New York: Routledge, 1995); and Terry Eagleton, *Literary Theory: An Introduction* (Minneapolis: University of Minnesota Press, 1983).
7. E.P. Thompson, *The Making of the English Working Class* (New York: Vintage, 1963); Gareth Stedman Jones, "Rethinking Chartism," and "Why is the Labour Party in a Mess?" in *Languages of Class: Studies in English Working-Class History, 1832-1982* (Cambridge: Cambridge University Press, 1983), pp. 90-178, 239-256.
8. For a discussion of this and other contemporary historiographic trends see Bryan D. Palmer, *Descent into Discourse: The Reification of Language and the Writing of Social History* (Philadelphia: Temple University Press, 1990).
9. See Russell Jacoby, "Marginal Returns: The Trouble with Post-Colonial Theory," *Lingua Franca* (September-October 1995): 30-37.
10. David Harvey, *The Condition of Postmodernity: An Enquiry into the Origins of Cultural Change* (Oxford: Basil Blackwell, 1989), pp. 116-17.
11. See Ellen Meiksins Wood, *The Retreat from Class: A New "True" Socialism* (London: Verso, 1986).
12. Patrick Joyce, *Democratic Subjects: The Self and the Social in Nineteenth-Century England* (Cambridge: Cambridge University Press, 1994), p. 2.
13. Marx and Engels, *The German Ideology* (New York: International, 1969), p. 39; *The Eighteenth Brumaire of Louis Bonaparte*, in *Selected Works* (Moscow: Progress, 1968), p. 103.
14. Leon Trotsky, *The Revolution Betrayed* (New York: Merit, 1965), p. 254.
15. Leon Trotsky, *In Defense of Marxism* (New York: Pathfinder, 1973), p. 178.

Against social de(con)struction of science: cautionary tales from the third world

MEERA NANDA

> People resisting despotism and its lies need ideals of one truth, one reason, one reality and on occasion, one science. To be able to be critical of the unities is a luxury and let us never forget it.
>
> —IAN HACKING, 1996[1]

1

One of the most remarkable—and the least remarked upon—features of the "radical" movement engaged in deconstructing natural science is how it ends up denying the unity (i.e., universality) of truth, reason, reality, and science precisely in the name of those who need these unities most urgently—the "people resisting despotism and its lies." These would include those of us from non-Western societies fighting against the despotism of some of our own cultural traditions, and the untested and untestable cosmologies that are used to justify these traditions. A loose and varied assortment of theories that bear the label of social constructivism have declared the very content of modern natural science to be justified, in the final instance, by "Western" cultural values and social interest. Once modern science in seen not as a universally valid knowledge about the natural world, but a particular or "ethno"-construct of Western society, it becomes easy to see science as part of the imperialistic West's despotism, which the West's "Others" must resist in the name of cultural survival and anti-imperialism. Modern science thus becomes a despotism, an *object* of resistance rather than an *ally* of those resisting despotism.

My goal in this paper is to cast a critical look at the anti-realist and relativist assumptions of the skeptical theories of social construction of science that have gained wide currency in the postmodern academy; and I want to look at them from the perspective of the people's science movements in non-Western countries. These theories—unlike the Marxian idea of the social mediation of knowledge with which they are often confused—have eroded the distinction between scientifically justified beliefs and folk beliefs and/or ideology. What has undermined these distinctions is the fundamental thesis of social constructivism which states that *all* beliefs alike are justified by the community consensus, which is itself based upon social power, rhetoric, and custom. There is no objective truth about the real world which scientifically justified knowledge can aim toward, but rather, all "truth" about "reality" is literally constructed out of choices between different equally justifiable interpretations that a "thought collective" makes. These choices, in turn, are driven by the conscious and unconscious biases and interests of the members of any given community of inquirers. Though varied in emphases and details, constructivist theorists agree that there simply is no truth, or even reality, that can transcend the local social context of inquiry. The "unities" of truth and reason that Ian Hacking speaks for (above) are treated in the constructivist discourse as remnants of the imperialistic impulse of the Enlightenment which sought to impose the West's own peculiar stories about truth and reality on the rest of the world.

Such a view of knowledge justifies itself in the name of cultural autonomy, tolerance, and respect for non-Western ways of knowing the world and living in it. But I will argue that in actual practice, such "tolerance" has only ended up providing theoretical grounds for, and a progressive gloss on, the fast growing anti-modernist, nativist, and cultural/religious revivalist movements in many parts of what used to be called the third world. These movements seek to subordinate scientific rationality to local traditions, and thus are incapable of critically interrogating these same traditions, many of which are patently illiberal and oppressive to women and other marginalized groups in non-Western societies.

Almost in direct proportion with the rise of nativist anti-modernist social movements in the third world, which correspond with the ascendance of social constructivist theories in academia globally, many parts of the third world have seen a decline and stigmatization of people's science movements. The people's science movements seek to appropriate the contents and methods of modern science in order to bring traditional knowledge under empirical scrutiny and critique. In the part of the third world that I am most familiar with—my native India—people's science movements have come to be eclipsed by the highly visible and vocal transnational alliance that has emerged around the idea that modern science is Western, and that the non-West needs its non-Western "ethno"-sciences. Affirmed and emboldened by the most avant-garde intellectuals in the West and at home, these nativist movements tend to label any critique of traditional knowledge from the vantage point of modern science as a sign of Western imperialism, or worse, a hangover from the old, "discredited" and "Western" Enlightenment (although, interestingly, they continue to applaud the attack on "Western" science from the perspective of ethno-sciences as anti-Eurocentric, and therefore progressive).[2] Indeed, I believe that the recent electoral victory of the religious right (the BJP) in my native India has definitely benefited from the cultural climate in which even supposedly Left-inclined intellectuals and activists tend to treat all liberal and modern ideas as "Western," inauthentic, and thus inappropriate for India. Thus I will try to show that although the animus against the rationality of modern science is justified in the name of anti-imperialism and egalitarianism, its real beneficiaries are not the people but the nativists and nationalists of all stripes, religious or "merely" cultural/civilizational.

Perched rather comfortably in the academe, the critics of science in the West tend to applaud the efforts of indigenous science movements in the ex-colonial world to produce, in Donna Haraway's phrase, "situated knowledges"—e.g., "Islamic" science, "Vedic" mathematics, "Indian" science, "third world women's" science, etc. They tend to see these movements as a justifiable reassertion of long-silenced traditions and as heroic attempts by the once colonized civilizations to accommodate forces of modernity on their own terms. There is undoubtedly some truth in this perception: the memory of colonialism with all its economic exploitation and cultural denigration and the fear of the fast encroaching "McWorld" have indeed lent a sense of urgency to the third world's search for alternatives.

But if one examines the actual track record of the social movements that seek to encourage and implement culturally "authentic" science and technology, a very different and much more worrisome picture emerges. At their best, the indigenous science movements have spawned neopopulist, antimodernization and anti-state agitation targeted indiscriminately against modern institutions and ideologies of third world states (as in India), and at worst, they have actively joined forces with religious fundamentalists, as in most Islamic countries (and to some extent, at least indirectly, in India as well). Indeed, it is becoming harder by the day to discern much difference between the positions of the religious (and generally on the right) and the secular (generally on the left) critics of science, technology, and modernity in India and elsewhere in the third world.

Against these rather dangerous political developments, this paper can be read as an appeal from an "other," in whose name the deconstructivists in the Western academe justify their reduction of modern science to a "Western" cultural construct, an "ethno-science" like any other, to rethink how their epistemological egalitarianism is impeding the urgent task of actually changing the oppressive social structures and cultural values in non-Western societies. I believe it is time the proponents of "de-Westernization" of knowledge asked themselves: Is such a project a step forward for the disadvantaged groups in the non-Western societies? And is it time the rest of us asked if the project of de-Westernization deserves the support of progressive, left-inclined intellectuals?

This paper is written out of a strong belief that a cultural nationalism that turns against the internationalism of science is completely devoid of any progressive impulse, and for all its populist rhetoric, can only keep the people it claims to speak for in the bondage of age-old oppressions justified by ancient superstitions. As a third world woman trained in "Western" science, I wish to reaffirm the words of Abdus Salam, the Pakistani Nobel Laureate in physics, that "there is only one universal science, its problems and modalities are international and there is no such thing as Islamic science, just as there is no Hindu science, no Jewish science, no Confucian science, nor Christian science" ... nor, indeed, "Western" science.[3]

It may be appropriate here to disclose my personal investment in the defense of the universality of scientific knowledge and a scientific way of thinking. I learned to do science as a young woman in India, received a doctorate in molecular biology, and later worked as a science writer in close collaboration with people's science movements in India and also in the United States.[4] Although I know that science can be mobilized in support of oppressive power, I sense a deep epistemological connection between modern science and a principled dissent from, and opposition to, *all* arbitrary authority, be it the authority of traditions, family, community, or the state. It was this connection between a scientific skepticism and dissent that I intuited when I left the lab for the newspaper office and for science activism. And it is this connection that I now want to defend—more self-consciously this time, now that I have the advantage of hindsight—against the radical science critics who would deny it.

2

The idea that science, like all human knowledge, is socially and culturally mediated has a history that long predates postmodernism, but there are critical differences between today's social constructivism and earlier theories. The thesis *social construction of scientific knowledge* traces its ancestry to the tradition of sociology of knowledge that includes such seminal figures as Karl Marx, Karl Mannheim, and more contemporaneously, Robert Merton. There are undoubtedly connections between these scholars and their latter-day, "post"-marked progeny—but with two *crucial* differences. None of the classical sociologists of science was an anti-realist. None of them ever denied that science, though always situated in specific social contexts, nevertheless helps us understand the reality that exists independently of our practices. And none treated the truth of scientific ideas as relative to the "prevailing regime of truth," which in the last instance is a matter of social power, as the current Foucaultian social theory would have it. While all classical sociologists of knowledge believed, with different theoretical emphases, that the logic of science works through context-bound social practices and institutions, they equally firmly held that the logic of science was, in the final instance, justified by empirical evidence from the real world, which could be checked independently of antecedent theoretical and social assumptions. Thus, while they made room for the undeniable fact that competing social interests could generate competing theories, they simultaneously believed that these theories were sooner or later settled by the universalistic facts of nature which are consonant with one and not with another theory.

Post-al sociologists sometimes like to drape themselves in the mantle of Marx, even as they declare Marxism to be essentialist, determinist, and hopelessly passé. Marx certainly holds the view that knowledge is socially mediated and that science is a social practice. But scientific knowledge for him always implies the *objectivity of the material world,* i.e., the independent reality of natural, and the (relatively) independent reality of social, forms. Scientific knowledge emerges from an interplay between the social practices of science—the socially and historically located labor or cognitive work that goes into producing knowledge—and the material world that exists independently of human cognition. The *historicity of knowledge,* for Marx, is always in an ever-changing dialectical relation with the objectivity of the material world: a constant give-and-take between our historically located categories of thought and the world that exists independently of these categories continually transforms our categories of thought, putting them to the test of scientific experiment and anchoring them with an increasing accuracy to the objects of the material world. As the physicist and Marxist historian of science J.D. Bernal clearly saw, science is a "human activity, linked to all other human activities and continuously interacting with them." Yet science also "transcends the means or the motives that helped step by step to build it up ... [because] it is securely anchored in the material world, in the properties of animate and inanimate things."[5]

The social constructivists ostensibly retain Marx's emphasis on the historicity of knowledge, *without* his emphasis on either the objectivity of material reality, or our ability to arrive at increasingly truthful accounts of that reality through a constantly self-correcting social practice. We begin to encounter a full-blown constructivist view of science in the early 1970s when, citing the ideas of Thomas Kuhn and Ludwig Wittgenstein, social theorists associated with the Edinburgh University, especially David Bloor and Barry Barnes, began to propound what they call the "Strong Programme" (SP) of sociology of scientific knowledge. The SP and the various schools of science critique it helped to bring about (including the feminist and cultural studies of science) are strong on the historicity but weak on the objectivity of scientific knowledge, to the point that it has become impossible to discern any traces of the latter in their accounts of science. In fact, as other essays in this volume show, the paradoxical effect of postmodernist constructivist conceptions of history is to make history itself unintelligible, so that we now have a conception of "historicity" without a conception of history. Postmodernism gives us neither the epistemological standards to judge, say, Galileo's astronomy as better than pre-Copernican science, nor the means to situate the development of science in an intelligible historical process.

The net result is that constructivists end up admonishing us to give up such outmoded notions as *truth as a correspondence with a mind-independent reality*. All knowledge claims should be explained "symmetrically" regardless of their truth or falsity.[6] The demand for symmetry means that one's reason for holding a belief is to be explained in terms of locally operating (sociological) causes and not in terms of the character of the belief (e.g., whether true or false in terms of correspondence with an element of reality). An explanation based on the latter terms would amount to an a priori assumption that it is the reality that fixes beliefs and would rule out an impartial examination of how social relations allowed a statement to be "stabilized" as true.

This stabilization or "entrenchment" of some beliefs in a community's particular web of beliefs, furthermore, is seen as a highly flexible process in which the inquirers have an active role to play. At all stages of a scientific inquiry—from coming up with a hypothesis, to testing it through an experiment, to reading the results of the experiment—scientists are seen as active agents doing things, making choices, forming alliances, pursuing local goals, advancing career interests, and so on.

All the choices are made in a rich field of social, cultural, institutional, and political forces, which are seen as directing the choices scientists make at every step. These choices are said, in the final instance, to constitute the very content of science. Scientists have this "interpretive flexibility" presumably because reality and the evidence thereof can never *compel* what we can say about it: observations are theory-laden (start with different theories, you will see different things) and all theories are underdetermined by evidence (any set of observations can justify more than one hypothesis).[7] At every step of the way, scientists have options open to them, and the choices they make are not forced by reality.

It is this assumption of interpretive flexibility that severs the connection between the real world and the social location of the knower. The idea that natural scientists interpret experimental data depending upon their social interests and assumptions makes experiments circular and question-begging: scientists practically "see" relationships and properties in nature depending upon their social location. This flexibility makes the active and socially conditioned choices of scientists internal to the very logic of science, thereby turning contextual values into the constitutive values of science. Science is thus relativized "all the way down," or as the popular constructivist slogan would have it, "science *is* social relations."[8]

How do these constructivist theses lead to the idea of different sciences for different people? Once the contextual values become the constitutive values of science—that is, once the content of science is seen as constituted by social values—it follows that different social-cultural groups would hold different "facts" about the world. It is only when this dynamic is accepted that it becomes possible to talk of a "Hindu science," "non-Western science," "feminist science," all claiming objectivity from their own internal standards.

The relativistic and pseudo-radical logic of social construction was revealed for all to see by the tongue-in-cheek postmodern rendition of a "liberatory" quantum gravity by the physicist Alan Sokal which appeared recently in *Social Text*, an avant-garde journal of cultural critique. So taken for granted is the postmodernist incredulity aboutthe ability of human reason to understand the causal mechanisms of the physical world that the following (intentionally) outrageous claim by Sokal failed to raise any warning flags for the eminent editors of *Social Text*:

> It has become increasingly apparent that physical "reality," no less than social "reality" is at bottom a social and linguistic construct; that scientific "knowledge," far from being objective, reflects and encodes the dominant ideologies and power relations of the culture that produced it, that truth claims of science are inherently theory-laden, and that the discourse of the scientific community, for all its undeniable value, cannot assert a privileged epistemological status with respect to the counter-hegemonic narratives emanating from dissident or marginalized communities.[9]

The ideas Sokal *satirizes* are exactly the ideas that the cultural nationalists from the third world uncritically and respectfully *borrow* from the social constructivists and other radical historicists of science (although it is heartening to find that progressive Indian scientists have begun to use Sokal's demonstration of the hollowness of social constructivist claims to combat the nativist critics of science).[10] As the self-appointed representatives of "dissident or marginalized communities," third worldist intellectuals argue that if modern science "encodes the dominant ideologies and power relations of the culture that produces it," its claim to objectivity is a ruse, an ideological ploy that the West needs for its own self-image as rational as compared to the irrational and superstitious "other."[11]

Thus it has come to pass that amid self-righteous chants of anti-imperialist solidarity with the West's silenced and exploited "other," the social constructivist, postmodern, and self-professed "postcolonial" academics and activists in the West and in the third world are united in the idea that modern science is not a unity. Rather they see it as merely an "ethno-science" of the West, constituted out of the contextual values of the West, and thus without any justifiable claim to truth beyond the supposed boundaries of its birthplace, "the West."[12] As a Western discourse, modern science is seen as "inherently" inimical to the development and flourishing of other local knowledge systems, which are assumed to be grounded in the supposedly more benign assumptions of non-Western social orders.

Seen in this light, it makes sense that third world people should fashion a science that is appropriate to their own civilizational imperatives, cultural meanings, and ways of knowing. One demand that recurs time and again with desperate urgency in the fast-growing genre of postcolonial science critique is to give up the modernist attempts to assimilate modern science into local cultures, and to create entirely new sciences in which the very facts of nature will be different, for they will derive their legitimation as facts from a worldview that is organically and authentically related to the "way of life" of people living in these societies. The new non-Western sciences will operate with different criteria of rationality, objectivity, and truth, criteria furnished by their own aims, values, and conceptual categories. Thus it is not the case that these sciences are any less objective or factual, but only that the validity of their truth must be judged not in comparison with the Western sciences but "in their own terms."[13]

As we shall see in the next section, the political implications of this "radical" equation of modern science with the West are not lost on the resurgent neotraditionalist and religious fundamentalist movements. These movements seek salvation not in a rational worldview locally and a democratic internationalism globally, but in assertions of civilizational autonomy through a reconstruction of their own respective ethno-knowledges. When modern science is understood as local knowledge, at all times perfectly porous to the social assumptions of the imperializing West, it is not surprising at all that the opposition to imperialism should turn into an opposition to modern science and technology, as has increasingly happened in the alternative science movements in the third world. I will try to argue, next, that whatever else it may be, this project of social deconstruction of science is no friend of the people of the third world, who need to appropriate modern science in order to question and get rid of *all* oppressive ideas and structures, be they Western imports or authentic domestic products made of "their own" assumptions and values.

3

In defending both scientific rationality and its crucial importance for social change, I am in a way defending a personal and deeply transformative experience I have had of doing science and working as a science popularizer.

I count doing science as one of the most formative experiences of my life. Indeed, it would be no exaggeration to say that training in modern science marked the beginning of humanism and feminism for me. My training in biology demolished once and for all ideas of social hierarchies and differences that were deeply entrenched in my middle-class Hindu milieu.[14]

My double consciousness of tradition and modern science is in fact quite commonplace in the rapidly changing societies of the third world. Like many of my fellow first-generation, post-independence citizens of once-colonized countries, I came of age in India in a thoroughly hybrid cosmopolis: the education in modern "Western" sciences that I was fortunate enough to receive shaped my ideas of the natural order—the *cosmos*—while the social order—the *polis*—of my birth, and my place in it as a woman of my caste and class background, were grounded in thc local, largely Hindu, customs and knowledge systems.[15]

This hybrid cosmopolis, far from being an impossibility (as the holists among sociologists suggest), or a prison-house of Western-masculinist imperialism (as the cultural nationalists among third world intellectuals claim), was experienced by some of us as truly emancipatory. Our scientific understanding of the *cosmos* gave us the resources to question the grounds of some of the cultural practices of our *polis,* and to win a modicum of autonomy for ourselves. Contrary to those who see science as "inherently Western," science made perfect sense to me, growing up in my small and rather provincial city in Punjab. I did not find scientific explanations of the natural world alien or oppressive. Sure, they did not sit well with the traditional rationalizations of Karma, caste, and the inferiority of women as "facts of nature." But if this is what "violence" and cultural dissonance caused by "Westernization" is all about, I suggest that we have more of it!

More seriously, I am perfectly aware of the risk I am running of being misunderstood as lumping those who critique modern science with a better future society in mind, together with those who defend the status quo with all its injustices. I know, moreover, that in the atmosphere of distrust of science that pervades the academe today, my defense of science as a necessary (though not sufficient) agent of progressive social change could well be put aside as a mere throwback to the simplistic, culturally insensitive, authoritarian attempt characteristic of the much-derided Enlightenment. To put such worries to rest, let me assure the reader that I fully recognize that the secular social critics of science and modernity in the West and in the third world are no apologists for the traditional naturalizations of inequities. They are as much—if not more—actively engaged in a variety of new social movements against social injustices based on identities (gender, caste, and ethnicity) that the traditional, more class-based progressive movements had failed to address directly. Indeed, both through personal associations and through their written works, I know the critics of science to be motivated by deeply egalitarian, democratic, and anti-racist sentiments. As far as I know, major alternative science movements (in India, at least) have no overt sympathy and/or working relations with the religious conservatives and their divisive agendas, and most of them (again, speaking only of India), have been at the forefront of feminist, civil rights, and anti-communal movements. Those among the new social movements that take the anti-essentialism of postmodernist ideas seriously, moreover, have no truck with the false unified civilizational imperatives that the religious fundamentalists are projecting onto the diverse and plural polities of places like India.

Thus, I have no intention whatsoever of playing a game of more-progressive-than-thou with those whose views on science I disagree with. What I *do* intend is to ask: Can the means they have chosen actually realize the political ends they favor? That is, can the idealistic, antirationalist and antirealist theories of knowledge they have come to embrace advance their political goals, which presumably include full autonomy of the individual and a society without prejudice and injustice? Is it not more likely that by relativizing all knowledge to the existing cultural discourses and social arrangements, they are depriving themselves of any ground to stand upon from where to critically appraise the existing cultural traditions that are not hospitable to these political ideals?

I wholly agree with the critics of science in that modern science will never give us the ultimate and final answers to the mysteries of the world, and that human relations should not be patterned after the mechanisms of nature revealed by science. I also see, of course, the many ways in which modern science can be and has been used destructively. Yet the fact remains that modern science has developed a method of constant self-critique in light of systematic observation and experimentation on nature that gives us good reasons to reject some views as false reports of the world. I believe that progressive politics is impossible without a sifting of truth from falsehood. A discursive egalitarianism that refrains from critiquing objectively false beliefs because they happen to be held by the more traditional "masses" actually impedes the struggle for real and substantive equality. Egalitarianism and truth need each other, and if truth is left to be decided by the often deeply inegalitarian standards of the community that holds it, it is not clear how these standards themselves can ever be questioned.

To return to my own experience with science as a source of personal values and social philosophy: my experience of finding personal courage and intellectual strength in science and my disillusionment with the elitist agenda of the scientific establishment in India inclined me to take an active interest in people's science movements. The early 1980s (when I was completing my Ph.D.) were a time of soul-searching in the scientific community in India, with many active "science for people" groups springing up on university campuses and in scientific research institutions. These groups provided working scientists an opportunity to participate in the life of the community through active alliances with consciousness-raising and educational initiatives in villages and urban slums.[16]

This was also the time, it must be mentioned, when the first audible rumblings of the organized nationalist/culturalist opposition to science and modernity began to be heard in the form of an active opposition to the idea of a "scientific temper" from well-known neo-Gandhian intellectuals in Delhi and Madras.[17] In the intervening decade and a half, political upheavals (above all the disappearance of the Soviet Union), problems thrown up by rapid and uneven modernization, and the "post"-marked intellectual trends that emphasize cultural autonomy over cosmopolitanism have all contributed to the ascendancy of the cultural nationalist, "patriotic science" tendency which is critical of modern "Western" science and technology as "inherently" anti-people.[18] The people's science movements are berated as holdouts of die-hard rationalists and "communists" who do not understand and respect the cultural traditions and religiosity of the people, with even sympathetic critics urging an accommodation with the "patriotic" tendencies.[19]

Such dismissals of people's science movements ignore the countless young and idealistic men and women in India from all walks of life, including my colleagues in research institutions, who may not be card-carrying members of any political party but who are drawn to these movements in the hope of using the findings of modern "Western" science to rationally critique the grounds of some of the most illiberal elements of their local traditional values and social arrangements.

"Science for social revolution" is the motto of one of the most prominent people's science movements in India, the Kerala Sastra Sahitya Parishad (KSSP) with 40,000 active members and nearly 1,500 science clubs in small towns and villages in the state of Kerala. There are many other science-based, consciousness-raising groups, some of them recognized nationally for their innovative educational methods in science, especially the central India-based Eklavya and the now-closed Kishore Bharati, which in 1972 nucleated the Hoshangabad Science Teaching Program (HSTP), a program that has now spread to more than 500 schools. For each such nationally recognized program, there are numerous others working in relative anonymity.[20]

The objective of groups like KSSP, HSTP, and other such groups is to develop a critical scientific attitude that puts inherited knowledge to the test of empirical evidence. Toward that end, these groups promote education in modern scientific ideas, especially those derived from modern "Western" biology (spontaneous generation vs. germ theory, the genetic basis of the sex of the fetus, the similarity of the genetic material in all life, etc.), the theory of evolution, and the Newtonian laws of physics, and relate them to the everyday life of people through all available cultural means, from classrooms to art fairs, songs, street corner theater, and "science processions." Illustrative examples include KSSP offering thousands of astronomy classes in rural areas when Halley's comet came close to the earth in 1986, or the Hoshangabad groups encouraging local students to trace the parasite that had caused a nationwide panic over a "curse" on green vegetables. Although they make no secret of their support of a scientific temperament, these groups are careful not to present science as a complete polar opposite of religion, but to suggest that deeply religious people like Isaac Newton, C.V. Raman, or Ramanujan could be great scientists as well. Neither can these groups be seen as uncritical science enthusiasts; instead, their emphasis is on wise and egalitarian uses of science, which sometimes leads them to actively oppose some ecologically disastrous development projects. The overall project of "science for social revolution" is similar in spirit to feminist consciousness raising, only in this case it takes place mostly in non-metropolitan areas, in villages, in small make-shift schools in rural and urban areas, among women in the slums, among farmworkers and among bonded laborers. It is no different in spirit than the coffee houses, learned academies, salons, and lending libraries that sprung up all across Europe, not just among the urban elite but also in rural areas and small towns during the Enlightenment.

It is both the desirability and the very possibility of just such a critical empiricism—a scientific temper—that has been severely questioned by the rise of the social constructivist theories of science among academics and activists alike. In tune with, and often borrowing from, the Western critics of the Enlightenment—from (the all too well understood) Heidegger, Nietzsche, Foucault, to (the much misunderstood) Kuhn and the post-Kuhnian feminist and ecological critics which abound in the academy—Indian, Islamic, and other non-Western critics have declared faith in the power of reason to know the truth about the world as the *cause* and not the solution of the "pathology" of modern western scientific thinking. They see the people's science movement's emphasis on critical rationality as an indicator of the "contempt" alienated modern intellectuals have for the traditions of the masses, and science as simply a Western superstition which the modernizers wish to substitute for the popular superstitions that give meaning to people. The solution, both for the West and the rest, is to turn to the "older civilizations" where rationality is subordinated to other cultural imperatives and values—including, of course, the values prescribed by religion, mysticism, and the lost Gnostic traditions.[21]

Yet, the critics of modern science and science for people movements stoutly deny that they oppose science and modernity, or that their view of science leads to a serious relativism.[22] Rather, they claim that they "only" want to redefine science in their own cultural terms. (This parallels feminist critiques of science which claim to strengthen the objectivity of science by explicitly acknowledging the role of emotions and progressive political values in doing science.) The problem with this manner of redefining science is that it leaves out precisely what is distinctive about science: the possibility of separating "facts" from "values." It has, of course, long been recognized that the fact/value distinction is not a simple matter, and I have no wish to seem naive about it here. But these critics of science are not just pointing out the difficulty of separating facts from values. In a sense, the problem simply does not exist for them, because values are for them the arbiters of facts. When they speak of redefining science in their own cultural terms, they are not simply trying to find ways of rendering scientific principles more congenial to their particular cultures. Instead, for them, the test of a theory is its correspondence to their own cultural values and predispositions rather than to some objective and independent reality.

While intellectual discourse has taken such a turn toward a "re-enchantment" and subordination of scientific reason to the authority of traditions, it should come as no surprise that the religious revivalists have begun to dominate politics in many parts of the non-Western world. While the Indian left has been busy theorizing the "decolonization of knowledge," the revivalist Hindu forces have succeeded in actually carrying out a decolonization of mathematics and history of science. In the states where they came to power, the Hindu revivalist parties decreed the replacement of modern mathematics with an apparently fraudulent version of "Vedic mathematics." Likewise, the revivalists have succeeded in revising the history of science and technology in order to incorporate more nationalistic elements in it.[23] But this is only a mild case of re-enchantment as compared to the situation in Pakistan, where the clergy has a lot more say in what will be taught and how, including, according to the physicist Pervez Hoodbhoy, strictures on weather and astronomical predictions.

The intellectual climate in many non-Western countries, as Hoodbhoy puts it in an understatement, is "not particularly propitious for free thinking and science."

4

I reject the idea that scientific knowledge is a social and cultural construct of the West for one very simple reason: it completely misdescribes the science I did in the lab and the science I did on the streets as an activist and a writer in New Delhi, circa mid-1980s. The various "post"-marked theories of social construction of science, and their more popular versions circulating among the alternative science movements in the third world simply have *no theoretical and normative categories to explain the project of science for social revolution.* The sociology of scientific knowledge lacks the vocabulary to describe the hybrid vigor of the cosmopolis that I and others in the science for people movements experienced. The most avant-garde constructivist theorists of science, who claim to speak in the name of deeper democracy and fuller human emancipation, *completely invalidate* the very real and very liberatory experience of those of us in progressive science movements.

If these theories are right, then I and my comrades who sought to use science to challenge our own inherited knowledge systems and myths were not only misguided, but we were actually doing the imperialists' dirty work.

If, when all is said and done, it is the social interests and cultural conventions that lead inquirers to accept some belief as a fact about an element of reality—that is, if scientific facts are *constituted* by the social relations in which science is done—then obviously we were not confronting our local knowledges with a better and truer understanding of the world, as we thought we were. Rather, we were universalizing the perspectives constituted by the capitalist and patriarchal social conventions of Western white men over our own people. This is exactly what the cultural nationalists and traditionalists in India have always accused us of. The sad irony is that we now have the most "radical," cutting-edge thinkers in the West giving intellectual ammunition to our nativists.

It is one thing to embrace a "cultural relativism" that respects the variety of human culture. It is quite another to adopt a relativism that makes these varied cultural values the sole or principal standard of truth, so that truth is simply what coheres with a particular system of beliefs, instead of what corresponds to the world that exists independently of our beliefs. Postmodernist critics of science have tended to adopt the second kind of relativism, which is indistinguishable from epistemological relativism. According to their type of relativism, a correspondence theory of truth, which inevitably makes universalistic claims, does violence and is the source of intolerance, colonialism, and even totalitarianism. The only solution they favor is to recognize the situatedness and partiality of all knowledge, including that of modern science—and then let a thousand sciences bloom. For obvious reasons, the epistemic charity the social constructivists extend to other knowledge systems has a great attraction for those who wish to replace "Western" science with their own sciences. But this charity is of the most dubious variety and I will argue that the third world must stoutly refuse any part of it.

This kind of relativism is precisely the reason why social constructionism fails to empower those—e.g., non-Western peoples—whose beliefs it wishes to affirm: it ends up telling them that there is no right or wrong picture of the world, that they are okay as much as anyone else is or could be. Such "affirmation" may affirm the cultural chauvinists, but it is far from liberatory: people fighting for their right to a decent life do not need condescending affirmations of their ways of knowing, as much as they need new cultural discourses that will open up new possibilities for new kinds of social relations. This struggling humanity needs a richer kind of empathy that includes respect but also critique; love but also anger. Because relativism is generous with the first but stingy with the second, it ends up subverting its own progressive impulses. It ends up providing aid and comfort to any particularistic cosmology which may demand that it be judged on its "own terms" of what constitutes justified belief. Understood purely from within a given framework, and with no external standard of truth, it is hard to see how *any* view could be wrong and *any* practice unjust. Indeed, as Norman Geras points out, if truth is wholly internalized to particular discourses or social practices, we cannot recognize injustice in victims' reports of their suffering; they become only so many *stories* of injustice.[24]

Most social constructivists don't deny that external reality exists, and that scientists interact with it in their experiments, and discourse about it through their publications, conferences, etc. They only deny that external reality determines, in the last instance, the truth or falsity of scientific knowledge. Of course they admit that the real world exists and that the real physical world is independent of what we think about it. But the acknowledgment of the real world is only an idle addition—a "fig leaf," as the philosopher Michael Devitt has called it—to the constructivist view of knowledge, for it serves a small and diminishing role in fixing scientists' beliefs.

But social constructivists, like all of us, would not want to defy the law of gravity by jumping out of the twenty-first floor of a building, as Alan Sokal keeps reminding them: they are perfectly aware of the bounds set by the real world in most of our activities, interpretations, and choices. How, then, do they justify reducing the real world to a fig leaf when it comes to scientific knowledge? The answer lies in what the British realist philosopher Roy Bhaskar calls the "epistemic fallacy": the failure to distinguish between an objective reality and the ways in which we represent or describe it, or as the introduction to this volume puts it, the conflation of the forms of knowledge with its objects. Here, the "real" world does not act as a check on our knowledge. On the contrary, our historically and culturally variable knowledge constitutes reality—or as Steven Woolgar proclaims, "How we know determines what exists." In that sense, social constructivists allow no difference between laws of physics and socially created objects (say a dollar bill or the rules of baseball): both are what they are because we agree to think of them as such. It is as if not only the science of physics were historically located and changeable, but the natural objects to which it refers were historically variable too.

The epistemic fallacy connects theories of social construction with postmodern theories of knowledge more generally. Both share one fundamental assumption, the assumption Philip Kitcher has dubbed as "IRA," the "Inaccessibility of Reality Argument," which holds that we cannot step out of language (or more broadly, our conceptual framework) to see reality in itself. "There is no God's eye view," as one often hears in postmodern discourse. IRA directly leads to the epistemic fallacy for it makes the boundaries of the real, knowable, and, in Kantian terms, the phenomenal world coincide with the boundaries of our socially limited and context-bound frameworks. Anything falling outside of our discourses is treated as the Kantian *noumena,* a thing-in-itself, which cannot be known by human reason. This makes the ordinary work of science seem god-like—impossible, transcendent, and full of hubris.

Given the assumption that the real is what we can know about it and say of it, social constructionism presents itself as the only humanly possible, socially situated and nontranscendental, naturalistic account of science. (That is why, as became obvious in the recent flap over Sokal's hoax, science studies scholars bristled at the notion that they were against science). But my problem with this account of science is that it removes from science all that makes it worth doing and all that makes it empowering for those questioning the despotism of superstitions all around the world.

5

What can be done? What is the way out of the quandary?

Social constructivists have led us into a blind alley, but the philosophical problems they invoke to make their case are by no means trivial. It *is* a fact, long recognized by the critics of empiricism (notably Karl Popper) much before postmodernism appeared on the scene, that there are no theory-free observations. Observations *don't* just jump out of the real world and compel our inferences. It *is* a fact that sensory perception by itself is not sufficient to give us access to the unobservable world of atoms and DNA and tectonic plates that science claims to have discovered. We *do* see the world through conceptual categories that we have access to in any given place, culture, and time. We cannot indeed strip ourselves of all assumptions and rise above it all to see the world in its own terms and compare it with what we think about it, and then decide if we are right or wrong, whether our facts match with the world or not.

A return to naive empiricism which takes observation to be innocent of theory and social assumptions is neither possible nor needed. I believe that it is possible to accept all these assumptions and *yet* affirm that science can give us an explanation of the causal mechanisms of the real world, which exists apart from our views about it; or deny that scientific knowledge is made up of contextual values and choices of culture-bound scientists. A relativist social constructionism is not the only alternative left after the realization that all thought is socially mediated, and all observations derive their evidentiary force from the theoretical assumptions of the inquirer. A third alternative to both empiricism and social constructionism exists, namely, contextual realism.

I have offered a philosophical defense of a contextual realism elsewhere, and I can only say this much about it here.[25] I believe that it is perfectly possible to defend a realism that can distinguish truth from superstition, and justify preferring the former not simply in terms of coherence (or "solidarity" as Rorty calls it) with a particular community of knowers (i.e., Western scientists), but in terms of how accurately it maps onto, and—yes—corresponds to some part of what there is in the world.

The contextual realism I defend argues that, contrary to postmodernist assumptions, such a mapping between our theories and the world does *not* require us to secure an Archimedean point, or a God's eye view which is outside of all social practices, language, and cultural categories. Indeed, postmodernists have sent us on a fool's errand by making such impossible demands on scientific knowledge.

Scientific objectivity need not satisfy an impossible ideal of neutrality. History- and context-bound inquirers, with all their biases, interests, and other flaws can still get to know the world through a process of constant revision of our conceptual schemes and our observations of the world in light of each other. Through a relentless critique and revision of our conceptual categories based on new evidence (which is justified with the introduction of some other theories in the web of theories that make up a science), it is perfectly possible to transcend the limits of our inherited frameworks and to obtain a more complete picture of the natural and social world whose validity transcends the context of its production.

Even if one fully accepts (as realists always have) that evidence is never innocent of a theoretical standpoint and the knower's location at a certain point in history and society, observation and experiment can still be independent of the theory under test (although not from other theories). There is a way in which natural science *can* connect with the elements of the real world in a non-question-begging way. The independence of observation from the theory, when coupled with a free and open scientific community, is sufficient to make a dialectical self-correction and growth of knowledge possible. Contextual realism is not unlike reading a book written in an unfamiliar language: like the translator of such a book, a scientific community comes to understand the meaning or the plot of the book of nature by a constant back-and-forth between deciphering the marks on the pages (observations) in light of the context established by other recurrent marks, and revising and understanding the context better through new and better understanding of the marks.[26]

I will end here by arguing that we all—in the East or in the West—share the same natural world. Any advance in deciphering the common book of nature anywhere is an advance for all of us.

Notes

I am grateful to Ellen Meiksins Wood for her encouragement and insightful critique. An earlier version of this paper was presented at the American Philosophical Association (Eastern Division) in December 1995.

1. Ian Hacking, "The Disunities of Science," in Peter Galison and David Stump (eds.), *The Disunity of Science: Boundaries, Contexts and Power* (Stanford: Stanford University Press, 1996), p. 41.
2. For a recent representative of this kind of third worldism, see Sandra Harding, "Is Science Multicultural? Challenges, Resources, Opportunities, Uncertainties," *Configurations* 2 (1994): 301-330. See also Ziauddin Sardar (ed.), *The Revenge of Athena: Science, Exploitation and the Third World* (London: Mansell Publishing Ltd., 1988); Z. Sardar (ed.), *The Touch of Midas* (Manchester: Manchester University Press, 1984); Ashis Nandy (ed.), *Science, Hegemony and Violence: A Requiem for Modernity* (Delhi: Oxford, 1990); and Vandana Shiva, *Staying Alive* (London: Zed Press, 1988).
3. Abdus Salam, foreword to Pervez Hoodbhoy, *Islam and Science: Religious Orthodoxy and the Battle for Rationality* (London, Zed Press, 1991).
4. I got my Ph.D. in biochemical engineering from the Indian Institute of Technology, New Delhi, and later worked as a science correspondent for *Indian Express* in New Delhi. In the United States, I was associated with the sustainable agriculture movement and edited a resource guide to sustainable farming practices in the third world.
5. J.D. Bernal, *Science in History* (London: 1965), pp. 910 and 924.

6. The third tenet of the Strong Programme states: "[Sociology of Scientific Knowledge] would be symmetrical in its style of explanation. The same type of cause would explain, say, true or false beliefs." see David Bloor, *Knowledge and Social Imagery* (Chicago: University of Chicago Press, 1991 [1976]).

7. Now, it is true that facts are theory-dependent and that theories are "under-determined" by evidence, but in actual lab work, this by no means makes the enterprise of science as circular and question-begging as social constructivists assume. Despite solid arguments and evidence against it, interpretive flexibility continues to serve an important role in social constructivist theories.

8. I have admittedly used a broad brush here, but the picture I have painted is by no means a caricature. It can be fully substantiated, in letter and in spirit, from the writings of well-known social constructivists, including David Bloor, Barry Barnes, H.M. Collins, Knorr Cetina, Steve Woolgar, and Bruno Latour. Even though feminist critics of science, including Sandra Harding, Helen Longino, and Evelyn Fox Keller have tried to distance themselves from the relativist implications of the sociologists of science, they too accept the basic assumptions of symmetry and interpretive flexibility.

9. See Alan Sokal, "Transgressing the Boundaries: Toward a Transformative Hermeneutic of Quantum Gravity," *Social Text,* Spring/Summer 1996: 217-218. In this hilarious parody of a postmodern perspective on quantum gravity, Sokal strung together arcane, jargon-ridden abstractions from an extremely specialized area of quantum physics, peppered with pieties about contextual, nonlinear, and liberatory science.

10. T. Jayaraman, "Exposing Anti-Science: The Sokal Affair," *Frontline,* Vol. 13 (21 September-4 October 1996): 95-97.

11. Sandra Harding, among many others, has claimed that any demarcation between science and non-science is "necessary to preserve the mystique of the uniqueness and purity of the West's knowledge-seeking.... the self-image of the West depends upon the contrast between rational and irrational." See Harding, "Is Science Multicultural?" pp. 309-10.

12. Sandra Harding, "Science is 'Good to Think With,'" *Social Text,* Spring/Summer 1996.

13. See the essays especially by Glyn Ford, M. Ahmad Anees, and Ziauddin Sardar for this view in Sardar (ed.), *The Revenge of Athena.*

14. My training in science gave me enough self-confidence to defy the community norm of early and arranged marriage. I went to New Delhi and got my Ph.D. But the process of getting to Delhi and the experience of doing research in an elite institution changed my relationship with science: Ibecame more interested in making science more widely available to those who had been left out. As a result, I did not continue to work as a biologist, but worked off and on as a science teacher for disadvantaged children and found work as a science

writer for *Indian Express*, a national newspaper. As a journalist, I saw myself as a partisan of science for the people movements and sought to popularize their ideas.

15. Stephen Toulmin defines *cosmopolis* simply as: "cosmos + polis = cosmopolis." See his *Cosmopolis: The Hidden Agenda of Modernity* (Chicago: University of Chicago Press, 1990), p. 68. While for Toulmin the social order and the natural order are seen as organically related, I find Paul Gilroy's celebration of "double consciousness" more useful. See Paul Gilroy, *The Black Atlantic: Modernity and Double Consciousness* (Cambridge, MA: Harvard University Press, 1993).
16. Like the "Society of Young Scientists" at the All-India Institute of Medical Sciences which I was a member of, and many similar societies in Delhi University and later at Indian Institute of Technology as well. Members of these groups volunteered at schools, clinics, projects for appropriate technology, and other socially relevant projects.
17. Although in India, given the influence of Gandhian philosophy, there is a generalized and pervasive distrust of modern ideas. Ashish Nandy, India's foremost critic of modernity, led the polemical attack on a "Statement of Scientific Temper" put forward by a group of scientists and humanists in 1981. Nandy and his associates at the well-known Center for Study of Developing Societies in Delhi, in cooperation with the Gandhian "Patriotic People's Science and Technology," produced polemical attacks on modern science as "instruments of exploitation and violence" against the masses.
18. For a generally favorable account of the rise of new social movements in India, see Gail Omvedt, *Reinventing Revolution and the Socialist Tradition in India* (Armonk, NY: M.E. Sharpe, 1993). For an anguished statement of the rise of Islamic science in Pakistan, see Pervez Hoodbhoy, *Islam and Science*. For a recent and critical review of Islamic science, see Bassam Tibi, "Culture and Knowledge: The Politics of Islamization of Knowledge as a Postmodern Project?" *Theory, Culture and Society* 12 (1995): 1-24.
19. See Matthew Zachariah, *Science for Social Revolution? Achievements and Dilemmas of a Development Movement: The Kerala Sastra Sahitya Parishad* (London: Zed, 1994), p. 156.
20. For a recent review, see Zachariah, ibid., and Anita Rampal, "Innovative Science Teaching in Rural Schools in India: Questioning Social Beliefs and Superstitions" in Joan Solomon and Glen Aikenhead (eds.), *STS Education: International Perspectives on Reform* (New York: Teachers College Press, 1994).
21. For a representative attack on science and people science movements in India, see Claude Alvares and others in Nandy (ed.), *Science, Hegemony and Violence*.

22. For a call for re-integration of knowledge and Islamic values, see Munawar Anees and Merryl Davies in Sardar (ed.), *The Revenge of Athena*. For a call for re-integration with Brahminical/Hindu values, see Shiva, *Staying Alive*.
23. Meera Nanda, "Science Wars in India," *Dissent*, Winter 1997.
24. Norman Geras, *Solidarity in the Conversation of Humankind: The Ungroundable Liberalism of Richard Rorty* (London: Verso, 1995), p. 107.
25. Meera Nanda, "Restoring the Real: Rethinking Social Constructivist Theories of Science," forthcoming in *The Socialist Register 1997*.
26. A lucid exposition of just such a contextual realism is provided by Peter Kosso in his *Reading the Book of Nature* (Cambridge: Cambridge University Press, 1992).

3: POSTMODERNISM AND MOVEMENTS

Issues of class and culture

AIJAZ AHMAD

An interview conducted by Ellen Meiksins Wood

Q: In your book, *In Theory: Classes, Nations, Literatures* you observe that American literary theory in the last two decades has been remarkably devoid of influences from the major work in Marxist political economy that has been done in the United States, not least by *Monthly Review* and its publishing house. Why is this significant? Why does literary theory need Marxist political economy?

Ahmad: The latter part of your question can be answered more briefly. Culture is not reducible to those processes that Marxist political economy studies for its own purposes, but culture *is* embedded in those processes. The so-called mass culture today is quite inseparable from processes of mass production, marketing, profiteering, systems of mass communication, etc. Every social practice and all material production involves signification, but neither communication nor fashion nor any other of those things that Cultural Studies takes as its specific object of study is merely or even mainly a signifying practice. Nor can the relation between cultural production and its basis in economic and political processes be read off anecdotally or epiphenominally; it has to be studied rigorously and structurally. You can't just throw in a bit of economics here, a bit of technology there; you have to be able to locate individual facts in a complex historical process, and for that you need very considerable theoretical preparedness. In its beginnings Cultural Studies was quite aware of all this, and some have sought to remain true to those very prosaic origins. In the main, though, Cultural Studies has itself become one of those many styles of consumer capitalism that it sets out to study.

But my reference to *Monthly Review* that you have recalled meant a great deal more than that. Implied in it was my own sense of the overall structure of the output—in the journal and from the press—that one associates with *Monthly Review*. It seems to me that in the postwar United States *Monthly*

Review has been the only institution of the left which provides a full-fledged narrative of the world, for the very period in which this institution has functioned. One doesn't have to agree with all aspects of this narrative, but what I want to emphasize is that there is a narrative of the world more comprehensive than any that has come from any other source in the Anglophone world, and this narrative includes, equally, the structures of advanced capitalism as well as the attempts to overthrow it or at least transform it. In scope, this output has been less occupied with Western Europe and Japan, and the latter I think is a special lacuna; but this narrative includes comprehensive histories of people's struggles—specifically revolutionary struggles—a matter that stands in sharp contrast to the output of the *New Left Review* and its press, the only institution of the left over the past three decades, albeit outside the United States, that may be compared with *Monthly Review* either in ambition or in achievement. It is interesting to me that *Monthly Review* has been relatively less concerned with Western Europe, which has been *New Left Review's* special provenance.

This narrative has some specific features. One is that although it broke with what became of the Soviet state with Stalin and thereafter, it did not become hostile to the myriad Communist movements as such, be they in Cuba, Vietnam, Angola, India, or anywhere else, not to speak of the many revolutionary movements which were not formally Communist but were of that kind of inspiration. The criterion of solidarity was not that a movement be Stalinist or Trotskyist or Maoist or Guevarist or whatever, but that it be revolutionary in a sense that would be recognizably so from a Marxist perspective. I don't mean that I agree with every judgment *Monthly Review* made based on this principle (its treatment of the Chinese Cultural Revolution is a case in point) but I do greatly support the principle. This remarkable combination of nonsectarianism and profound respect for the revolutionary enterprise gave to the principal tendency of *Monthly Review* also a remarkable resilience against the two great temptations of our time: social democratic degeneration on the one hand, romance of the national bourgeoisies on the other—and this without devaluing either the importance of whatever reform the working people might be able to win or the importance of anti-imperialist nationalism in the imperialized world. I might add that the editors of *Monthly Review* have had an exemplary commitment to a certain level of linguistic communication that is necessary for socialist activism. I think that in these times of professionalized jargons on the left it needs to be said that those "Review of the Month" essays, in which [Paul M.] Sweezy and [Harry] Magdoff [co-editors of *Monthly Review*] have over the years given us such lucid analyses of intricate details of high capitalist finance, are gems of English prose. That prose should be compulsory reading for Derridians.

I remember teaching [Harry] Braverman's great book [*Labor and Monopoly Capital* (New York: Monthly Review Press, 1974)] to undergraduates who had no background in economics and communicating to them something essential, something concrete about what has happened to the American working class in this century. I think a profound sensitivity to work of that kind would yield us a very different sense of what gets called "mass culture" in today's Cultural Studies. As I look back on that stream of books that came out of the Monthly Review Press about revolutionary struggles in a host of imperialized countries—Cuba, Vietnam, Guinea-Bissau, Brazil, Colombia, Chile, China, Egypt, and many others—I am firmly convinced that anyone who had seriously attended to the lessons of that documentation could never so easily downgrade the whole question of revolutionary class struggle in favor of "national allegory," "hybridity," "postcoloniality" or whatever else happens to be the fashion of the day. *Monthly Review* is of course not the only source for knowledge of that kind, but in the United States it has been the largest such source and comparatively the most reliable. So, I find it quite reprehensible that American leftists who want to do radical work in areas of culture and ideology, and who constantly make large statements about the politics of the modern world, especially "third world," have been so little engaged with the body of theory and information made available by this institution.

Since you have referred to my book, I might add that I have of course not written a book in the *Monthly Review* tradition, but some key sections of the book would be better understood in the United States if radicals in that country were better acquainted with this archive in their own national tradition. It interests me that my critics never engage with the two chapters, the introduction and the concluding chapter, which I take to be crucial in the very deliberate design of the book; they only go after the famous names—Said, Jameson, Rushdie—of the middle chapters. Now, the narrative of the postwar world that I provide there is of course not the narrative one would get from *Monthly Review*, but anyone familiar with the *Monthly Review* narrative would be well-equipped to make sense of the narrative I have assembled in summary. I think that readers who pay little attention to the actual struggles of the people around the world over the past fifty years or more, but who know their Benedict Anderson and their Gellner and their Subalternists, are very ill-equipped to understand my approach toward nationalism. For example, I view the question of nationalism *historically*. Consequently I may oppose many, many kinds of nationalism, but I also hold on to the importance of anti-imperialist nationalism in a world dominated by imperialism. Similarly, a good number of people can't quite figure out what kind of Marxist I am; they seem to have some very fixed categories in their head—Stalinist, Trotskyist, Eurocommunist, Maoist, what have you—and I don't fit any of those categories. This, then, is made worse by the fact that I write comprehensible prose, which probably means that I couldn't possibly be doing theoretical work; some people have actually declared that I am anti-theory. If U.S. radicals knew more about the *Monthly Review* tradition they would immediately see that I have *not* written a book in that tradition but they would also have a way of handling some of the things in the book that confuse them.

Q: In your recent article on the literature of "postcoloniality," you make some provocative suggestions about the current historical conjuncture, arguing that, while there has certainly been an increasing "globalization" of capital, there has, contrary to conventional wisdom, also been "an intensification of the nation-state form." Could you elaborate a bit on this and on the contradictory effects which, you argue, this combination is having on the realms of culture and ideology?

Ahmad: I don't want to repeat what I have said in that article on this issue. So, let me simply give the full reference; it was published in the London-based journal *Race and Class*, in the January-March issue, 1995.

The word "globalization" is, I think, a highly ideological word, and as such actually refers to quite a few different things. At one level, it simply means that with the collapse of the Soviet Union and the system of the states it represented there is now only one system, that of imperialist capital, and everyone better accept this fact. Those who celebrate "globalization" don't put it so brutally, but that's what they mean. Second, the term refers to the tremendous mobility of capital and commodities, the increased role of export/import trade in national accounts, the power of communication and transport technologies with unparalleled global reach, the enormous power of finance capital and speculation over and above industrial capital across national frontiers, the ability of new and centrally-produced cultural commodities to bypass national apparatuses of education and information through telecasting and information highways, the rise of production and management systems in which the production process itself can be fragmented and located in different countries and/or quickly moved from one to the other, and so on. Third, the term "globalization" is also a euphemism for the fact that a handful of imperialist institutional arrangements—the World Bank, IMF, GATT, etc.—are now determining national policies across the so-called third world. Fourth, it refers to the rapid penetration of all production by capitalism, hence by the world market. The World Bank calculated that by the end of the century only 12 percent of the economic production in the world will be outside the global capitalist market as such.

At the macroeconomic level, these are powerful tendencies and I do not wish to understate their importance. In some ways, none of this is very surprising. Capital has had a tendency toward transnationalization since its very inception, as not only Marx but also Luxemburg and Lenin knew very well. This is part of the story of colonialism, for example. Lenin's definition of imperialism would mean nothing without this historical tendency. What I am saying is something else. The first point is that there is another, equally powerful historical tendency, the one toward a far greater mobility of capital and relative *immobility* of labor, which still holds. One feature of this other tendency is that while capital seeks to travel across national frontiers, regimes of labor still continue to be national regimes. There is a pretense in most kinds of economics that prices are determined—perhaps brutally but "freely"—in the market. This simply is not so. Prices, especially the prices of labor, are determined *historically*, and the nationally constituted disciplines and regimes of labor are a fundamental component of that history.

Even in the most advanced capitalist countries, the nation-state is alive and well. Japanese capital is both transnational and aggressively Japanese. Germany has achieved its expanded national unification only recently, and one would have to be a fool not to see that there is a relationship between the German national interest and the Bundesbank. I also read somewhere that something like 95 percent of U.S. savings are invested inside the country. I might add that mutual accommodation of national interests is much more possible among the most advanced capitalist countries, and one may speak with relatively greater justice of a market of "free" exchanges among them. But as soon as you look at the "globalization" that connects the imperialist countries with the imperialized ones, you become much more aware of national differentiations and coercions.

Which brings me to the question of colonialism and the so-called post-colonialism. I mean, first of all, the hard materialities of it. How does U.S. capital arrive in Bangalore today, in the context of a sovereign Indian state, to exploit the cheaper labor and industrial plant there, including even intellectual labor? Is there a colonial empire to make free entry possible, as it was possible for British capital to come to India during the Raj? Or is there just an open global market for capital to travel on its own volition? Not at all. That capital must pass through the Indian nation-state, must rely on certain disciplines of labor, wage contracts, conditions of industrial peace, chances of repatriation of profits that only the Indian state can guarantee. The nation-state in this case is the articulating principle between global capital and national labor.

From whose point of view do you then read history? From the standpoint of capital that circulates globally, or from that of labor which is everywhere in chains? I think the metropolitan intellectuals who are such enthusiasts of globalization should organize a movement for the abolition of passports, so that we may actually have movements of labor almost as free as the movements of capital itself. Let all the U.S. capital come to India and all the Indian workers go to the U.S. to earn U.S. wages. Let there be a global equalization of wages and profits. Here I am not asking for socialism, only that the bourgeoisie be true to its word: free movements of people. The struggle for socialism would be, I think, easier in a world turned so upside down.

What does it mean for "realms of culture and ideology"? It depends on what sites of cultural and ideological production you have in mind. I think that the intellectuals in the metropolitan countries who speak of a "world culture," without emphasizing the fact that a "world culture" in this circumstance can only be the predominance of imperialist culture, are paving a way to hell with good intentions. As I look at this process from inside India, what I find is a powerful affirmation of the good old Marxist idea that economics and culture go hand in hand. In fact, the contemporary evidence is that one *experiences* the shifts in the realm of culture even before those shifts take hold fully in the economic realm. The Indian government, politically bankrupt to its core, has now had the policy of "globalization" and "liberalization" in the current sense for barely five years or so. During this time, very little Western investment capital has actually come in because they want even more favorable conditions. But the flooding of India with western cultural artifacts, from entertainment grids to consumption goods to ideologies of consumption, has been much more far-reaching.

In these circumstances, one is struck by two parallel developments in the ideological realm of what gets called Cultural Studies. There is the idea of the *discreteness* of identities, cultural, ethnic, or national; a kind of remorseless differentialism, whereby I am not permitted the claim that I may *understand* your identity but I am supposed to simply *respect* whatever you say are the requirements of your identity. In this ideology, any number of people celebrate hardened boundaries between self and other, denounce what they understand as the "universalism" of the Enlightenment, rationalism, and so on, while also fully participating in the globalization of consumption patterns and the packaging of identities as so many exhibits. At the same time and often from the same people, we also have the propagation of the idea of infinite hybridity, migrancy, choice of alternate or multiple identities, as if new selves could be fashioned in the instant out of any clay that one could lay one's hands on, and as if cultures had no real historical density and identities could be simply *made up, sui generis,* out of the global traffic and malleability of elements taken from all over the world.

Q: In the same article, you remark that "postcoloniality is also like most things a matter of class." This kind of emphasis on class is, of course, deeply unfashionable. Without dwelling on the notion of "postcoloniality" (if it isn't too frivolous to ask for an answer in such a limited space), would you care to justify the sweeping proposition that "most things" are a matter of class?

Ahmad: Let me first make explicit a rather memorable reference there. In her biography of Zhu De, the great commander of the People's Army during the revolution in China, Agnes Smedley recalls a moment when she had asked him about his having been a bandit and a thief in his youth. As Smedley tells it, Zhu De fell silent for a while and then said something like, "Theft, you know, is also a matter of class." I read that book when I was a very young boy, but the truth of that simple statement has stayed with me all these years, and in paraphrasing those words I just wanted to record my admiration for both Smedley and Zhu De.

But you have asked me to *justify* those words. I'm not sure how one justifies words so obviously true. India is said to have a population between 900 and 1,000 million. Roughly half of them are illiterate; but no bourgeois is illiterate anywhere in the world, and those who constantly speak of "the pleasure of the text" are never poor. Roughly half of the world's blind people live in India; but blindness too is a matter of class, in the sense that blindness is overwhelmingly a disease of the poor and in the sense that such high incidence of blindness has a lot to do with living in conditions that produce blindness, with the number and quality of hospitals, with the ability to pay for cure and care. What needs to justify itself is that other kind of blindness, which refuses to see that most things *are* a matter of class. That refusal is itself very intimately a matter of class.

The real question, then, is: why does one need to reiterate a truth so obvious? I think that the institutionalizing of certain kinds of radicalism has gone hand in hand with a certain sanitization of vocabulary, which is ultimately quite devastating for thought itself. One begins with the idea that there is some economic determination in social life but also that, as Althusser famously put it, "the lonely hour" of that final determination "never comes." In the next step, one forgoes the idea of economic determination altogether. Then, the critique of capitalism is sundered from any forthright affirmation of what might replace it. So, the more antibourgeois, and anticolonial, etc., one becomes, the less one talks about socialism as a determinate horizon. In the process, critiques of capitalism are also sundered from any necessity of working class politics. Indeed, one may use the word "bourgeois," in a cultural sort of sense, but the word "proletariat" makes one distinctly uncomfortable, as if using such words is some kind of antisocial activity. One may speak of any number of disorientations and even oppressions, but one cultivates all kinds of politeness and indirection about the structure of capitalist class relations in which those oppressions are embedded. To speak of any of that directly and simply is to be "vulgar." In this climate of Aesopian languages it is absolutely essential to reiterate that most things *are* a matter of class. That kind of statement is I think surprising only in a culture like that of the North American university in which radicalism has not had a powerful connection with movements of the working class for a long time. But it is precisely in that kind of culture that people need to hear such obvious truths.

Q: You have made some very trenchant criticisms of contemporary literary and cultural writings by thinkers who are very influential on the intellectual left. These criticisms have generated a great deal of controversy. What aspects of your criticisms seem to have been most difficult for people to accept? Why? Have you been surprised by the reaction? Have people been missing the point? What do you regard as most important about your criticisms? Do you want to set the record straight in any way?

Ahmad: I can say quite truthfully—I don't mean I am necessarily right, but I do think—that no real controversy on my book has ever taken place. I said earlier that so far as I am concerned, the burden of the main argument is contained in the Introduction and the last chapter. To my knowledge, no one has engaged with those in print. The chapter that has had the most electrifying effect in literary circles in India, the one on Indian literature, has never been discussed in the West; most people who have commented on my book there simply don't know what I'm talking about. Most critics latch on to the three middle chapters, about individuals and largely about individual texts, but in ways that I find bewildering. I have said that Jameson is to my mind the most important living literary theorist in the English language today, from whom I have learned a great deal, but I am writing critically about him because I reject the idea that *every* text from the third world is to be read as a "national allegory," and the further idea that nationalism is the determinate answer to what Jameson calls "American postmodern culture." This very high praise for Jameson—is he really that much better than Eagleton?—I am not inventing now, "to set the record straight"; it is there in the very essay I wrote in response to his essay. No one has yet refuted what I have actually said about "national allegory," etc; but it is alleged that what I have said amounts to "attack," "vilification," and so on—without any citation of any discourteous phrase I might have used about Jameson. The same sort of thing has happened about my criticism of Rushdie. I have been calling Khomeini a "clerical fascist" since the day he took power—when some of the more notable defenders of Rushdie were being very enthusiastic about the so-called revolutionary tradition of the Iranian clergy and were concentrating only on the misrepresentation of Islam in the U.S. media. You only have to look at Edward Said's *Covering Islam* and the issue of *Race and Class* which covered the Iranian Revolution at that time to see what I mean. But I am accused of waging a *jihad* against Rushdie, as someone has written in the prestigious U.S. journal, *Public Culture*.

So the matter boils down to the chapter on Edward Said. The last one-third of that chapter is a close scrutiny of two of Said's essays; I have never come across a single critic or reviewer who has engaged with that part of the chapter. Even about *Orientalism,* I think that the so-called "controversy" has never actually dealt with the main issues: Said's insistence on a remorseless continuity from Greek tragedy onwards; his uncertainty and even error in specifying the relationship between imperialism and the Eurocentric biases in modern European discourses about non-Europe; his privileging of written textuality in general and of literature in particular in this narrative of Europe's domination over non-Europeans; his neglect of the fact that much more than the Arab East, it is India, China, and generally the Far East that have been far more central in the system of knowledges that we can properly call "Orientalism"; his careless remarks about such key figures as Dante and Marx; his astonishing leveling of all kinds of European knowledges under the singular heading of Orientalism, whereas, for example, anyone who knows anything about India would find it scandalous that both William Jones and Macauley are so easily called "Orientalist," and so on. All kinds of historical specificities are sacrificed for the making of this construct called "Orientalism." I have never denied that in the Eurocentric atmosphere prevailing in the U.S. academy *Orientalism* has had quite considerable salutary effects, especially in areas of literary study and Middle Eastern Studies. I did not dwell on those positive aspects because they are well known. I thought, instead, that one should address some other aspects of that work which have indeed done very considerable harm. I must say that the substance of my argument, which I have illustrated here in the form of separate questions, was never answered. Looking back, I now think that there certainly were places where I mishandled the rhetoric, but it also interests me that verbal exaggerations of a negative kind were made the issue, but the same people never mentioned that I had praised Said in the highest terms for his personal courage and the work he has done on the issue of Palestine. So the reading of the rhetoric was itself tendentious. If you discount short reviews, Michael Sprinker is the only one among the critics who have written at any length about my book who has in fact addressed any of the issues that were central to its argument.

Was I surprised? Very much. By the attention that the book got, and then even more by the will of the detractors to personalize the whole issue, as if the book were nothing more than a "vilification" of a couple of individuals. It has been very discouraging for me that people who write about the book normally don't engage with the more substantive chapters: the Introduction, the last chapter, what I have to say about Marx or India or about Indian Literature—most of the basic issues I raise about the authors whose fame preoccupies those who usually feel constrained to write about my book. My chapter on *Shame* opens with a discussion of the connection there might be between the way the issue of "migrancy" gets posed in Rushdie's kind of fiction, the circulation of multinational capital, and of the personnel thrown to the whirlwind by that circulation, in our time—between the cultural "hybridity" that is celebrated these days, the fragmented and polyglot surface of literary texts made familiar to us by such masterpieces of modernism as *The Waste Land*, and the patterns of consumption symbolized by the supermarket in an age of globalized circulation of commodities. It has been both a surprise and a regret for me that the kind of "cultural studies" we now have just doesn't engage with questions of that kind, not when it comes to a serious discussion of a novel written by somebody who now commands an iconic status in the West thanks to his conflict with "Islamic fundamentalism." I find this kind of self-righteousness very amusing, considering that my own tussle with Islamism started much earlier.

Q: "Multiculturalism" is a major theme in U.S. intellectual life. Does this strike you as a useful concept? Does it denote a coherent educational or political project?

Ahmad: I believe that the logic of capital is to destroy the integrity of all use values and to impose exchange value upon all productions of value. Which then means that the cultural logic of capitalism is to produce a uniform culture of pure consumption, pure commodity fetishism. I don't mean that the actual, historically constituted cultures of capitalist societies are like that. Capital is never able to resolve the contradictions that it produces. But I do think that the *logical* tendency of capital is toward subsumption of all cultural value under commodity fetishism. I also speak and write constantly about absolutely necessary tensions between universality and particularity which cannot be resolved. Such tensions can only be lived, and the hope is that they shall be lived not destructively but in a productive relation. But I am under no illusion that this tension can ever be resolved or even need be resolved in any final sense, because both are intrinsic to human social life. With this kind of belief, no one could possibly be against the idea of the multiplicity of cultures or the need to devise educational and political agendas that recognize such multiplicities.

So one can't be against "multiculturalism" as such. But one can legitimately question, not just from the right but also authentically from the left, the way this concept has come into play in the United States. Chronologically, I think, this particular idea of "multiculturalism" has come *after* and in some covert way *against* the black insurgency and the women's liberation movement, and of course *after* the incipient and eventually unrealized anti-imperialist potentials of the antiwar movement. It serves to defuse and even derail the idea that empire and gender and race are *central* to the structure of differences in U.S. society in a way that differences among, say, the Italian, Jewish, and Polish ethnic groups are not. It denies, in other words, the idea that there is a hierarchy of determination in existing social relations which is an inevitable result of historical formation quite beyond any valuation that any individual may attach to them. It tends to push down in the scale of one's priorities the idea that, given the specific history of the United States, given the social structure bequeathed by slavery, the position of African-Americans is *unique* and cannot be collapsed into generalities of ethnicities, difference, and "multiculturalism." In other words, this kind of relativism tends toward the obliteration of actual, historically given relations of power in favor of a leveled-out notion of multiplicity and difference in which everyone becomes, sooner or later, everyone else's "other" and, by the same token, a member of a minority and even of a "subaltern" group. Such definitions tend to privilege the idea of culture as signifying system over the idea of culture's embeddedness in material life. They tend to assert the discreteness of cultures within a national space, and to privilege ethnicity in the constitution of each culture. A Jewish peddler on New York's Lower East Side then comes to have something more fundamentally in common with a Jewish magnate on Wall Street than all the peddlers from different ethnic groups could ever share.

At one end of this ideology, we have the abrogation of any normative sense of cultural value whereby judgments of right and wrong can be made; each culture, as discrete ethnicity, is said to have its own structure of identity formation. At the other end, the ideology of multiculturalism tries to reconstruct, on campuses that have seen intense confrontations on the issue of fatally unequal distributions of power, a celebratory version of U.S. pluralism whereby there is always enough in the basket to go around for everyone and all differences can be accommodated in a non-antagonistic fashion. So in the process of being granted their autonomous spaces, differences are also trivialized. In the actual syllabus formation, this kind of relativism and pluralism typically leads to either a very hardened version of discrete identities, whereby entire courses can be structured around distinct identities, or to sheer randomness in which today's text may illustrate one identity and tomorrow's another, and so on. This kind of multiculturalism in the U.S. college system has had the effect of greatly diluting the original purpose of cultural studies.

Q: Some kinds of "relativism"—cultural, even moral—used to seem progressive, in the sense that they resisted various claims to moral or cultural superiority which could be used to justify domination, oppression, imperialism, and so on. Today, the socialist left often finds itself defending "universalist" principles against new forms of particularism and relativism; and you, for example, have had some very strong things to say about poststructuralist and postmodernist particularisms, "identity" politics, extreme forms of "cultural differentialism," and so on. Can you offer any simple rules for negotiating the difficult transactions between "universalism" and "particularism?" Is there a way of granting recognition to human "difference" without giving up the kinds of universal principles that used to underlie the socialist project of a general human emancipation?

Ahmad: Let me first tell you something about my *experience* before going on to history and theory. I was born and bred in a society with a phenomenal range of diversities of all kinds. The Anthropological Survey of India tells us that there are today some 3,000 distinct communities in India, something like 360 languages and dialects. It might also interest you that according to the same survey, 60 or so percent of the Indian people think of themselves as migrants, as having come from elsewhere in the country. Historians of Early Medieval India tell us that the people who do *not* believe in any grand religions—Hinduism, Islam, Christianity, etc.—have always been the majority in this country. Meanwhile, a sense of a subcontinental entity also begins early. I think it has something to do with geography, with being bounded by very tall mountains on one side and a vast ocean on the other, and with the massiveness of alluvial plains and the riverine systems. This sense of an entity is there even in the territorial expanse over which the stories of the *Mahabharatha* unfold. Some of it gets embedded in the Early and Medieval imperial consolidations. By the time of the devotional theisms of medieval times a certain sensibility can be found among the popular classes across India, grounded in regional idioms but profoundly humanist and universalist. In the more recent centuries, the generalization of capitalist market, the national anticolonial movements, and then, since independence, a system of representative government based on a universal franchise, not to speak of modern travel, communication, etc., has also produced a profound sense of a modern polity and a territorial nation.

In a nation so very heterogeneous, negotiations between universality and particularity, between migrancy and a sense of place, is a daily experience; even the Constitution of India has to recognize twenty national languages against one in the United States or two in Canada. One has a profound sense of belonging to all of it, yet the knowledge that one would not understand even a fraction of it, even in the simple sense of exchanging mutually intelligible words. So, when these same issues surface in such facile ways in the exhortations of "identity politics," as if these were grand discoveries of the postmodern, I don't quite understand—I understand cerebrally but I don't understand in the gut—what the fuss is all about.

I don't mean that everyone in India lives like that. All sorts of abominable things happen. I meant to say something about my own experience and the experience I share with other progressive people like myself, and there *are* millions of us, I don't know how many but a great many—and about the very textures of daily life that people share without having actually theorized about it. And what I meant to say was that in this life, and in the lives of countless people, generation after generation, there have been so many ways, traditional ways and modern ways, of reconciling "universalism" and "particularism" that there have been, for me, many quite concrete ways of negotiating my own experience. These ways are quite different from the way this question gets posed in societies like those of North America which have very brief histories and which carry such burdens of racial genocide, slavery, and migration—societies that have relatively little that is older than a capitalist ethic and not much of a communist tradition.

In more impersonal terms of history and theory, I would again bring up the issue of *rights,* about which I write and speak constantly because I think it *is* important to come at it from different angles. I think that there is a terrible distortion in the way the history of "universalism" gets recounted in the polemics against the Enlightenment, post-Enlightenment, etc. In such accounts, the discourse of rights remains where it began, namely in the proposition that the locus of all rights is the individual, that this individual has no attributes other than that of citizenship, that the structure of universal rights must follow the logic of universal laissez-faire which itself emanates from the pre-Ricardian notions of the so-called free market. I don't think that the debate has been frozen at that point of origin for all these years. Rather, there have been constant struggles. In our own time, a whole range of theories—Marxist certainly, but even liberal-feminist, secular, anticolonial and antiracist theories, not to speak of the extremely complicated discourses of minority rights—have amply demonstrated that the supposedly attribute-less individual that laissez-faire liberalism proposes is, under the ideological surface, none other than the white bourgeois male, and that even liberal theory must face up to the fact that the individual who might be not-male, not-white, not-bourgeois cannot be called upon to surrender her attributes to an abstract universality.

The whole issue of the commensurability of universal rights with rights of various kinds of minorities is at least as old as Locke. Historically, the capitalist state has of course not granted to workers or women the rights that should be theirs, but an idea is commonly held that there *are* rights that are specific to workers as workers and to women as women. There is an idea of the right of historical redress, in the form of affirmative actions, for sections of the population whose present disadvantage is rooted in the accumulated oppressions of the past. In the advanced capitalist countries, the state is in the process of being pushed to accommodate itself to the rights of the elderly, the physically handicapped. Everywhere in the world, the illiberal as well as the liberal are being called upon to accommodate themselves to the rights that are specific to what remains of those indigenous peoples whose lives are constantly shattered by capitalism's conquest of nature. A recognition is beginning to dawn upon political theory that situations of individuals and communities are so various that the secondary structure of particular rights will cumulatively far surpass the underlying structure of universal rights. Neither the beginning of trade union rights in the nineteenth century nor the expanding structure of women's rights in the twentieth, neither the civil rights legislation in the United States nor the ideology of the welfare state in Western Europe, would be conceivable outside the extremely difficult problematic of reconciling, on the terrain of practical social covenants, the universal and the particular.

None of it has given us anything resembling what I might mean by socialism, but there have been people's struggles and those struggles have sought a simultaneity of both universal and particular rights. I think we do a great disservice to the memory of those struggles when we speak only of what they *failed* to achieve and not of what they *did* achieve. And we do a great disservice to *ourselves* because that *is* our own history. The common people, the people who fought for a decent life, always said, let's all have equal rights but let's also take care of those who have special needs. They didn't have fancy language, but they knew what we, as intellectuals, mean by "universal" and "particular."

What I am trying to say, I think, is that we certainly need the most rigorous of theories, but we also need to have memories of the traditions of mercy and the struggles for justice. It is only there that any true reconciliation of the universal and particular is really possible.

The mirror of race: postmodernism and the celebration of difference

KENAN MALIK

The postmodern critique of racial discourse flows out of its hostility to universalism. For postmodernists, the Enlightenment project of pursuing a rational, scientific understanding of the natural and social world, and of deriving certain universal principles out of a fragmented experience, is not only a fantasy, but a dangerous fantasy. It is a fantasy because the world is too complex and too varied to be subsumed under a single "totalizing" theory. It is dangerous because universalism is a Eurocentric viewpoint, a means of imposing Euro-American ideas of rationality and objectivity on other peoples. Universalism is racist because it denies the possibility of non-European viewpoints. The intellectual arrogance of universalism, argue such critics, has led to the attempt to eliminate not just non-European thought but non-Aryan *peoples* too. Not just for postmodernists, but for many postwar social theorists, the road that began with Enlightenment universalism ends in Nazi death camps.

I want to argue in this article that the postmodern critique of universalism, far from establishing a critique of racial theory, in fact appropriates many of its themes and reproduces the very assumptions on which racism has historically been based. In its hostility to universalism and in its embrace of the particular and the relative, postmodernism embodies the same notions of difference as are contained in nineteenth-century Romantic racial theories. To understand better the relationship between the two, I want in this article to look at two key aspects of anti-universalism which are central to its critique of race: the opposition to essentialism, on the one hand, and to humanism, on the other. Through the first I want to show the irrationalism of postmodern discourse, its affinity to racial theory and its hostility to equality. Through the second I will show how the experience of political defeat has influenced postmodern theory and produced a convergence with reactionary and antidemocratic attacks on humanism, "modernity," and "mass society."

In the course of this critique, I will be examining the ideas of a number of writers from a variety of theoretical outlooks—structuralism and poststructuralism, post-Marxism and deconstructionism, phenomenology and postmodernism. My intention is not to erase the differences among the authors or their ideas, nor to ignore the often heated debates that have taken place among the various protagonists. Rather, it is to demonstrate the common threads that link the diverse strands of contemporary theory and to suggest that these commonalities far outweigh in importance the differences that are often expressed. In this spirit, I shall use the terms poststructuralist and postmodernist interchangeably to refer to discourses and theorists influenced by the works of such writers as Claude Lévi-Strauss, Jacques Lacan, Jacques Derrida, Michel Foucault, and similar thinkers. Their work, though varied and often conflictual, is characterized by a number of common themes, including a critique of reason, a rejection of humanism, an anti-realist epistemology, and a radical relativism.

"Essentialism" and identity

"Poststructuralist thinking," sociologists David Bailey and Stuart Hall have argued, "opposes the notion that a person is born with a fixed identity—that all black people, for example, have an essential underlying black identity which is the same and unchanging. It suggests instead that identities are floating, that meaning is not fixed and universally true at all times for all people, and that the subject is constructed through the unconscious in desire, fantasy and memory."[1]

The reminder that our identities are not naturally given but socially constructed is a useful antidote to the idea that human differences are fixed and eternal. But by insisting that society is inherently and irreducibly heterogeneous and diverse, and by rejecting any idea of "totality" that might allow us to see the commonalities or connections among heterogeneous and diverse elements, poststructuralist discourse has undermined its own capacity to challenge naturalistic explanations of difference. The paradoxical result, I shall argue, is a conception of identity scarcely different from that of nineteenth-century racial theory.

The problem can be seen in the very concept of "anti-essentialism" as understood by postmodernist thinkers. Sociologist Ali Rattansi has described anti-essentialism as a "manoeuvre cutting the ground from conceptions of subjects and social forms as reducible to timeless, unchanging, defining and determining elements or ensemble of elements—'human nature,' for example, or in the case of the social, the logic of the market or mode of production."[2]

Rattansi seems at first to define anti-essentialism simply as opposition to an ahistorical understanding of social phenomena, hostile to the idea of timeless or unchanging social forms. But he slides from this rejection of ahistorical explanation to a repudiation of social "determinants" altogether. He rejects any idea that social forms can be explained by reference to forces or pressures like the "logic of the market" or the "mode of production" which permeate and shape the social order, even if these determinants are conceived as historically specific. A non-essentialist understanding of society is apparently one that denies any unifying patterns or processes among the diverse and constantly shifting fragments that constitute society. In other words, Rattansi identifies anti-essentialism with an insistence on indeterminacy. In this he reflects much postmodern thinking which finds the meaning of social forms not in *relations* but in *differences*.

But this kind of indeterminacy is precisely the foundation of ahistorical explanations. How, for instance, can we understand the historical nature of capitalism as a specific social form without identifying the specific determinants that distinguish it from other social forms, in other times and places? We could argue about whether the "essence" of capitalism should be seen in the logic of the market, in the particular mode of production, in some other aspect, or in some combination of these. But unless we can characterize the fundamental specificity—the "essence," if you will—of capitalist society, its distinctive "laws of motion" or systemic logic, we cannot distinguish it from other types of societies. How, then, should we analyze race in modern capitalist societies? If we treat race as just an "identity" detached from any specific social determinants, then race becomes not a historically specific social relation but an eternal feature of human society—just as it is in reactionary biological theories of race, in which racial divisions are a natural and permanent necessity.

This may seem an odd conclusion to draw from postmodern anti-essentialism, because its roots lie precisely in a hostility to naturalistic explanations of social phenomena, particularly positivism, which reduce social laws to natural laws, treating the laws that govern human relations as quantifiable and permanent, just like the laws of nature. Because the positivist view of society underpinned nineteenth century racial theories, opponents of racial theory have always been hostile to naturalistic theories of society.

But in its haste to dispatch naturalistic theories, poststructuralist discourse (and indeed much of modern sociology) takes up arms against not simply naturalistic explanations of society, but against *any* causal explanation, or at the very least, any explanation that assigns priority to certain causes over others. Any idea of determination—even in its non-reductionist sense, having to do with what E.P. Thompson often calls the "logic of process" or Raymond Williams (in *Marxism and Literature* [1978]) describes as "a complex and interrelated process of limits and pressures"—is considered to be essentialist and therefore illegitimate. Postmodern anti-essentialists hold that theory can have no recourse to determinants beyond empirically given phenomena. Essences and forces, whether natural or metaphysical, spiritual or historical, are fictitious. At best social "laws" are convenient fictions that allocate an order to empirical phenomena. At worst they are self-serving illusions which disguise some sinister interest or power. For poststructuralists, then, social phenomena cannot be explained by reference to another property that bestows meaning on them. This kind of anti-essentialism renders all determinate relations contingent, bereft of any inner necessity.[3]

Poststructuralists deny the concept of an "essential" identity and stress instead "the phenomenon of multiple social identities." As Robin Cohen puts it, "the modern study of identity has ... dished the old 'essentialisms'—for example the Marxist idea that all social identity could essentially be reduced to class identity." Instead it holds that "there are competing claims for affiliation that cannot be reduced to epiphenomena" and that "gender, age, disability, race, religion, ethnicity, nationality, civil status, even musical styles and dress codes" are all "very potent axes of organization and identification."[4]

The recognition that human beings are subject to conflicting claims and identities is clearly important. The problem arises, however, when all "identities," of whatever form, are treated as equivalent, so that personal lifestyle preferences such as "musical styles" are given the same weight and significance as physical attributes such as "disability" or social products such as race and class, while, at the same time, each identity is conceived in isolation from specific social relations. In fact, there is already a problem in conceiving race or class as an "identity" in the first place. Social relations such as racial oppression become not social relations at all but personal attributes, or even lifestyle choices. When race is equated with "musical styles" or "dress codes," the "social" seems to mean nothing more than a particular decision that any individual may make, and "society" is reduced to the aggregate of individual identities.

The consequence of the poststructuralist notion of society is that many contemporary writers treat social distinctions as personal or political choices. There is a scene in Woody Allen's film *Bananas,* in which our luckless hero, played by Allen, bemoans the fact that he dropped out of college. "What would you have been if you had finished school?" someone asks him. "I don't know," sighs Allen. "I was in the black studies program. By now I could have been black."

This seems to be the essence of the contemporary view of identity. As Robin Cohen observes, postmodernists seem to believe that "an individual constructs and presents any one of a number of possible social identities, depending on the situation. Like a player concealing a deck of cards from the other contestants, the individual pulls out a knave—or a religion, or an ethnicity, a lifestyle—as the context deems a particular choice desirable or appropriate."[5]

In this spirit an increasing number of writers now view racial division as the result of a deliberately chosen cultural exclusiveness. Winston James, employing Benedict Anderson's notion of an "imagined community," argues that, "Like all nations, nationalities and ethnic groups, Afro-Caribbean people in Britain have erected boundaries in relation to those with whom they identify."[6] The suggestion is that Afro-Caribbeans have chosen to establish distinctive cultural patterns, that they have asserted their right to be different, as a way of confirming their "imagined community," of establishing what James calls a "new sense of fellowship."

If this were true, however, racism would not be a problem. If we could choose identities in the way we choose our clothes every morning, if we could erect social boundaries from a cultural Lego pack, then racial hostility might be no different from disagreements between lovers of Mozart and those who prefer Charlie Parker, or between supporters of different football clubs. In other words, racial differences would not be *social relations* which exist apart from the preferences of any given individual. They would simply represent prejudices born out of a plurality of tastes.

But we know that in reality racial divisions *are* social relations, that they are not simply the product of personal preferences, and that blackness amounts to more than a semester on a black studies program. It is not Afro-Caribbeans, or any other racialized group, who have "erected boundaries" separating them from the rest of society. These boundaries are socially constructed not just in the sense that they are culturally specific, like personal tastes in music or clothes, but in the sense that society has systematically racialized certain social groups and signified them as "different"—as James himself acknowledges when he notes "the powerful centripetal forces of British racism."[7] Black youth in Brixton or the Bronx have no more "chosen" their difference than Jews did in Nazi Germany.

Certainly oppressed communities have often reacted to racial division by adopting particular cultural forms. In his autobiography, Miles Davis recounts how black jazz musicians in the forties responded to racism by developing bebop as a style that would exclude white players.[8] Similarly many Jews today continue to observe Jewish cultural rituals less out of religious faith than in response to anti-Semitism and in memory of the victims of the Holocaust. But such cultural assertion is not the cause of racial identification, it is its product.

This is one of the fundamental contradictions at the heart of postmodernism. Insisting on the "discursive" or "social construction" of all knowledge and identity, under the cover of "anti-essentialism" it ends by effectively denying determinate historical relations altogether and thus effectively abandons its original principle that identity and the human subject are socially constructed. Poststructuralist discourse reduces (or deconstructs) society to the accidental interaction of individuals and removes the subject from the terrain of the social. Determinate social relations are reduced to individual, personal attributes or at best to contingent relations between individuals. There can be no "social construction" when the "social" itself has no existence apart from "discursively constructed" individual identities.

Against "totality"

The postmodernist celebration of indeterminacy is reinforced by hostility to universalizing theory, or ideas of totality. Indeed the stress on indeterminacy arises from the belief that we cannot comprehend social reality in any holistic sense. In poststructuralist theory all attempts at grasping social reality as a totality are rejected. All such attempts are "totalitarian," ethnocentric, and racist, because they impose a single vision of the world upon what is in fact a plurality.

Here, postmodernists fall into another confusion. Their rejection of universalism and "totalizing" theories draws on some well-established epistemological principles, which they take to extreme—and illogical—conclusions. There has long been a widely accepted epistemological convention, even a truism, that "facts" do not present themselves to us unmediated, unaffected by our social experience and without selection or interpretation. This is, of course, even more the case when we are dealing with very complex social "facts" and when powerful ideological factors intervene. For example, by conventional measures of intelligence, African-Americans as a group have a lower I.Q. than white Americans. That is a fact. But what that fact means is not apparent from the fact itself. For some authors, like Richard Herrnstein and Charles Murray in their infamous *The Bell Curve,* the difference in I.Q. is an indication that black and white Americans are naturally different in their intellectual abilities. For others it means that I.Q. tests are a poor measure of intellectual ability. For yet others, the difference between the I.Q. scores of black and white Americans is a product of their differential treatment by society.

This obvious epistemological point does not necessarily mean that there is no basis for judging one interpretation as better than another. Many—probably most—historians and social scientists have long acknowledged that their knowledge is mediated in various ways; but they have not necessarily felt obliged to conclude that there are no standards of historical truth, or plausibility, against which to measure one account of history or social experience in comparison to others. Such people have commonly recognized that there can be different accounts, seen from the perspective of different places, times, or social groups, and that these accounts can even all be valid in relation to the particular experience and needs of those that propound them; but they have not necessarily felt obliged to conclude that there can never be a common standard to adjudicate among these different accounts, no basis for comparing them, or even a common vantage point from which to communicate between them or accommodate them to each other. As E.H. Carr understood:

> It does not follow that, because a mountain appears to take on different shapes from different angles of vision, it has objectively either no shape or an infinity of shapes. It does not follow that, because interpretation plays a necessary part in establishing the facts of history, and because no existing interpretation is wholly objective, one interpretation is as good as another, and the facts of history are not amenable to objective interpretation.[9]

But postmodernists have indeed jumped to such extreme and absurd conclusions. They have seized upon the multiplicities of meaning in order to reject not only common standards of judgment but the possibility of any commensurability between different worlds of meaning.

Postmodernism claims to situate "facts" in their specific social and historical context, but that is precisely what it fails to do. The very nature of deconstructionist methodology imposes an eternal framework on its object of investigation. The starting point of poststructuralism is the search for difference. As Derrida has put it, it is futile to ask who or what differs, since difference is prior to any subject.[10] But this is to smuggle the conclusion of the investigation into the method. If you set out to find difference in anything and everything, then that is exactly what you will find. If you begin with the premise that there is nothing but difference, then it goes without saying that you will never find commonalities or relations between things that are irreducibly different, let alone totalities in which these different things are linked together. Difference becomes the absolute in history. It plays the "essentialist" role in poststructuralist discourse that Nature played in nineteenth-century positivism.

The paradox of poststructuralist anti-essentialism, then, is this: it is an outlook that arises from a desire to oppose naturalistic explanations and to put social facts in a social context. But by celebrating indeterminacy and by opposing the idea of totality, all in the name of anti-essentialism, it has undermined its own ability to explain social facts historically. Facts wrenched from their living context are apprehended only in their isolation. The irony is that this methodology resembles nothing so much as the radical empiricism of the positivists, the very theory of knowledge that anti-essentialism sought to overturn.

This is not the place to resolve all the difficult epistemological questions involved in the debate between postmodernism and its critics. Some of these questions are dealt with elsewhere in this book. But we are entitled to ask whether postmodernists can sustain an anti-racist project on the basis of their own, supposedly anti-racist, assumptions. Can their epistemological assumptions support their own professed opposition to racial oppression? How, for example, would they distinguish between a racist history and a non-racist one? On postmodernist premises, each would be valid in its own context. The capacity of postmodernists to challenge racist discourse is undermined by their own belief in the relativity of meaning. If we want to argue that a racist and a non-racist interpretation of history are not equally valid, we are required to choose between them, to decide which is true and which is not, and that means we are obliged to accept that there is some standard against which we can judge them. What postmodernists dismiss as "totalizing" theories do not require us to encompass every possible "fact," as some postmodernists maintain, but they do give us some basis for choosing.

Anti-essentialism is supposed to be the very foundation of postmodernist anti-racism, but anti-essentialism as postmodernists define it ends by disabling any anti-racist project. Antiracism, for example, surely requires some commitment to equality. It is certainly true that "equality" is a historically specific idea, which has had different meanings in different social contexts. But the historicity of this idea does not change the fact that a commitment to equality, and especially racial equality, presumes the existence of a "human essence." Without such a common essence, equality among different "identities" or social groups would be a meaningless concept. If humanity did not constitute a single category, if in Foucault's words "Nothing in man—not even his body—is sufficiently stable to act as this basis for self-recognition or for understanding other men,"[11] then equality between different human individuals and groups would be as meaningless as equating apples and oranges or, to use Lévi-Strauss's analogy in his critique of Sartre, such "different domains" as "natural and irrational numbers."[12]

The postmodernist might reply that the principle of "difference" implies a truly radical egalitarianism, because it recognizes no standard by which one individual or group can be judged as better than another. But the point is that this principle of difference cannot provide any standards which oblige us to respect the "difference" of others. At best, it invites our *indifference* to the fate of the Other. At worst, it licenses us to hate and abuse those who are different. Why, after all, should we *not* abuse and hate them? On what basis can they demand our respect or we demand theirs? It is very difficult to support respect for difference without appealing to some "totalizing," universalistic principles of equality or social justice. We can acknowledge that the concept of "rights" is historically specific and socially constructed; but any argument in favor of equal rights, in whatever form, invariably brings us back to what postmodernists would call an "essentialist" explanation. Once such explanations, whether natural or social, are excluded, the very idea of equality also becomes subordinate to the "contingency of prevailing identities."

If the appearance of difference is taken at face value, in the absence of any common "essence" beyond or beneath that appearance, then the *appearance* of difference must be taken as evidence that there are indeed many different categories of humanity and that they have nothing fundamentally in common. This is precisely the method employed by positivist racial theory, which deduced from the appearance of difference (skin color, head form, and so on) the division of humanity into different categories or "races." Of course, contemporary theorists of difference deny that superficial biological differences define categorical distinctions, preferring instead to emphasize historical or cultural factors. But cultural formalism is in substance no different from racial formalism. Both move from the apprehension of formal difference to posit the existence of different ontological categories. This is why the anti-essentialist tendencies of poststructuralist thought inevitably puts in question equality itself.

The sources of antihumanism

Anti-essentialism reveals the commonality between postmodern and racial discourse, a commonality which lies in the common distrust of universalism, a fundamental ahistoricism, and the embrace of a radical empiricism. Now, I want to consider the social factors that gave rise to the postmodern outlook, by looking at the evolution of a second key component of postmodern antiracism—its unremitting hostility to humanism.

"[T]hose universal features which define the human," argues Robert Young, "mask over the assimilation of the human itself with European values." The category of the human, he believes, "however exalted in its conception," is "too often invoked only in order to put the male before the female, or to classify other 'races' as sub-human, and therefore not subject to the ethical prescriptions applicable to humanity at large."[13]

This kind of hostility to humanism, while central to much of contemporary social theory, is relatively new. An anthropocentric outlook underpinned the scientific and philosophical revolution unleashed by the Renaissance and the Enlightenment and has been central to all progressive Western philosophies and political movements. At the heart of humanism lie two key beliefs. First, humanists hold that human beings, while an inherent part of nature and subject to its laws, nevertheless have an exceptional status in nature because of their unique ability, arising out of human reason and sociability, to overcome the constraints placed upon them by nature. Second, humanists believe in the unity of humankind, holding that all humans possess something in common, a something which is often described as "human nature."

The humanist outlook has expressed itself in a variety of political forms, from liberalism to Marxism. Liberal humanists tend to view human nature as a static, eternal quality given by nature. David Hume, for instance, argued that "there is a great uniformity among the acts of men, in all nations and ages, and that human nature remains the same in its principles and operations."[14] (Hume himself occasionally lapsed into "Eurocentric" or even apparently racist language, nor was he alone in his contradictions—which may not be unrelated to the static, ahistorical conception of human nature characteristic of the tradition to which he belongs.)

Marx on the other hand always situated the human essence in a social and historical context. In his *Theses on Feuerbach,* for example, Marx criticized the German philosopher Ludwig Feuerbach for "abstract[ing] from the historical process" and assuming that the human essence was "an internal dumb generality which naturally unites the many individuals." But, argued Marx, "the human essence is no abstraction inherent in each single individual. In its reality it is the ensemble of the social relations."[15] In other words, "historical humanism," as Lukács called it, sees "man" not as naturally given but "as a product of himself and of his own activity in history."[16]

Whether liberal or Marxist, underlying all humanistic strands is a belief in human emancipation—the idea that humankind can rationally transform society through the agency of its own efforts. Indeed, no emancipatory philosophy is possible without a humanist perspective, for any antihumanistic outlook is forced to look outside of humanity for the agency of salvation—if earthly salvation is possible at all.

Antihumanistic strands developed from the Enlightenment on, largely in opposition to the idea of rational human emancipation. Just as there have been a number of different strands of humanism, so there have been a number of different strands of antihumanism, ranging from the conservatism of Burke, the Catholic reaction of de Maistre, to the nihilism of Nietzsche and the Nazism of Heidegger. All rejected Enlightenment rationalism and the idea of social progress because they despaired of the capacity of humankind for such rational progress, a despair that was in general an expression of either fear of or contempt for the masses, who were seen as irrational, atavistic, and a threat to civilized society. Antihumanism rejected ideas of equality and human unity, celebrating instead difference and divergence and exalting the particular and the "authentic" over the universal.

Antihumanism developed therefore as a central component of elite theories. In the postwar era, however, antihumanism came to represent a very different tradition—the liberal, indeed radical, anticolonialist and antiracist outlook. In the hands of such critics of Western society as Frantz Fanon, Michel Foucault, Jacques Derrida, and Louis Althusser, among others, antihumanism became a central thread of structuralist and poststructuralist theories, and a key weapon in the interrogation of racist and imperialist discourses. Even Jean-Paul Sartre, in his famous preface to Fanon's *The Wretched of the Earth,* wrote that "Humanism is nothing but an ideology of lies, a perfect justification for pillage; its honeyed words, its affectations of sensibility were only alibis for our aggression." Elsewhere he claimed that "Humanism is the counterpart of racism: it is a practice of exclusion."[17]

How did a philosophical outlook which originated within conservative anti-emancipatory politics, and which was a key component of racial theory, become a central motif of radical antiracist, anti-imperialist doctrines? And how did philosophers such as Nietzsche and Heidegger, whose work had previously been seen as paving the way for twentieth century racist and fascist ideologies, become icons of antiracist discourse?

There were two main strands to postwar radical antihumanism. One developed out of anticolonial struggles, the other through Western (and in particular French) academic philosophy and was subsequently elaborated by the "new social movements" such as feminism and environmentalism. In *The Wretched of the Earth,* Fanon gave voice to the rage of colonial peoples against their inhuman treatment at the hands of the imperialist powers. The humanist idea of "Man," wrote Fanon, which lay at the heart of the Western post-Enlightenment tradition, was achieved through dehumanizing the non-Western Other. Europeans only became human, Fanon suggested, by denying humanity to their colonial Other. To maintain a belief in humanism while treating non-European peoples as animals, Europeans declared that non-Europeans were in fact subhuman. Herein lay the source of racial theory in humanism. At the same time, argued Fanon, humanists salved their consciences by inviting the subhuman colonial Other to become human by imitating "European Man."

The category "human" is empty of meaning, the critics asserted, because it is ahistorical. The invocation of a common human nature hides the fact that human nature is socially and historically constructed. According to the anthropologist James Clifford, "[I]t is a general feature of humanist common denominators that they are meaningless, since they bypass local cultural codes that make personal experience articulate."[18] When humanists assert the universality of human nature, what they are really talking about are the particular human values expressed in European society.

Third world critics, however—and some European critics like Sartre too—did not reject humanism in its entirety. Fanon, for instance, recognized that the contradiction lay not in humanism itself but in the disjuncture between the ideology of humanism and the practice of colonialism:

> All the elements of a solution to the great problems of humanity have, at different times, existed in European thought. But Europeans have not carried out in practice the mission which fell to them, which consisted of bringing their whole weight to bear violently upon these elements, of modifying their arrangement and their nature, of changing them and, finally, of bringing the problem of mankind to an infinitely higher plane.[19]

Fanon called therefore for a new humanism stripped of its racist, Eurocentric aspects:

> Let us decide not to imitate Europe; let us combine our muscles and our brains in a new direction. Let us try to create the whole man, whom Europe has been incapable of bringing to triumphant birth.[20]

For Fanon, then, the humanist idea of "the whole man" was key to emancipation. Despite the critique of Western humanism as a camouflage for the dehumanization of non-Western peoples, humanism remained a central component of the ideology of third world liberation struggles of the postwar era, virtually all of which drew on the emancipatory logic of universalism. Indeed, Western radicals were often shocked by the extent to which anticolonial struggles adopted what the radicals conceived of as tainted ideas. As Claude Lévi-Strauss noted ruefully, the doctrine of cultural relativism "was challenged by the very people for whose moral benefit the anthropologists had established it in the first place."[21]

The willingness of third world radicals to maintain at least a residual support for a humanistic outlook stemmed from their continued engagement in the project of liberation. Postwar radicals in the West, however, increasingly rejected humanism, not simply in its guise as a cover for racism and colonialism but in its entirety. For postwar European intellectuals the most pressing problem was not that of establishing the ideological foundations of liberation struggles but rather of coming to terms with the demise of such struggles in Western democracies. Western intellectuals had, on the one hand, to excavate the social and intellectual roots of the Nazi experience, an experience that more than any other weighed upon the European intellectual consciousness in the immediate postwar period; and on the other, to explain why the possibilities of revolutionary change, which had seemed so promising in the early part of the century, appeared to have been extinguished. For many the explanation seemed to lie in some deep-seated malaise in European culture.

Postwar radicals asked themselves why it was that Germany, a nation with deep philosophical roots in the Enlightenment project and a strong and vibrant working class movement, should succumb so swiftly and so completely to Nazism. The answer seemed to be that it was the logic of Enlightenment rationalism itself and the nature of democratic politics that had given rise to such barbarism. As Theodor Adorno and Max Horkheimer put it in their seminal work, *The Dialectic of Enlightenment,* "Enlightenment is totalitarian."[22] Adorno and Horkheimer develop the two motifs—a critique of Enlightenment rationality and social progress, on the one hand, and of mass society, on the other—which became central themes of the Frankfurt school and which were to become immensely influential in shaping postwar discourse.

The idea that the Holocaust—and indeed all Western barbarism—had its roots in Enlightenment rationalism and humanism became a central tenet of postwar radicalism. The Enlightenment ambition of mastering nature, of setting humanity above nature, inevitably had destructive consequences for humanity itself. A humanity which could enslave nature was quite capable of enslaving fellow human beings. As David Goldberg has put it, "Subjugation ... defines the order of the Enlightenment: subjugation of nature by human intellect, colonial control through physical and cultural domination, and economic superiority through mastery of the laws of the market."[23] Mastery of nature and the rational organization of society, which in the nineteenth century was seen as the basis of human emancipation, now came to be regarded as the source of human enslavement.

The idea that technological and social progress could be the cause of barbarism has led many critics to find evidence not simply of humanism but the whole project of "modernity" behind the Holocaust. Zygmunt Bauman has suggested that the Final Solution was the "product" not the "failure" of modernity and that "it was the rational world of modern civilisation that made the Holocaust thinkable":

> The truth is that every ingredient of the Holocaust—all those many things that rendered it possible—was normal ... in the sense of being fully in keeping with everything we know about our civilisation, its guiding spirit, its priorities, its immanent vision of the world—and of the proper ways to pursue human happiness together with a perfect society.[24]

Bauman's argument that the Holocaust became thinkable only in the conditions of modernity may fall short of actually blaming that horror on Enlightenment principles of rationality; but his hint that "civilisation" itself may have been responsible for the barbarism of the "Final Solution" is made explicit by Richard Rubinstein who (in a phrase approvingly quoted by Bauman) argues that the Holocaust "bears witness to the advance of civilisation":

> The world of death camps and the society it engenders reveals the progressively intensifying night side of Judeo-Christian civilization. Civilization means slavery, wars, exploitation, and death camps. It also means medical hygiene, elevated religious ideas, beautiful art, and exquisite music. It is an error to imagine that civilization and savage cruelties are antithesis... Both creation and destruction are inseparable parts of what we call civilization.[25]

This comes very close to saying not just that modernity makes death camps possible but that it makes them necessary and inevitable. This proposition is deeply questionable in many ways, but for our purposes, the first question that comes to mind is this: what does it mean to suggest that barbarism is a product of civilization? To suggest that "the advance of civilization" inevitably leads to "slavery, wars, exploitation, and death camps" can only mean that barbarism is an ineradicable part of human nature. Yet is this not to posit a concept of a human nature that is as ahistorical as that supposedly held by humanists? Condemning civilization as forever imbricated with inhumanity is certainly an argument that sits uneasily with a critique of humanism which claims that an ahistoric notion of "Man" has been used to deny humanity to the West's Others.

To argue that humanism and rationalism (or "modernity") are the causes of the Holocaust is to turn logic on its head. The discourse of race was a product not of Enlightenment universalism and humanism but of its degradation. Scientific racism was not the application of science and reason to the question of human difference but the use of the discourse of science to give legitimacy to irrational, unscientific arguments. The "Final Solution" was implicit in the racial policies pursued by the Nazis. To engage in mass extermination it was necessary to believe that the objects of that policy were less than human. But to say that it was a rationally conceived plan is to elevate the prejudices of the Third Reich to the status of scientific knowledge—in other words to accept as true the very claims of racial discourse.

The critique of "mass society"

The second motif in the Frankfurt school analysis of fascism which came to dominate postwar thought was the critique of mass society. The concept of mass society began to win acceptance among sociologists in the 1950s. Stuart Hughes has pointed out both the ambiguity and irrationality of the concept and the underlying disillusionment with the soullessness of modern capitalist society which it expressed.[26] For the sociologists of the mass society, technological progress and mass democracy had combined to debase society, creating a mass of people with little intellectual depth, spiritual involvement or cultural profundity. The creation of such a mass society had taken humanity to the abyss of barbarism. Behind the rise of Nazism lay the willingness of the unthinking masses to follow herd-like demagogic leaders such as Adolf Hitler.

The critique of Enlightenment rationality and the critique of mass society became fused into the "totalitarian" theory of fascism. Popularized by Hannah Arendt in her book *The Origins of Totalitarianism,* the theory suggested that fascism was a species of totalitarianism, similar to the Soviet Union, Communist China, or (a comparison that later totalitarianism theorists would make) the Ayatollah Khomeini's Iran and Saddam Hussein's Iraq. The components of a totalitarian state were a herd-like mass, a compelling totalizing ideology that subsumed all under its cold logic, and a machine-like society that effaced all individuality in the name of a higher rationality. For Arendt totalitarianism represented the "madness of the mob," the "refuse of all classes," falling under the leadership of declassé intellectuals.[27] The mob sought to merge into something larger than themselves, to give up their individualism to belong to the mass. The critique of totalitarianism—and of totality—was to become a defining feature of poststructuralist discourse.

The irony in this is that the critique of totalitarianism is in substance a reworking of the nineteenth century critique of Enlightenment rationalism and of mass society pursued by philosophers such as Nietzsche and Heidegger, whose work flowed from the hostility of the intelligentsia to equality and mass democracy.[28] Arendt's theory of totalitarianism carries over the main themes of Heidegger's thought in its anti-mass character, its incipient anti-rationalism, and in particular its hostility to the Enlightenment as the embodiment of both.

The idea of the authoritarian personality, and of the masses as the "refuse of all classes," has close parallels with the themes of crowd psychology, such as those expounded by Gustav LeBon.[29] Both are a cry against what Heidegger called the "anonymity of the They: an endless etcetera of indifference and always-the-sameness ... the domination of the indifferent mass ... that destroys all rank and every world-creating impulse of the spirit."[30] The antihumanist belief that the technical forms of modernity arising from human mastery of nature underlay the implementation of the Holocaust are also taken from Heidegger.

> Agriculture is now a mechanised food industry; in essence it is no different from the production of corpses in gas chambers and death camps, the embargoes and food reductions to starving countries, the making of hydrogen bombs.[31]

Compare Heidegger's analysis, above, of the barbarism of the twentieth century with a sociological interpretation of the same, from Edmund Stillman and William Pfaff:

> There is more than a wholly fortuitous connection between the applied technology of the mass production line, and its vision of universal material abundance, and the applied technology of the concentration camp, with its vision of a profusion of death.[32]

I find it odious that scholars can in all seriousness equate mass extermination with the production of McDonald's hamburgers or of Ford Escorts, or make a comparison between technology aimed at improving the material abundance of society and political decisions taken to annihilate whole peoples and destroy entire societies. But what is interesting is that the second quote, from Edmund Stillman and William Pfaff, comes from a liberal interpretation of the Holocaust, while the first quote, from Heidegger himself, comes from an apologia for his Nazi past.

Heidegger had been an active member of the Nazi Party until 1943. After the war he attempted to rehabilitate his reputation, and in the document *Rectoral Addresses—Facts and Thoughts* he marshaled the arguments which he hoped would distance him from the Third Reich. The key piece of evidence for the defense was the assertion that Nazism was simply another manifestation of the spirit of modernity. According to Heidegger there existed a "universal will to power within history, now understood to embrace the planet," and that "everything stands in this historical reality, no matter whether it is called communism, fascism or world democracy."[33] It is a telling measure of the degree of confusion in postwar theory when liberal and Nazi explanations of the Holocaust can barely be pried apart.

Heidegger's ideas, which originally sought to articulate national socialism, went on, through the totalitarian thesis, to shape the interpretation and critique of fascism after its defeat. The antihumanism of Heidegger and his fellow thinkers became a central theme of poststructuralist and postmodernist discourse, of colonial discourse analysis, and of the theories of difference and cultural pluralism. There is more than a touch of irony in considering how, through the rehabilitation of antihumanist thinkers such as Heidegger and Nietzsche, the rejection of barbarism should preserve the very prejudices that gave rise to it.

Underlying the commonality of themes in racial and poststructuralist theory is the attempt to come to terms with the same problem—the disjuncture between a belief in equality and progress and a society that can seem to deliver neither. Sartre's famous preface to Fanon's *The Wretched of the Earth* makes this clear:

> Liberty, equality, fraternity, love, honour, patriotism and what have you. All this did not prevent us from making anti-racial speeches about dirty niggers, dirty Jews and dirty Arabs. High-minded people, liberal or just soft-hearted, protest that they were shocked by such inconsistency; but they were either mistaken or dishonest, for with us there is nothing more consistent than a racist humanism since the European has only been able to become a man through creating slaves and monsters.[34]

Nineteenth century thinkers who held fast to Enlightenment principles—whether liberal or revolutionary—argued that the disjuncture could be closed by social transformation. By the end of the century, however, liberals had by and large come to despair of the possibility of any such transformation and were drifting over to the long-held conservative belief that inequalities were both inevitable and necessary. By the midpoint of this century, the experience of Nazism and the defeat of working class movements had led radicals to similar pessimistic conclusions. As Stuart Hughes observes in his wonderfully lucid study of postwar intellectual thought, there was within the radical intelligentsia a widespread "disappointment in the course of recent history, in the strategy of the political parties that laid claim to the inheritance of Marx, and, most particularly, in the proletariat itself. The class which Engels had celebrated as the 'heirs of classical philosophy' had failed to perform in the style expected of it."[35]

Postwar developments entrenched such views. The experience of the failure of the student revolts of May 1968, the collapse of both Stalinist and social democratic parties in the eighties, and the demise of third world liberation movements all added to the belief that social transformation was a chimera.

The very goals of "modernity" seemed unattainable. As Bauman has put it, "Postmodernity is modernity coming to terms with its own impossibility: a self-monitoring modernity, one that consciously discards what it was once unconsciously doing."[36] For postwar theorists the gap between belief and reality could be closed not by transforming the reality but by relinquishing their beliefs. Despairing of social change, poststructuralist and postmodernist thinkers asserted instead that equality and humanity had no meaning, and that difference and diversity should be our goal.

Despair about social transformation also led postwar theorists to see the barbarism of the twentieth century not as a product of specific social relations but unspecifically as the consequence of "modernity." The claim that the categories of modernity necessarily give rise to a racial division of humanity conflates two different meanings of "modernity." On the one hand there is modernity in the sense of an intellectual or philosophical outlook which holds that it is possible to apprehend the world through reason and science—what has come to be called the Enlightenment project—and the technological advance that such an outlook has engendered. On the other hand modernity has also come to mean one particular society in which these ideas found expression—in other words capitalism.

By conflating the social relations of capitalism with the intellectual and technological progress of "modernity," the product of the former can be laid at the door of the latter. The specific problems created by capitalist social relations become dehistoricized. In poststructuralist discourse racial theory, colonialism, or the Holocaust are not investigated in their specificity, as products of distinctive tendencies within capitalist society, but are all lumped together as the general consequence of "modernity." In this way the positive aspects of "modern" society—its invocation of reason, its technological advancements, its ideological commitment to equality and universalism—are denigrated while its negative aspects—the inability of capitalism to overcome social divisions, the propensity to treat large sections of humanity as "inferior" or "subhuman," the contrast between technological advance and moral turpitude, the tendencies towards barbarism—are seen as inevitable or natural.

NOTES

This essay is based on my book, *The Meaning of Race* (New York: New York University Press, 1996), where some of the arguments are developed in greater detail.

1. David Bailey and Stuart Hall, "The Vertigo of Displacement," *Ten8* 3, no. 3 (Spring 1992).
2. Ali Rattansi, "'Western' racisms, ethnicities and identities," in Ali Rattansi and Sallie Westwood (eds.), *Racism, Modernity and Identity: On the Western Front* (Cambridge: Polity Press, 1994), p. 29.
3. For a useful discussion of poststructuralist conceptions of the "social" see James Heartfield, "Marxism and Social Construction" in Suke Wolton (ed.), *Marxism, Mysticism and Modern Theory* (Basingstoke: Macmillan, 1996).
4. Robin Cohen, *Frontiers of Identity: The British and the Others* (London: Longman, 1994), p. 205.
5. Ibid.
6. Winston James, "Migration, Racism and Identity Formation: The Caribbean Experience in Britain" in Winston James and Clive Harris (eds.), *Inside Babylon: The Caribbean Diaspora in Britain* (London: Verso, 1993), p. 266; Benedict Anderson, *Imagined Communities: Reflections on the Origins and Spread of Nationalism* (London: Verso, 1983).
7. James, ibid.
8. Miles Davis (with Quincy Troupe), *Miles: The Autobiography* (London: Macmillan, 1989).
9. E.H. Carr, *What is History?* (Harmondsworth: Penguin, 1987 [first published 1961]), pp. 26-27.
10. Peggy Kamuf (ed.), *Between the Blinds: A Derrida Reader* (Brighton: Harvester Wheatsheaf, 1991), pp. 66-67.
11. Cited in Mark Philp, "Michel Foucault" in Quentin Skinner (ed.), *The Return of Grand Theory in the Human Sciences* (Cambridge: Cambridge University Press, 1985), p. 78.
12. Claude Lévi-Strauss, *The Savage Mind* (London: Weidenfeld and Nicholson, 1966), p. 260.
13. Robert Young, *White Mythologies: Writing History and the West* (London: Routledge, 1990) pp. 122, 123.
14. David Hume, *Inquiry Concerning Human Understanding* (Oxford: Oxford University Press, 1994 [originally published 1748]).

15. Karl Marx, "Theses on Feuerbach" in Karl Marx and Frederick Engels, *Selected Works* (London: Lawrence and Wishart, 1968), p. 29.
16. Georg Lukács, *The Historical Novel,* translated by Hannah and Stanley Mitchell (London: Merlin, 1962), pp. 28-29.
17. Jean-Paul Sartre, "Preface" in Frantz Fanon, *The Wretched of the Earth* (Harmondsworth: Penguin, 1967 [originally published 1961]), p. 21; *Critique of Dialectical Reason,* Vol. 1: *Theory of Practical Ensembles,* translated by Alan Sheridan Smith (London: New Left Books, 1976), p. 752.
18. James Clifford, *The Predicament of Culture: Twentieth Century, Ethnography, Literature, Art* (Cambridge, MA: Harvard University Press), p. 263.
19. Fanon, *The Wretched of the Earth,* p. 253.
20. Ibid., p. 252.
21. Claude Lévi-Strauss, *The View from Afar,* translated by Joachim Neugraschel and Phoebe Hoss (Harmondsworth: Penguin, 1987 [originally published 1983]), p. 28.
22. Theodor Adorno and Max Horkheimer, *The Dialectic of Enlightenment* (London: Verso, 1979 [originally published 1944]), p. 6.
23. David Theo Goldberg, *Racist Culture: Philosophy and the Politics of Meaning* (Oxford: Blackwell, 1993), p. 29.
24. Zygmunt Bauman, *Modernity and the Holocaust* (Cambridge: Polity Press, 1989), pp. 6, 13, 8.
25. Richard L. Rubinstein, *The Cunning of History* (London: Harper & Row, 1978), pp. 91, 95.
26. H. Stuart Hughes, "The Sea Change," in *Between Commitment and Disillusionment* (Middletown, CT: Wesleyan University Press, 1987), pp. 134-35.
27. Hannah Arendt, *The Origins of Totalitarianism* (New York: Harcourt, Brace & Javonavich, 1973), p. 309.
28. See Kenan Malik, *The Meaning of Race,* pp. 104-14.
29. Gustav LeBon, *The Psychology of Peoples* (New York: G.E. Stechert, 1912 [originally published 1894]).
30. Martin Heidegger, *Introduction to Metaphysics* (New Haven, CT: Yale University Press, 1959), p. 85.
31. Martin Heidegger, cited in Jean-François Lyotard, *Heidegger and the "Jews"* (New Haven, CT: Yale University Press, 1994), p. 85.
32. Edmund Stillman and William Pfaff, *The Politics of Hysteria* (New York: Harper & Row, 1964), p. 34.
33. Cited in Thomas Rockmore, *On Heidegger's Nazism and Philosophy* (Berkeley: University of California Press, 1994), pp. 93-94.

34. Sartre, "Preface" in Fanon, *The Wretched of the Earth*, p. 22.
35. Hughes, "The Sea Change," pp. 135-36.
36. Zygmunt Bauman, *Modernity and Ambivalence* (Cambridge: Polity Press, 1991), p. 272.

Postmodernism, Feminism, and Marx: Notes from the Abyss

CAROL A. STABILE

For over a year, the trial of O.J. Simpson was headline news, not only for the tabloids but for the mainstream press as well. In the days following the grisly murders of Nicole Brown Simpson and Ron Goldman, the case was the hot topic on almost all television or radio talk shows; it appeared on the covers of popular magazines such as *Time* and *Newsweek,* and was featured regularly on the front page of major newspapers. Shock radio host Howard Stern, after playing the now infamous 911 tapes, suddenly discovered domestic violence, while millions of television viewers tuned in to watch the Los Angeles Police Department's stately pursuit of Simpson's white Bronco.

The story had a surrealistic air to it from the beginning, a distance from the real event that ended the lives of Simpson and Goldman, as well as from the realities of race, class, and state repression in L.A. As the weeks lengthened into months, the distance between the event and media coverage grew wider, while the case itself overshadowed healthcare, the passage of Proposition 187, and the "Contract with America." Domestic violence dropped out of the picture as coverage focused on the trial as game, sporting event, or performance. The question became less and less Simpson's guilt or innocence—what really happened—and more and more how the defense and prosecution would play their respective hands. Few in the mainstream media mentioned economic privilege, but race and gender were repeatedly raised as "issues," first in relation to Simpson and Nicole Brown Simpson, then as the court became a battleground between Johnnie Cochran, the African-American head of the defense team, and Marcia Clark, the white chief prosecutor. In the coverage of the case, the lines between information and entertainment, reality and fiction, weren't just blurred: they disappeared.

Welcome to postmodernism: world of the media spectacle, the disappearance of reality, the end of history, the death of Marxism, and a host of other millenarian claims. While celebrity trials have provoked sensationalized coverage historically, few would deny that the media themselves have undergone massive changes in the past decades, or that the media now control and manipulate vast flows of information. But while some of us might want to offer a historical and materialist explanation for these changes, for postmodernists the disappearance of the line between reality and fiction that allegedly constitutes "popular culture" today actually is the reality of the late twentieth century. There's nothing to explain, in other words, because the media's representations and fictions are all there is to know, all we *can* know. Society has moved to the edge of a now flattened world, postmodernists claim, and the only fact we can know with certainty is that we cannot understand what has moved us there or what lies down below, in the abyss.

It would be easy to dismiss or explain postmodernism's apocalyptic vision of society as just another instance of intellectuals' divorce from reality. In this essay, however, I want to treat this trend not just as an intellectual abstraction but as a historical phenomenon and as an intellectual retreat from politics. In particular, I want to consider the points at which postmodernism intersects with contemporary feminism and the political implications of that intersection.

What is postmodernism?

Let me first try to define these two very broad and often incoherent terms, "postmodernism" and "feminism," at least as they are used today in the academy. Postmodernism is loosely identified with a historical epoch, the condition of postindustrial, post-Fordist, or even postcapitalist society. "Contemporary" relations of production (if one can still call them that) are variously described as fragmented (this applies to both the social fabric and the mode of production), diffused or disorganized (in the sense that systemic power relations are everywhere and nowhere, pervasive but with no identifiable source), and ultimately unhinged from historical and economic determinants. Consumption has overtaken production, making class struggle (or even the notion that society is antagonistically divided into workers and capitalists) an obsolete concept. People no longer identify themselves with, or as, a class, but through various, more particular identities (e.g., woman, lesbian, gay, African-American, Latina), identities that are not only, or not at all, economically defined. Oppression, in short, has no systemic material foundation.

Central to the postmodernist understanding of society is the belief that the "grand," or totalizing, principles of modernity and the Enlightenment—

including appeals to rationality, progress, humanity, justice, and even the ability to represent reality—have been fatally undermined. This line of reasoning emerges from poststructuralist critiques of language, subjectivity, and representation; but where poststructuralism refers to theory, postmodernism is the practice. In other words, where poststructuralists criticized the foundations of modernism, postmodernists read these critiques as mandates for rejecting foundations altogether.

For postmodernists, then, the system—rarely (if ever) named as "capitalism"—has become so diffuse and heterogeneous that it not only surpasses understanding but no longer offers any point from which it can be opposed. Indeed, capitalism's "disorganization" signifies that there is no central point, or system, to oppose. In a media-saturated age in which no one knows, with any degree of certainty, what's really real, representation—whether political or artistic—has become impossible. Capitalism, now fragmented and lacking any organic unity, is no longer comprehensible as a system; and, in any case, the very grounds for understanding or knowing have been swept away.

European postmodernists, like Jean-François Lyotard, have expressed the belief that Marxism, like the Enlightenment in general, culminated in Stalinism because of its "totalizing" impulses. Some postmodernists, especially in the United States, have gone much further than this identification of Marxism with Soviet-style systems, holding Marxism responsible for all kinds of oppression. "Twentieth-century Marxism," maintains Linda Nicholson, "has used the generalizing categories of production and class to delegitimize demands of women, black people, gays, lesbians, and others whose oppression cannot be reduced to economics."[1] This kind of judgment dramatically displays yet another feature of postmodernism: its historical amnesia. An argument like Nicholson's not only represses a rich history of democratic class politics, it is remarkably insensitive to the simple fact that Marxism and socialist organizations in general have been repeatedly marginalized and delegitimized by capitalism. The transplantation of postmodernist modes of thought from Europe to North America has tended to be doubly ahistorical, divorced from the historical and material conditions that first produced them, and then, in a climate of backlash against class-based political struggles, appropriated by a society whose history of class struggles has been assiduously repressed. It would seem ironic, if the political stakes weren't so high, that both postmodernists and the likes of George Bush and

Dick Armey seem to be arguing that we don't have classes in the United States.

Postmodernist social theory, and postmodernism in general, exist for the most part in humanities and social science programs in the university. Eschewing empiricism and quantitative methods (which assume the existence of some form of reality that can be represented), most postmodernists rely on interpretive methods borrowed from Saussurean linguistics and hermeneutics to support their often contradictory claims. Postmodernist social theorists, in replaying traditional debates within philosophy about idealism and materialism, haven't transcended the terms of the debate laid out by Marx and Engels in *The German Ideology*. Rather, they claim an absolute victory for idealism, as materiality and the economic base are consigned to the dumpster of history, and only language remains. Working from this "linguistic" foundation, postmodernist social theorists argue that politics, in the waning years of the century, can only work haphazardly, or through the fragmented, divided, and often conflicting categories with which people identify.

Despite its many contradictions and confusions, postmodernism does have some unifying principles: an uncritical and idealist focus on the discursive construction of the "real" (i.e., what is "real" is constructed in and by language, although no one really explains what this means) and a related privileging of the notion of "difference." If, in the end, we cannot point to any "real" interests that might unify "us," then the only form of political action conceivable is one based on "differences" in identity. As opposed to Marx's notion of unity in difference, or E.P. Thompson's "identity of interests," in which people share widely common interests which can be represented by political agencies, postmodernists reject any such representation in favor of particular and localized differences.

What is Feminism?

Feminism seems at first a more accessible category than postmodernism, since it apparently refers to women as a political category with an identifiable constituency. Although the dominant trends in "academic" feminism share with postmodernism a rejection of historical materialism as a method and Marxism as a political critique, poststructuralist critiques within feminism have followed a distinctive trajectory. Most significantly, and unlike postmodernism, contemporary feminist theory began not by rejecting the very idea of system or "totality" but, on the contrary, by elaborating its own systemic analysis, in which, at least at first, "patriarchy" was proposed as an alternative to, or occasionally the accomplice of, capitalism. In this theoretical framework, women were oppressed by a patriarchal system and had a common interest in opposing it. The project for feminism has been both intellectual and political: to raise women's consciousness of their oppression as women and promote social change through collectively organizing women as a distinct revolutionary class.

From the beginning, however, this project was rife with problems. The concept of women as a uniform group proved an inadequate foundation for feminists, either as a theory or a framework for activism, for although it cannot be denied that most women experience the effects of a profoundly misogynist system, they do so in various ways and to varying degrees. An academic's experience of sexism, for example, however viscerally lived, is mitigated by the resources she possesses by virtue of her class position and is far different from that experienced by a working class woman or a woman on welfare. By substituting "women" for "working class," feminism tends to deny that not all women share an interest in liberation, much less a common ground for political action. Feminists of color and lesbian feminists have pointed out that exclusions and oppressive practices were built into the category of women as defined by many feminists, that certain groups of women benefit from the oppression of other women, and that women, like men, participate in racist, sexist, and homophobic practices. Postcolonial feminists have argued that not all "patriarchal" systems are the same: that "patriarchy" encompasses qualitatively different relations within different societies and that these relations are themselves subject to historical changes. As these examples suggest, for feminists to place exclusive emphasis on division between women and men was not only to deny divisions among women, but to reproduce a stereotypical view of female nature as caring, nurturing, and relational. In short, the concept of patriarchy has run the risk of reproducing sexist understandings of what it means to be female or male and could, therefore, be yoked to antifeminist, reactionary politics, as in the case of antiporn feminists' alliance with the Meese Commission in 1986.

During the 1980s, the debate within feminist theory revolved around essentialism (the argument that there is some foundation for the category "women," grounded in female nature) and anti-essentialism (the argument that "women" is a historically specific and socially constructed category).

For essentialists (and it is instructive that few feminists would claim this label, since it functions as a pejorative), women share common characteristics upon which political action can be based. For anti-essentialists, categories such as "female" and "male" are not fixed by nature and cannot be located in some unchanging natural essence. Instead, they are socially constructed and vary considerably across cultures and historical moments. If essentialism emphasizes differences with a capital "D," or the absolute difference between male and female, anti-essentialism stresses the plural, lower-case "differences" within the category "women."

The critique of essentialism has been important in identifying the exclusions upon which much feminist theory and practice were based, but the opposition between essentialism and anti-essentialism has exhausted whatever utility it once had. It is here that we can begin to notice the convergence of the dominant tendencies in academic feminism with postmodernism, insofar as both lead to the same political dead end. Anti-essentialist feminism, having taken note of the differences among women, has now moved on to something like the postmodernist blindness to anything *but* difference. In other words, just as postmodernists argue that "the real" no longer refers to any concrete, objective reality, current trends in feminism are dissolving the category "women" into a "discursive" construct, so fragmented and variable that it is hard to see how it could be the basis for a political project. It is not surprising that, as feminism adopts postmodernism's emphasis on language and discourse, the abstract opposition between essentialism and anti-essentialism has produced much theory but has precluded practice.

Despite these points of intersection between postmodernism and anti-essentialist feminism, some would argue that the main distinction between the two is that where postmodernism's critique culminates in the impossibility of politics, feminism remains committed to the emancipation of women (though by what means is unclear). Postmodernism is and always has been a hyper-intellectualized movement, while feminism's trajectory within the U.S. academy has maintained some connection to a political constituency. Where postmodernism can be dismissed as an elite disavowal of social and political realities, feminism's continuing political validity is guaranteed by its original, if now quite tenuous, connection to oppositional politics.

But as a word referring to an approach or even a political position, "feminism" has become ever more vague in recent years. One can be an explicitly postmodernist feminist, with a focus on gender-constitution, language, and representation. One can also be a socialist-feminist, an antiporn feminist, an anti-antiporn feminist, a liberal feminist, a cultural feminist, or an ecofeminist. And while it was once understood that feminism unilaterally stood for reproductive freedom, there are now anti-abortion feminists within the academy and "Feminists for Life" outside.

In spite of these seemingly contradictory impulses within feminism, certain commonalities can be observed at the intersection of anti-essentialism and postmodernism. For example, although anti-essentialists claim a connection to feminist politics, the category "politics" (like the term "women") is often emptied, as is postmodernism in general, of any connection to material struggles or, indeed, any connection to social relations, since the "social" is collapsed into the "discursive," and social relations into linguistic patterns. In arguing for differences, individualized power relations are emphasized, to the exclusion of their systemic interconnection; and, of course, as any systemic source of power disappears, so too does the capitalist mode of production (not to mention any understanding of how academic feminists themselves fit into it). The upshot of this micropolitical focus is that a politics of identity based on "lifestyle," consumption, and individualism has replaced a politics of common interest and collective social struggle.

When political struggle is reduced to abstractions based on language and language-games, there is no way to identify the system against which people must struggle or the revolutionary agencies that might conduct such a struggle. Postmodernists openly concede—in fact, they insist—that there will be no site from which any antisystemic struggle can emanate, because (even if "systems" exist) identities are infinitely fragmented and mobile. Certain feminists continue to dodge such nihilism by invoking patriarchy, but some fundamental differences among women must be set aside if all women are to be treated as primarily and uniformly oppressed by the patriarchal system. It will seem a truism to those working within socialist organizations (or, incidentally, those who are working class) to observe that those groups of women who benefit from the exploitation of other human beings occupy a more privileged class position than those who are exploited. But anti-essentialist feminists can only take class position into account by introducing a theory of economic determination that they have worked very hard to deny, a move that would undermine their own theoretical foundations.

Why not Marxism?

To explain the origins of postmodernist trends, we would have to explore both the successes of capitalism in the 1950s and the 1960s (the rise of "consumer capitalism," or the so-called "affluent society") and its failures in the 1970s and 1980s. We would also have to examine changes in the conditions of academics in those decades. These complex developments are beyond the scope of this article, but it is not so difficult to describe the conditions in the academy today that have helped promote the intellectual centrality of language and "identity," divorced from economic, social, and political contexts.[2]

The trend away from "economistic" concerns has a long history on the intellectual left. The current displacement of productive activity by intellectual practice can be traced to earlier, more prosperous periods of capitalism, when many people were convinced that consumer capitalism had won the hearts and minds of the working class. Since then, the changing structure of capitalism, the increased mobility of capital, and the growth of the "consumer society" have contributed to a conception of identity as shifting and variable, subject to changes in "lifestyle" and consumption patterns (at least for those who can afford it). For others, the power of capital, and its vicious attacks on the working class and the poor, have made change appear to be impossible. But if capitalist success had something to do with current trends, today these tendencies have been strengthened by capitalist decline, not least by the financial squeeze on the academy itself.

As education itself is increasingly subject to commodification and the economic imperatives of capitalism, job opportunities for academics are becoming much more limited and insecure. While the academic profession remains a privileged career, graduate students today, many of whom have already worked in low-wage and insecure jobs outside the academy, are likely to end up in debt, in temporary and insecure academic work, or in chronic unemployment. There is a powerful incentive for junior faculty to "distinguish" themselves by adopting ever more fashionable, sexy, and "cutting-edge" theories. Theories that elaborate the grim, monotone realities of class struggle and capitalist exploitation don't sell very well, especially when contrasted with, say, Madonna's "resistant" feminism. And this kind of "resistance," based on lifestyle and consumption, seems radical without being threatening. In addition, the pressure to publish has speeded up the production process, favoring sheer quantity over quality, as well as work emphasizing topical, contemporary issues, which is easier and cheaper to produce, over carefully researched analytic work, based on historical accounts or fieldwork.

Given this more direct experience of economic realities, academics today, and feminists in particular, should find a critical analysis of capitalism especially compelling, since the contradictions confronting them are becoming ever more evident. But in the academy, it has become a kind of intellectual common sense to dismiss Marxism and its methods *in toto* as "totalizing" (because it seeks to explain society through an analysis of its mode of production—capitalism), "reductive" (because economic structures are said to shape legal, political, and cultural structures), or "universalizing" (because class is said to shape consciousness). A main feminist critique has been that women and female labor were excluded from analysis. These knee-jerk responses have become so pervasive that it is no longer necessary to explain what "totalizing," "reductive," or "universalizing" mean—in fact, they are just understood. For a younger generation of scholars, whose formative political experiences have been in various feminist movements, the rejection of Marxist-oriented political activism is based on a set of myths about the masculinist virulence inherent in Marxism.

How justified is this rejection of Marxism? Let's look at the three main charges leveled against it by many feminists: that it is "reductive," that it is too "universalistic," and that it fails to consider female labor. On the first point, the general claim is that historical materialism reduces structures of oppression to class exploitation, thereby ignoring or minimizing sexism, racism, and homophobia. While it is certainly true that historical materialism places relations of production at the foundation of society, there is nothing simple or reductive about how these relations structure oppressions. Rather, historical materialist analyses, instead of examining only one form of oppression—like sexism, racism, or homophobia—would explore the way they all function within the overarching system of class domination in determining women's and men's life choices. Sweatshop workers in New York City, for example, experience sexism and racism in quantitatively and qualitatively different ways than do middle class women. The racism directed at poor African-American youths occurs in a different context than that directed at African-American women in the academy. This is not to claim that the latter forms of oppression do not exist or are inconsequential, but by situating both forms within the material context and historical framework in which they occur, we can highlight the variable discriminatory mechanisms that are central to capitalism as a system.

The charge of reductivism might be leveled more accurately against anti-Marxist feminism. For although feminists have been forced to confront the inequalities that exist among and between women, some have been less than careful in considering the inequalities that exist among and between women and men. Isn't it reductive to suggest that the oppression I ostensibly suffer as an educated, middle class woman should be accorded primacy over the oppression of working class men? It may very well be the case that some working class men are sexist, but to what extent does a focus on "their" sexism work to erase my class privilege, as well as the fact that the most powerful and oppressive forms of sexism are wielded by capitalists rather than disempowered workers? In short, while experiences of sexism, racism, and homophobia vary in intensity and extremity across class lines, those very class lines (demarcated by relations of production) remain much more rigid and inflexible. It takes a certain distance from economic hardship to claim that relations of production and class position are unimportant, so it is not surprising that the claims of economic reductivism invariably issue from more privileged class positions.

The charge of "universalism" is closely related to that of reductivism. This objection starts with the critique of modernity (including Marxism) on the grounds that its conceptions of truth, reason, and justice (in fact, its conception of "humanity" itself) are too universalistic, too insensitive to the many differences among human beings. This critique has been valuable in challenging capitalism's oppressive uses of concepts like "justice" and "reason," or the destructive applications of science and technology in the name of rationality and progress. But at the same time, it poses some serious problems for feminists. First, if there can be no standards of truth, justice, or reason, we cannot appeal to them as criteria of judgment or action. In fact, postmodernists, including postmodern feminists, have often been criticized on the grounds that, without the kind of standards they are so swift to reject, they themselves can have no basis for supporting or justifying resistance to oppression. Second, the possibility of opposition to oppression is also undermined by the presumption that the common interests among human beings are so narrow and fleeting that any politics beyond the most particularistic and narrow forms of resistance are impossible. Accordingly, people can struggle against "power" (defined provisionally and contingently) only through single-issue politics, and the best that can be hoped for is piecemeal reform. Since power can no longer be located or identified, since "real" unifying interests are a colonizing fiction, a part of a uniformly oppressive Enlightenment worldview (to which Marxism also belongs), then an organized opposition is neither feasible nor desirable. Politics, let alone revolution, is reduced to a turf war among "discourses."

The third charge against historical materialism—that it has excluded female labor from its analysis—has always been debatable.[3] While it may be true that women's unpaid domestic labor wasn't systematically integrated into classical Marxist analyses of the mode of production (although both Marx and Engels discuss the sexual division of labor), from the 1970s on there have been Marxist revisions of this concept, particularly within anthropology and economics. In addition, while anti-essentialist feminists have been swift to appropriate and revise poststructuralist theories (that either neglect gender or deal with it in profoundly sexist ways) in order to further analyses of gender, only Marxism seems to be singled out for rejection on the grounds of this alleged omission.

At any rate, the development of contemporary capitalism has to some extent made this question moot. With the increased blurring between the public and private spheres, the heightened commodification of previously unpaid female labor (care of the elderly, child care, cooking, cleaning, etc.), and the wholesale entry of middle class women into the labor force, women's conditions are more obviously determined by relations of production in a very Marxist sense. Non-Marxist feminism, with its lack of attention to relations of production, is beginning to look far more inadequate than even the most gender-blind Marxism in explaining the conditions of women.

The limits of conventional feminism

The inadequacies of conventional feminism, both in explaining the conditions of women as workers and in constructing a foundation for effective political action, are illustrated by the narrowness of the struggle over abortion rights. This has, of course, been the central issue for mainstream women's movements for the last thirty years. There is room for argument about the importance of this issue in relation to others that affect women, but the point I want to make here has to do not so much with the relative importance of this question as with the angle from which it has been approached. For example, the passage of the Hyde Amendment in 1977 (which effectively closed off economic access to abortion for poor women) generated very little feminist opposition compared to the more recent Webster Decision (1990). Abortion "rights," in this context, seem to mean the rights of more privileged women. The very fact that abortion rights have emerged as the defining focus of mainstream feminist activism, to the exclusion of both economic access to abortion and economic support in the form of day care and subsidies for those women who continue to mother, suggests a narrow conception of feminist interests.

In the winter of 1994, I was involved in organizing a reproductive rights coalition, the goal of which was to break out of the abortion/anti-abortion deadlock by emphasizing economic issues such as healthcare (including both prenatal and postnatal care, as well as abortion services), daycare, and welfare. Several members of the coalition, sympathetic to NOW and Planned Parenthood, suggested that we focus our energies on supporting the passage of the Freedom of Access to Clinic Entrances Act (FACE). Others objected, voicing concern about how this legislation might be used against striking workers and political protesters in general. Although this predictably elicited heated commentary about unions and sexism, what emerged most forcefully from this debate was that the "rights" we were being asked to endorse were viewed from a privileged perspective. Because the state was perceived as an ally which promoted the particular interests of the more economically privileged, these women could overlook the fact that at the same time (and often in the very same places), the state was brutally dismantling and repressing the rights of the vast majority of women and men. The struggle for "rights" was being viewed apart from the larger system of power and privilege in which those rights were situated.

Similar points could be made about the struggles against sexism and homophobia in the military. Of course, struggles for the democratization of any institution should be welcomed by socialists, but there is something profoundly disturbing about an attempt to democratize the inner workings of an institution like the military while ignoring, even accepting, the anti-democratic and oppressive functions of the institution itself. And lifting the ban on combat cannot change the fact that many women (who may have little interest in career advancement within the military) enlist because it is, as a friend of mine once put it, a steady gig with good benefits for those who have few economic opportunities.

The defense of "rights," abstracted from historical, political, and economic contexts, has weakened feminist politics and contributed to a general sense that feminism serves only narrow and privileged interests.

Historical materialism offers the possibility of coalitions based on a broader understanding of the exploitative nature of capitalist relations of production, enlisting women and men in struggles against family violence, further cuts to already severely diminished social programs, and, moreover, against the system that benefits from these ills. Furthermore, it proposes that women's liberation—if it is to include all women—is incompatible with capitalism.

Historical materialism has the advantage of offering the kind of self-reflexivity—so lacking in postmodernism and contemporary feminism—that I've tried to underscore in this essay. It at once forces us to understand our theories, our practices, and our positions in relation to the dominant structure of power, and provides a much more effective basis for an understanding of the positions of both women and men within multinational capitalism and of contemporary shifts in these positions.

Consider, for example, the debate about "family values." The conventional feminist argument is that the New Right's call for a return to family values is simply a backlash. On the one hand, this backlash is said to represent an attempt to reinstate a traditional version of the nuclear family in order to force women out of the labor force and back into the home. On the other hand, it is seen as a measure of the effectiveness of the feminist movement, insofar as women now have the "choice" of working. What disappears from view in these analyses is the fact that economic conditions have forced upon middle class women the dubious advantage of working one or more full-time jobs in addition to domestic labor, and that this social change benefits capitalism, and not individual men. Poor and working class women (many of them women of color) have long worked outside the home, although few of them would call their alienated and often desperate labor a matter of "choice." What is being represented as a gain for women simply means that middle class women are now being compelled by the necessities of capitalism to make the "choice" that has traditionally been available to poor and working class women. To argue that the debates about family values are intended to force women back into the domestic sphere overlooks the fact that there can be no return to the traditional nuclear family because it is no longer economically feasible. To argue that these debates about family values were provoked by feminist successes is to accept the ideological mystification that treats the economic mandates of capitalism as if they were free life-style "choices."

I would like to believe that feminists are, in fact, committed to revolutionary social change, but there's another, less pleasant possibility to contemplate—one that points to the dangers of ignoring class position. It could be that many who call themselves feminists are interested only in maintaining their own class privilege or in gaining celebrity status. From that point of view, Marxism is a serious threat not only because it represents a challenge to the theoretical foundations of a postmodern feminism, but also because it reveals the historical, material, and class foundations of certain forms of knowledge. It is fairly clear how women such as Katie Roiphe, Naomi Wolf, and Camille Paglia use feminism as a marketing strategy to promote their books, images, and careers, instead of promoting equality and social justice. But as long as so many feminists refuse to acknowledge their own privilege and the ways in which we all "benefit" from the exploitation of less-privileged women and men, feminism in general will be in danger of becoming a professional strategy rather than a political project.

Let's return briefly to the world of the media spectacle and the trial of O.J. Simpson. The trappings of stardom and courtroom melodrama aside, the courtroom seemed to stand in for a multicultural society—a place where identities flourished. Most of the jury members were African-American, the key participants in the debate were a woman and an African-American man, and a stern Asian-American man presided over the courtroom. But do people really buy into the spectacle at a time when a massive consolidation of capitalism is taking place at the top of society? Do people actually buy into the image of the multicultural society at a time when black unemployment is more than twice that of whites, when the rights of women, men, children, and their families are being dismantled in such an open and brutal manner, when lesbians and gays are under attack throughout the United States, and when striking workers are being pepper-gassed by police in places like Decatur, Illinois?

In the end, the media spectacle tells us nothing at all about what people want or how they identify. Few, in fact, can afford to blur the division between reality and fiction during a time in which reality bears so little resemblance to its media representations. Those who continue to believe in the possibility of revolutionary social change cannot abandon a belief in the power of critical consciousness and the tools that enable people (particularly those facing an unstable economic future) to make sense of their situation and learn how best to fight against it, and not simply make their peace with it. If feminist analyses are to maintain any claim to analytic and political coherence (not to mention efficacy), then we need to understand better how the projects some of us promote—postmodernist, feminist, or some combination thereof—may actually feed into and reinforce capitalism. By repudiating the very categories of analysis that might enable understanding, these projects obscure our own positions within relations of systemic exploitation and preempt any project of social transformation.

Instead of seeing the fragmentation of identities as a cause for celebration, we should try to understand how identity has been transformed into a commodity for those with the capital to consume it, and how the capitalist system has worked (and will continue to work) against the organization of socialist politics. In place of an identity politics that serves only to pit groups against one another in a never-ending litany of competing claims to oppression, we need a more cogent understanding of the systemic nature of oppression. We need to consider the extent to which the politics of identity represents not a challenge to, but a product of, the system, a manifestation of market segmentation and the commodification of identity produced by the globalization of capital as a world system. For what appear to be oppositional strategies may very well turn out to be the symptoms of oppression.

Notes

I would like to thank Mark Unger, Sudeep Dasgupta, Jonathan Sterne, the members of my graduate seminars on postmodernism at the University of Illinois and the University of Pittsburgh, and Anthony Arnove, Dan McGee, Gretchen Soderland, and Elizabeth Terzakis.

1. Linda Nicholson, *Conflicts in Feminism* (New York: Routledge, 1990), p. 11.
2. See Ellen Meiksins Wood, *The Retreat from Class* (London: Verso, 1986) for the most sustained analysis of these points. See also Wood, "A Chronology of the New Left and Its Successors, or: Who's Old-Fashioned Now?" in *Socialist Register* no. 35 (1995): 22-49.
3. Ruth Schwartz Cowan's *More Work for Mother: The Ironies of Household Technologies, From the Open Hearth to the Microwave* (New York: Basic Books, 1983) illustrates how historical materialism offers a powerful tool for understanding the relationship between household and industrial labor.

Marx and the Environment

JOHN BELLAMY FOSTER

It has become fashionable in recent years, in the words of one critic, to identify the growth of ecological consciousness with "the current postmodernist interrogation of the metanarrative of the Enlightenment." Green thinking, we are frequently told, is distinguished by its postmodern, post-Enlightenment perspective. Nowhere is this fashion more evident than in certain criticisms directed at Marx and Engels. Historical materialism, beginning with the work of its two founders, is often said to be one of the main means by which the Baconian notion of the mastery of nature was transmitted to the modern world. The prevalence of this interpretation is indicated by its frequent appearance within the analysis of the left itself. "While Marx and Engels displayed an extraordinary understanding of and sensitivity toward the 'ecological' costs of capitalism," socialist ecofeminist Carolyn Merchant writes, "... they nevertheless bought into the Enlightenment's myth of progress via the domination of nature."[1]

It is of course undeniable that many of those who claimed to be following in Marx's footsteps treated nature as an object to be exploited and nothing more. It is common for today's critics, however, to argue that the worldview of Marx and Engels themselves was rooted before all else in the extreme technological subjugation of nature, and that despite the ecological sensitivity that they displayed in particular areas, this remains the primary context in which their theoretical contributions must be judged. Marxism and ecology are therefore never fully compatible.

The chief complaint upon which this general criticism is based is that Marx adopted what the socialist environmentalist Ted Benton—himself a critic of Marx in this respect—has called a "Promethean, 'productivist' view of history." Reiner Grundmann concurs, writing in his *Marxism and Ecology* that "Marx's basic premiss" was "the Promethean model" of the domination of nature—a position that Grundmann attempts to defend. For liberal Victor Ferkiss, no defense is possible: "Marx's attitude toward the world always retained that Promethean thrust, glorifying the human conquest of nature." Social ecologist (ecological anarchist) John Clark goes further:

> Marx's Promethean ... "man" is a being who is not at home in nature, who does not see the Earth as the "household" of ecology. He is an indomitable spirit who must subject nature in his quest for self-realization.... For such a being, the forces of nature, whether in the form of his own unmastered internal nature or the menacing powers of external nature, must be subdued.[2]

There are of course other common environmental criticisms directed at Marx and Engels (not to mention Marxism as a whole) in addition to this one. Benton, for example, argues that Marx was "unmistakably anthropocentric" and that he resisted any framework that would recognize the natural limits to economic advance. Marxian value theory, we are frequently told, designated labor (power) as the source of all value, thereby denying any intrinsic value to nature. Then there is the dismal ecological performance of the Soviet Union and other Eastern European regimes before the fall, which is seen as a general reflection of Marx's failure to incorporate ecological concerns into his master narrative.

Yet it is the charge of Prometheanism that occupies central place in green criticisms of Marx. True environmentalism, we are led to believe, demands nothing less than a rejection of modernity itself. The charge of Prometheanism is thus a roundabout way of branding Marx's work and Marxism as a whole as an extreme version of modernism, more easily condemned in this respect perhaps than liberalism itself. Thus postmodern environmentalist Wade Sikorski writes that, "Marx ... was one of our age's most devout worshipers of the machine. Capitalism was to be forgiven its sins because ... it was in the process of perfecting the machine."[3]

This claim that Marx's work was based on a crude "Prometheanism," it is worth recalling, has a very long history. Bourgeois critics of Marxism have long sought to use Marx's frequent literary references to Aeschylus's *Prometheus Bound* to demonstrate that underneath his apparent commitment to scientific understanding lay a "mythical-religious" foundation. Yet it is crucial to remember that Marx was not the only thinker attracted to the Greek myth of Prometheus, who was the predominant cultural hero of the entire Romantic period, and who stands in Western culture not only for technology but even more for creativity, revolution, and rebellion against the gods (against religion). Rubens, Titian, Dante, Milton, Blake, Goethe, Beethoven, Byron, Shelley, and numerous others incorporated Prometheus as a central motif in their work.[4]

In Marx's own work, Prometheus is invoked more often as a symbol of revolution than as a symbol of technology. It is true that in Greek mythology the Titan (or demigod) Prometheus brought fire to humanity. But more important to Marx was the fact that Zeus in retaliation bound Prometheus in chains for eternity, from which he sought to free himself. For the great tragedian Aeschylus, as Ellen Meiksins Wood observes in *Peasant-Citizen and Slave,* Prometheus is "the personification of the Athenian opposition to servitude and arbitrary rule, as he resists the tyranny of Zeus and scorns the servility of the god's messenger, Hermes." Moreover, what is celebrated in Aeschylus's *Prometheus Bound,* a version of the Promethean myth reflecting the values of Athenian democracy, is not technology as it is now understood but the gift of labor, craftsmanship, and creativity—the practical arts underpinning democracy. So central was the myth of Prometheus to ancient Athens that the class opposition between laboring citizens in the democracy and the aristocratic opponents of democracy can be seen in the radically different treatments of this myth, as represented respectively by *Prometheus Bound* and Plato's use of the same myth in his *Statesman.* Understanding the revolutionary class character of this conflict within antiquity, Marx clearly identified with the Prometheus of Aeschylus rather than Plato.[5]

All of this, though crucial for understanding Marx's own references to Prometheus, may seem irrelevant, since none of this rich cultural background, stretching back over millennia to the very beginnings of Western civilization, exists at all in the work of those among today's cultural and environmental critics who now commonly level the charge of Prometheanism at the entire Enlightenment tradition and at Marx and Engels in particular. Shorn of most of its historical and cultural meaning, the myth of Prometheus has been transformed, in the work of such critics, into a cultural symbol of modernity itself, standing for extreme productivism and the domination of nature (including human nature). Indeed, the fact that the very idea of human creativity, as symbolized by the Greek myth of Prometheus, has come to be identified in the eyes of many of today's postmodern critics with crude productivism and the technological subjugation of nature provides a startling indication of the extent to which the dominant worldview of capitalism has penetrated such thinking.

The classic reformulation of the Promethean myth along these lines is to be found in Herbert Marcuse's *Eros and Civilization,* which argued that Prometheus, "the predominant culture-hero" of European culture,

> is the trickster and (suffering) rebel against the gods, who creates culture at the price of perpetual pain. He symbolizes productiveness, the unceasing effort to master life.... Prometheus is the culture-hero of toil, productivity, and progress through repression.

In opposition to this one-sided emphasis of Western modernity, Marcuse insisted that

> another reality principle must be sought at the opposite pole. Orpheus and Narcissus ... stand for a very different reality. They have not become the culture-heroes of the Western world: theirs is the image of joy and fulfillment.... They recall the experience of a world that is not to be mastered and controlled but liberated.[6]

Marcuse was developing a critique of the instrumental rationality that characterized Western industrial culture as a whole (encompassing both capitalism and what Roy Medvedev has called "barracks pseudosocialism"). His argument was, however, seen by some as a "trenchant criticism" of Marx in particular. Marcuse's text is interpreted in precisely this way in Marshall Berman's *All That Is Solid Melts into Air,* which nonetheless argues that it is wrong to see Marx as a proponent of crude Prometheanism. According to Berman,

> If Marx is fetishistic about anything, it is not work and production but rather the far more complex and comprehensive ideal of *development*—"the free development of physical and spiritual energies" (1844 manuscripts).... Marx wants to embrace Prometheus *and* Orpheus; he considers communism worth fighting for, because for the first time in history it could enable men to have both.... He knew that the way beyond the contradictions would have to lead through modernity, not out of it.[7]

It is certainly possible to argue, as socialist environmentalist Kate Soper has in her essay "Greening Prometheus," that there was a certain "ambiguity" in "Marx's Prometheanism" that one can exploit to develop a green interpretation of his thought. However, what seems to be mere "ambiguity" on the surface is more adequately understood as a dialectical tension resulting from Marx's attempt to transcend the usual ways in which human production and the mastery of nature were depicted in the Enlightenment tradition. As Marcuse's student William Leiss has observed in his indispensable study *The Domination of Nature,* such phrases as "the mastery of nature," "the control of nature," and "the domination of nature" were almost universal within nineteenth-century thought, and as such took on varied and complex forms. The mere use of such terms on occasion by Marx and

Engels does not therefore establish that they adopted an extreme productivist point of view. Indeed, taken together, the writings of Marx and Engels, Leiss contends, "represent the most profound insight into the complex issues surrounding the mastery over nature to be found anywhere in nineteenth-century social thought or *a fortiori* in the contributions of earlier periods."[8]

What was clear from Marx's analysis was that humanity and nature were interrelated, with the historically specific form of production relations constituting the core of that interrelationship in any given period. As he wrote in the *Economic and Philosophic Manuscripts of 1844,*

> Man *lives* from nature, i.e., nature is his *body,* and he must maintain a continuing dialogue with it if he is not to die. To say that man's physical and mental life is linked to nature simply means that nature is linked to itself, for man is a part of nature.[9]

Far from being mere worshipers of productivism, Marx and Engels were two of its foremost critics. As the young Engels wrote in 1844, "To make the earth an object of huckstering—the earth which is our one and all, the first condition of our existence—was the last step toward making oneself an object of huckstering." Under capitalism all natural and human relationships, Marx argued, have been dissolved into money relationships. Rather than a society ruled by "callous 'cash-payment'" and by the necessity for continual increases in productivity, he looked forward to a social order that would promote the many-sided development of human capacities and the rational human relation to the nature of which we are a part. The further growth of human freedom, he wrote in the final part of the third volume of *Capital,* consists in "socialized man, the associated producers, rationally regulating their material interchange with nature and bringing it under common control, instead of allowing it to rule them as a blind force."

The human community, Marx believed, can no more free itself from the need to control its interaction with nature than it can free itself from the need to take into consideration the natural conditions of human existence. Yet rational control of the relation between nature and humanity is inherently opposed to the mechanistic domination of nature in the interest of the ever increasing expansion of production for its own sake. In a society of freely associated producers, Marx argued, the goal of social life would not be work and production, in the narrow forms in which they have been understood in possessive-individualist society, but the all-around development of human creative potential as an end in itself, for which "the shortening of the working-day is a basic prerequisite." This would set the stage for the achievement of a realm of freedom in which human beings would be united with each other and with nature.[10]

The realization of these conditions, Marx recognized, necessitated a radical transformation in the human relation to nature. With the elimination of private ownership of land and the development of a society of freely associated producers, global sustainability in the relationship to nature would become feasible for the first time. Pointing to the imperative of protecting the globe for future generations Marx stated:

> From the standpoint of a higher economic form of society, private ownership of the globe by single individuals will appear quite as absurd as private ownership of one man by another. Even a whole society, a nation, or even all simultaneously existing societies together, are not the owners of the globe. They are only its possessors, its usufructuaries, and like *boni patres familias* [good fathers of families], they must hand it down to succeeding generations in an improved condition.[11]

It was the proper purpose of agriculture, Marx argued, "to minister to the entire range of permanent necessities of life required by the chain of successive generations"—in contradiction to "the whole spirit of capitalist production, which is directed toward the immediate gain of money." There was thus a direct conflict between capitalism's short-sighted expropriation of the earth's resources and the longer term character of truly sustainable production. Economic advance in a society of freely associated producers, Marx insisted again and again, would have to occur without jeopardizing the natural and global conditions upon which the welfare of future generations would depend. This is precisely the definition now given to the concept of sustainable development, most famously in the Brundtland Commission report, *Our Common Future,* which defined it as "development that meets the needs of the present without compromising the ability of future generations to meet their own needs."[12]

Although Marx did not concentrate on the ecological critique of capitalism in his writings—no doubt because he thought that capitalism would be replaced by a society of freely associated producers long before such problems could become truly critical—his allusions to sustainability indicate that he was acutely aware of the ecological depredations of the system. Central to his concerns in this respect was the effect of capitalist industrialization on the degradation of the soil. The best known passage in this regard, from *Capital,* vol. I, is to be found in the section on "Large-Scale Industry and

Agriculture," which constitutes the final, culminating part of Marx's key chapter on "Machinery and Large-Scale Industry" (on the effects of the Industrial Revolution). There Marx argues:

> All progress in capitalist agriculture is a progress in the art, not only of robbing the worker, but of robbing the soil; all progress in increasing the fertility of the soil for a given time is progress towards ruining the long-lasting sources of that fertility. The more a country proceeds from large-scale industry as the background of its development, as in the case of the United States, the more rapid is this process of destruction. Capitalist production, therefore, only develops the techniques and the degree of combination of the social process of production by simultaneously undermining the original sources of all wealth—the soil and the worker.[13]

These were not casual or isolated comments but reflected careful study of the work of the German agrarian chemist Justus von Liebig, often known as the founder of soil chemistry. Until the early 1860s, Marx thought that the progress of capitalist agriculture might be so rapid that it would outpace industry. By the time he wrote *Capital,* however, his studies of the work of Liebig and other agronomists had convinced him otherwise. "Large landed property," he explained in the conclusion to his most important chapter on capitalist agriculture ("The Genesis of Capitalist Ground Rent"),

> reduces the agricultural population to a constantly falling minimum, and confronts it with a constantly growing industrial population crowded together in large cities. It thereby creates conditions which cause an irreparable break in the coherence of social interchange prescribed by the natural laws of life. As a result, the vitality of the soil is squandered, and this prodigality is carried by commerce far beyond the borders of a particular state (Liebig).

Large-scale industry and large-scale agriculture under capitalism thus had the same results: both contributed to the ruining of the agricultural worker and the exhaustion of "the natural power of the soil." The "moral of history," Marx observed,

> is that the capitalist system works against a rational agriculture, or that a rational agriculture is incompatible with the capitalist system (although the latter promotes technical improvements in agriculture) and needs either the hand of the small farmer living by his own labor or the control of the associated producers.

For Marx "the rational cultivation of the soil as eternal communal property" was "an inalienable condition of the existence and reproduction of a chain of successive generations of the human race."[14]

Marx and Engels did not confine their discussions of ecological limits to the issue of the soil, but also explored numerous other issues of sustainability, in relation to forests, rivers and streams, the disposal of waste, air quality, environmental toxins, etc. "The development of culture and industry in general," Marx wrote, "has ever evinced itself in such energetic destruction of forests that everything done by it conversely for their preservation and restoration appears infinitesimal." With regard to industrial waste, he argued for "economy through the prevention of waste, that is to say, the reduction of excretions of production to a minimum, and the immediate utilization of all raw and auxiliary materials required in production."[15]

The chief source of ecological destruction under capitalism, Marx and Engels argued, was the extreme antagonism of town and country, a characteristic of capitalist organization as fundamental to the system as the division between capitalist and laborer. "When one observes," Engels wrote,

> how here in London alone a greater quantity of manure than is produced by the whole Kingdom of Saxony is poured away every day into the sea with an expenditure of enormous sums, and what colossal structures are necessary to prevent this manure from poisoning the whole of London, then the utopia of abolishing the antithesis between town and country is given a remarkably practical basis.[16]

Such ecological insights, so unusual among nineteenth-century thinkers, all derive from Marx and Engels's early recognition of the essential point that sustainability must lie at the core of the human relation to nature in any future society.

It is therefore wrong to argue, as Ted Benton has, that Marx and Engels "sustained and deepened *those aspects* of capitalist political economy which exemplified its hostility to the idea of natural limits to capital accumulation." To be sure, they had little to say about the *absolute* natural limits of the globe. In this sense, some, Benton included, have viewed Marx's analysis as ecologically inferior to that of Malthus, who emphasized the growth of population in relation to food supply (not primarily from an ecological or carrying capacity perspective but in order to justify subsistence wage levels and the dismantlement of the English Poor Laws). Yet Marx and Engels were unusual in the degree of emphasis they placed on the natural conditions of production, and in their recognition of the fact that a sustainable economy demanded a sustainable relation to nature on a global basis. In this sense, natural limits are very much a part of their argument.

As with other natural limits, limits to population growth, to the extent that they existed, Marx and Engels believed, only reinforced the case for socialism. "Even if Malthus were completely right" (with respect to the relation between population and food supply), the young Engels had observed in his very first essay on political economy, this only provided a further argument for a "social transformation": for the creation of a society in which the "production and destruction" of human beings would no longer be a mere commodity relation dependent "on demand." Of course, neither Marx nor Engels believed that Malthus was "completely right." Malthus's expectation that population would outpace food supply because of the inexorable nature of the former and the limited supply of cultivable land had, as Marx and Engels understood, underestimated the dynamism of capitalist agriculture unleashed by the commercial, agricultural, and industrial revolutions. Ironically, it is mainly because Malthus's expectations were *defeated* and the age-old cycle of famine (what Fernand Braudel has called "the biological *ancien régime*") was transcended for the first time in human history beginning in the late eighteenth century, that population has grown since Malthus's time to the point that overpopulation now poses a serious threat to the ecology of the planet as a whole. Moreover, if there is reason to believe that agriculture today is increasingly incapable of supplying the basic needs of a still growing world population, this is more related to Marx's analysis of the unsustainability of capitalist agriculture, which robs the soil itself, than to Malthus's more abstract notion (following Ricardo) of the diminishing marginal productivity of agriculture as more and more marginal land is brought under cultivation.[17]

No less mistaken is the criticism of Marx for—in the words of socialist ecologist Jean-Paul Deléage—attaching "no intrinsic value to natural resources" in his theory of value. For Marx, the law of value was a historically specific feature of capitalist society. Marx's comments on value relations no more indicate support for this setup (and the denial of intrinsic value) than they indicate support for capitalism itself (and the denial of the prospect of a non-alienated society). In Marx's theory, it is explicitly stated that capitalist value relations treat nature as a "free gift," as something given to capital "gratis." This was not at all inconsistent, however, with Marx's other point that the land and soil were "robbed"—or, in other words, that conditions of sustainability, which must take account of the reproduction of nature, were expressly violated by the system.[18]

For Marx, material wealth in its widest conception (understood in terms of use values) has to be distinguished from value creation under capitalism (the world of exchange value). "Labor," he wrote, "is not the only source of material wealth, of use-values produced by labor. As William Petty puts it, labor is its father and the earth is its mother." It is a contradiction of capitalism that it pursues exchange value (profit) while largely ignoring the qualitative conditions associated with use value and wealth in its larger context, which includes the natural environment and the productivity of nature. Marx seems to have clearly understood the basic ecological principal that "nothing comes from nothing," popularized in recent years by Barry Commoner and others. As Marx himself wrote,

> What Lucretius says is self-evident: "nil posse creari de nihilo," out of nothing, nothing can be created. Creation of value is transformation of labor-power into labor. Labor-power itself is energy transferred to a human organism by means of nourishing matter.[19]

We can more fully understand the historical significance of Marx and Engels's ecological thought by comparing their ideas with those of the great Vermont environmentalist George Perkins Marsh, widely recognized as the foremost conservationist/ecologist of the nineteenth century and (in the words of Lewis Mumford) "the fountainhead of the conservation movement." In one of the best-known passages of his classic work, *Man and Nature* (1864), Marsh wrote:

> There are parts of Asia Minor, of Northern Africa, of Greece, and even of Alpine Europe where the operation of causes set in action by man has brought the face of the earth to a desolation almost as complete as that of the moon; and though, within that brief space of time which we call "the historical period," they are known to have been covered with luxuriant woods, verdant pastures, and fertile meadows, they are now too far deteriorated to be reclaimable by man.... The earth is fast becoming an unfit home for its noblest inhabitant, and another era of equal human crime and improvidence ... would reduce it to such a condition of impoverished productiveness, of shattered surface, of climatic excess, as to threaten the depravation, barbarism, and perhaps even extinction of the species.[20]

This statement by Marsh can be compared to a closely related interpretation of long-term ecological developments put forward by Engels in his essay, "The Part Played by Labor in the Transition from Ape to Man," written in 1876:

> Let us not, however, flatter ourselves overmuch on account of our human conquest of nature. For each such conquest takes its revenge on us.... The people who, in Mesopotamia, Greece, Asia Minor, and elsewhere destroyed the forests to obtain cultivable land, never dreamed that they were laying the basis for the present devastated condition of these countries, by removing along with the forests the collecting centers and reservoirs of moisture. When, on the southern slopes of the mountains, the Italians of the Alps used up the pine forests so carefully cherished on the northern slopes, they had no inkling that by doing so they were cutting at the roots of the dairy industry in their region.... Thus at every step we are reminded that we by no means rule over nature like a conqueror over a foreign people, like someone standing outside nature—but that we, with flesh, blood, and brain, belong to nature, and exist in its midst, and that all our mastery of it consists in the fact that we have the advantage of all other beings of being able to know and correctly apply its laws.[21]

A close examination of these passages will reveal that there is a broad similarity in the way in which the issue of ecological destruction is approached by Engels and Marsh. Both refer in detail to great ecological disasters that have confronted civilizations. Both see this primarily as a question of sustainability. In Marsh's terms, such "improvidence" in the exploitation of nature must be ended, while Engels insists on the fact that we "belong to nature" and must "correctly apply its laws." Both adopt a broadly anthropocentric perspective, in the sense that they emphasize the consequences of such destruction for the fate of humanity.

The point here is not that Marx and Engels singly or together were the equal of Marsh in their understanding of ecological science; they were not. Yet their views were by no means incompatible with that of the greatest (and still widely respected) ecologist of their day. Moreover, it is no mere coincidence that *Man and Nature,* the leading work on planetary ecological devastation to be written prior to the twentieth century, was published only three years before the publication of the first volume of Marx's *Capital* (1867). Both were responses (though Marsh's less consciously so) to the effects of the Industrial Revolution. Marx's work helped inspire working class revolts, while Marsh's ideas gave impetus to a wide-ranging struggle on behalf of nature. Only by combining the analyses represented by these works do we have anything like a complete ecological critique of machine capitalism. The reason for this, of course, is that while Marsh was the premier conservationist/ecologist of his time, it was Marx and Engels who most acutely understood the *historical conditions* underlying such ecological destruction in the nineteenth century. Indeed, since the roots of the global environmental crisis are to be found not in nature but in society, Marx and Engels may have much more to teach us today about what is necessary in order to address the ecological problem than what can be learned from Marsh.

The key to Marx and Engels's understanding of modern society lay in their critique of capital accumulation. They were convinced that capitalism was economically and politically unsustainable. It would eventually give rise to the revolutionary forces that would overthrow it. The same critique of capital accumulation led them to conclude—beginning with their very earliest writings—that the system lacked a sustainable relation to nature. In their analysis, however, this problem did not yet loom so large that it would affect the future of capitalism (which they thought would soon die a natural death as a result of its economic and political contradictions). If the issue of ecological sustainability was frequently raised in their works, this had more to do with their understanding of the needs of the future society of freely associated producers than with the conditions of capitalism's demise. The stability of any future society, Marx clearly recognized, would be dependent on the creation of a wholly new and more balanced relation to the natural world.

Today radical ecologists see things differently only in the sense that it is now understood that global ecological destruction will play a central role in capitalism's end game. We are for the first time in human history confronting the problem of ecological survival on a planetary scale—a problem that nineteenth-century thinkers, Marx and Engels included (though Marsh might be considered an exception to this), could scarcely have imagined. Nevertheless, we cannot even begin to understand the complex of problems that now face us unless we approach them as Marx and Engels did in relation to the critique of capital accumulation. It would be a mistake to see the answer to the ecological problem as one of rejecting "modernity" in the name of some abstract and amorphous "postmodernity," at the same time rejecting those modes of thought that provide a systematic critique of capitalism. Rather, we must recognize that it is necessary to come to grips with modernity—above all capitalist modernity—and transform it. Since the destruction of the living world as we know it is otherwise certain, the great mass of humanity has nothing to lose but its chains. It has a planet to save.

NOTES

1. Zaheer Baber, "The Vulnerable Planet" (review), *Contemporary Sociology* (January 1995): 82; Carolyn Merchant, *Ecology* (Atlantic Highlands, NJ: Humanities Press, 1994), p. 2.
2. Ted Benton, "Marxism and Natural Limits," *New Left Review* 178 (November-December 1989): 82; Reiner Grundmann, *Marxism and Ecology* (New York: Oxford University Press), p. 52, and "The Ecological Challenge to Marxism," *New Left Review* 187 (May-June 1991): 120; Victor Ferkiss, *Nature, Technology and Society* (New York: New York University Press, 1993), p. 108; John Clark, "Marx's Inorganic Body," *Environmental Ethics* 11, no. 3 (Fall 1989): 258.
3. Wade Sikorski, *Modernity and Technology* (Tuscaloosa: University of Alabama Press, 1993), p. 138.
4. Leonard P. Wessell, Jr., *Prometheus Bound: The Mythic Structure of Karl Marx's Scientific Thinking* (Baton Rouge: Louisiana State University Press, 1984), p. 3; Linda M. Lewis, *The Promethean Politics of Milton, Blake and Shelley* (Columbia: University of Missouri Press, 1992), p. 2.
5. Ellen Meiksins Wood, *Peasant-Citizen and Slave* (London: Verso, 1988), pp. 141-44.
6. Herbert Marcuse, *Eros and Civilization* (New York: Vintage, 1962), pp. 146-49.
7. Marshall Berman, *All That is Solid Melts Into Air* (New York: Simon and Schuster, 1982), pp. 126-29; Roy Medvedev, *Let History Judge* (New York: Columbia University Press, 1989), pp. 852-59.
8. Kate Soper, "Greening Prometheus," in Peter Osborne (ed.), *Socialism and the Limits of Liberalism* (New York: Verso, 1991); William Leiss, *The Domination of Nature* (Boston: Beacon Press, 1974), pp. 85, 198.
9. Karl Marx, *Early Writings* (New York: Vintage, 1975), p. 328.
10. Frederick Engels, "Outlines of a Critique of Political Economy," in Marx, *The Economic and Philosophic Manuscripts of 1844* (New York: International Publishers, 1964), p. 210; Marx, *Early Writings,* pp. 377-79; Marx and Engels, *The Communist Manifesto* (New York: Monthly Review Press, 1964), pp. 5-6; Marx, *Capital,* vol. III (New York: International Publishers, 1967), p. 820; Erich Fromm, *Beyond the Chains of Illusion* (New York: Simon and Schuster, 1962), pp. 36-37.
11. Marx, *Capital,* vol. III, p. 776.
12. Ibid., p. 617n. World Commission on Environment and Development (the Brundtland Commission report), *Our Common Future* (Oxford: Oxford University Press, 1987), p. 43.
13. Marx, *Capital,* vol. I, pp. 637-38.

14. Marx, *Capital,* vol. III, pp. 121, 812-13; Ronald Meek, "Introduction," in Marx and Engels, *Malthus* (New York: International Publishers, 1954), pp. 13-14, 28-31. For a brilliant analysis of the contributions of Liebig and Marx to the critique of capitalist agriculture see Kozo Mayumi, "Temporary Emancipation from Land: From the Industrial Revolution to the Present Time," *Ecological Economics* 4, no. 1 (October 1991): 35-56.
15. Marx, *Capital,* vol. III, pp. 101-103; Marx, *Capital,* vol. II (New York: International Publishers, 1967), p. 244.
16. Engels, *The Housing Question* (Moscow: Progress Publishers, 1975), p. 92.
17. Benton, "Marxism and Natural Limits": 64; Engels, "Outlines of a Critique of Political Economy," p. 221; Marx, *Capital,* vol. I, p. 505; Fernand Braudel, *The Structures of Everyday Life* (New York: Harper and Row, 1979), p. 70.
18. Jean-Paul Deléage, "Eco-Marxist Critique of Political Economy," in Martin O'Connor (ed.), *Is Capitalism Sustainable?* (New York: Guilford, 1994), p. 48; Marx, *Capital,* vol. III, p. 745; vol. I, p. 510. A similar interpretation to the one presented here has been developed in a forthcoming work by Paul Burkett.
19. Marx, *Capital,* vol. I (New York: International Publishers, 1967), pp. 43, 215n. While Commoner refers to the informal ecological law "there is no such thing as a free lunch," other ecologists have translated this as "nothing comes from nothing." See John Bellamy Foster, *The Vulnerable Planet* (New York: Monthly Review Press, 1994), pp. 118-20.
20. George Perkins Marsh, *Man and Nature* (Cambridge, MA: Harvard University Press, 1965), pp. 42-43; Lewis Mumford, *The Brown Decades* (New York: Dover, 1971), p. 35.
21. Engels, *Dialectics of Nature* (New York: International Publishers, 1940), pp. 291-92.

Northern intellectuals and the EZLN

DANIEL NUGENT

In recent decades, important trends in social and cultural analysis have been qualified with the prefix "post." Today social scientists, for instance, are expected to know something about poststructuralism, postmodernism, post-Fordism, and even something called post-Marxism. A situation once identified as "colonial" is said by some to have been supplanted by another, called "postcolonial." Whatever the virtues of these perspectives—for the challenges they present to conventional understandings, for generating new forms of critique—they are of little value for understanding contemporary historical developments; worse, they have introduced a vocabulary and form of presentation that obscure considerably more than they reveal.

Other essays in this volume have outlined the main characteristics of postmodernist discourse. For present purposes, it will be enough to cite a particularly compelling example to illustrate how this discourse is now being applied to what used to be called the third world. That example is found in the work of Gayatri Spivak, who once remarked that "Class is the purest form of signifier,"[1] implying that class is a "pure" linguistic sign in the sense that it has no concrete referent in the material world. From the point of view of the sort of linguistic theory on which so many postmodernist discourse analysts draw, the quality of the referent is less important than the location of concepts like class in relation to other "signifiers." So Spivak is able to say, for instance, that "socialism" has "no historically adequate referent" in India, by which she means that Indian socialism did not originate in a truly indigenous tradition of socialist discourse. Aijaz Ahmad has recently commented on this observation in a way that nicely captures the postmodernist notion of "history." To be told that socialism has no "historically adequate referent" in India, he remarks, would come as a big surprise to all those millions of Indians who, for reasons having to do with their own experience of their own domestic capitalism and their own situation in its class divisions, regularly vote communist. The "historical referent" for Indian socialism, in other words, is not some disembodied imperial "discourse" but Indian capitalism and a political practice "undertaken within India by Indian political subjects."[2]

That is one way of summing up the difference between postmodernism and Marxism. It isn't that Marxism is uninterested in language, discourse, or meaning, and the best historical materialist work deals precisely with the many different concrete referents that words like "class" or "work" can have in specific historical conditions. But here I simply want to underline that Marxism can understand the practices through which meanings are produced in relation to the actions of people on and in the world and not just in relation to other meanings. Practices are undertaken in particular places at particular times by particular subjects in particular conditions, and these have to be studied historically.

Revolution on the Internet

Say, for instance, we want to analyze Mexican society, whether viewed through the prism of the Mexican revolution of 1910, the neo-Zapatista revolution in Chiapas that started on January 1, 1994, or the crisis of the state and the ruling party in recent years. A starting point would be to recognize that Mexico has long been a "postcolonial society." Mexico has moved along temporally—if not developmentally—from an earlier colonial condition for almost two centuries. Yet one of the most striking features of the ways in which political power is organized socially and experienced subjectively throughout Mexico—whether in the "advanced" northern state of Chihuahua or the "backward" southeastern state of Chiapas—is that it is and remains a profoundly colonial or, in a pinch, *neocolonial* rather than unequivocally postcolonial form of power. Neither the Wars of Independence and the Wars of the Reform during the nineteenth century, nor the revolution of 1910 and the "reforms" of the *Salinastroika* period in 1988 to 1994, signaled irreversible, radical breaks with the past. Rather, they are moments in a sustained process of transformation. That series of political transformations was associated with a series of economic transformations that established the specific form of Mexican capitalism. The language of "pre" and "post," which pretends to be about historical change, actually *disguises* these processes of transformation by carving up history into discontinuous and disconnected units.

Nevertheless, the lure of intellectual fashion is so great that scholars who two decades ago worked with peasants in Mexico, and wrote about social movements, rural class formation, and the permanent character of the primitive accumulation of capital in dependent, peripheral states, now author postmodernist essays and books with titles (e.g., *Hybrid Cultures*) and themes (the metaphor of a salamander to organize reflections on Mexican history) that have more in common with magical realist literature than with historical materialist analysis. This is not to suggest that magical realism—say, the novels of Gabriel Garcia Marquez or Isabel Allende—has nothing to tell us, and that only historical materialism can reveal the Truth. It is only to underline the radical differences between literary and historical ways of relating to social reality.

Perhaps it should come as little surprise that some postmodern/postcolonial critics seem, or pretend, not to know that the arenas of discourse in which their work circulates are at several removes from the social reality they purport to represent. The privileges now enjoyed by intellectuals in the North have been so reduced that many seem to be compensating by providing to themselves an inflated sense of their own importance and exaggerating the significance of purely intellectual or "discursive" practices. Nonetheless, the distinction between *what* is being talked about and *how* it is being talked about remains important.

Yet postmodern concepts and assumptions, even casual turns of phrase, have a real seductive power over many intellectuals; and the freewheeling adoption of a postmodern vocabulary is having especially insidious effects on the study of current historical developments. This is particularly evident in the boatloads of material published about the EZLN uprising in Chiapas, the rebellion of the damned in the South that woke up the world on the first morning of 1994. In the rush to issue accounts of this seemingly unprecedented and original popular uprising, the expression "postmodern" fell quite easily from the pens and mouths of many commentators. More than a year after the EZLN challenged the power of the Mexican state, meanwhile, we read on the *New York Times* Op-Ed page that "the Mexican Meltdown of 1995 is the first postmodern economic crisis."[3]

Beside an unending stream of English-language publications providing profiles of the EZLN or its spokesperson Subcomandante Marcos, several computer networks devoted solely to distributing information about the EZLN appeared as well. It's as though the circulation of information, the communication and production of commentaries in English-language book and electronic media, is mirroring the production by impoverished Chiapan peasants-become-artisans of "Marcos" and "Ramona" dolls, the small wooden figures clothed not in traditional Mayan garb but in the outfits of the EZLN, complete with miniature ski masks and wooden rifles.

It is perfectly in keeping with the postmodernist worldview that a major theme in accounts of the Chiapan rebels has to do with the media of communication through which "we" in the North learn about, and relate to, the EZLN. "In Marcos's prose," writes one specialist, "one senses an expertise and familiarity with computer-based text, if not directly with e-mail."[4] Putting matters this way (which assumes that guerrillas are freely able to tap into electric power lines in a state in which, though it generates half the hydroelectric power in all of Mexico, most towns are not wired for electricity) diverts attention and analysis from an explicit consideration of the actual goals and accomplishments of the neo-Zapatistas and their connection to other currents within Mexican, Latin American, and North American society. It shifts attention instead toward the postmodern world of digital simultaneity. In being asked to assess "what effect the e-mail activity [has] had on actual events" we are presented with the image of "new icons of romantic rebellion" "bursting through ... TV screens" and the powerful effect of "the Zapatista presence on the Internet."

Asserting that the multiple messages resonating "within the nocturnal hacker community"[5] have a palpable historical effect fits perfectly the notion that neo-Zapatismo is indeed a "postmodern political movement." Focusing on, even celebrating the EZLN's use of modems, FAX machines, and e-mail suggests that their most distinctive feature as a political movement is to have shifted the object of struggle from control of the means of production to control of the means of communication; revolutionary ideals are to be advanced by the free exchange of rebel-friendly software and communications packages. But this way of thinking about the rebellion tends to block out the years of organizing that preceded January 1, 1994. To assert the fundamental "postmodernity" of the EZLN is not really to analyze "actual events" in Chiapas in 1994. It is more a way of allowing some intellectuals to *appropriate* these events, to situate these complex historical developments on their own (intellectual) terrain, to assimilate them to a discourse that permits computer-literate academics to feel good about themselves.

A postmodern political movement?

Particularly disconcerting is the manner in which claims regarding the postmodernity of the EZLN are repeated by people on the left. An example that springs to mind is Roger Burbach's essay on the "Roots of the postmodern rebellion in Chiapas" published in *New Left Review* during the summer of 1994, where the EZLN is described as "a postmodern political movement ... [which] attempt[s] to move beyond the politics of modernity."[6]

Once past these introductory remarks, Burbach presents a compelling, competent, and concise description of the neocolonial background to the 1994 uprising. Drawing on recent research by anthropologists, sociologists, and political scientists familiar with the region, Burbach presents an analysis that is not particularly "postmodern" in either form or structure. He demonstrates that the rebellion occurred in Chiapas when it did because a particular form of capitalism has been adopted in this region of the world. The alienation of the peasantry from the land, how commercial agriculture—especially of coffee—is buffeted by fluctuations in international commodity prices, and how strategic relocations of squatters are engineered by the Mexican state while large landowners and ranchers continue to rely on hired gun thugs, the *guardias blancas,* are all described, and their relations to labor migration outlined. Burbach gives substantive content to the notion of "combined and uneven development."[7]

Nevertheless, in its opening and closing paragraphs, where the assertion of the fundamental "postmodernity" of the EZLN is repeated time and again, the essay is *symptomatic* of what can happen when northern intellectuals, even those on the left, become enchanted by a sort of postmodernist identity politics. This adoption of postmodern vocabulary and categories of analysis winds up revealing more about academic politics in the North than it does about the situations these analyses are meant to explain. I think it is worth closely examining some of these passages in Burbach's article in order to fully appreciate the absurdities to which such analyses can lead.

The opening paragraph begins thus:

> The Indian uprising in Chiapas that burst upon the world scene in January is a postmodern political movement. The rebellion is an attempt to move beyond the politics of modernity....

It is difficult to see how a rebel army of peasants, aware of itself as the product of 500 years of struggle, that quotes from the Mexican Constitution to legitimize its demand that the President of Mexico immediately leave office, that additionally demands work, land, housing, food, health, education, independence, liberty, democracy, justice, and peace for the people of Mexico, can be called a "postmodern political movement." How can the EZLN move *beyond* the politics of modernity when their vocabulary is so patently modernist, and their practical organization so emphatically premodern? Their democratic command structure is a slow-moving form of organization—requiring as it does direct consultation and discussion with the base communities in five or six different languages—which is difficult to reconcile with postmodernist digital simultaneity. Do their demands include a modem and VCR in every *jacale* or adobe hut in Mexico? No. Is their chosen name "The postmodern army of multinational emancipation" or "Cyberwarriors of the South"? No. They are the Zapatista Army of National Liberation. Emiliano Zapata (not a "free-floating signifier" but a specific historical subject), who led the peasants of Morelos, from 1911 until his assassination in 1919, in recovering control of the land and driving out the *caciques*/foreign political bosses, is a very unlikely postmodern hero.

Here is the conclusion of the opening paragraph: "Even more fundamentally, [the rebellion] seeks to end the victimization of Indians by centuries of western modernization." Again, there is little particularly "postmodern" about struggling to that end (quite apart from the fact that premodern forms of exploitation are alive and well and continue to be major targets of struggle). Here it becomes increasingly difficult to get a grip on what is supposed to be postmodern. What is the "modernization" that the neo-Zapatistas are resisting? Does it have something to do with capitalism? Would any anticapitalist struggle be "postmodern"?

Nor is our understanding of postmodernity or of the EZLN much advanced by the following:

> The uprising led by the EZLN ... comes in the wake of the collapse of the "modern" bipolar world of the post-World War II era and the ideological exhaustion of most national liberation movements....

Burbach here appears to be assuming that the collapse of "the Communist world" signaled the end of modernism. But it is not at all clear what is supposed to be postmodern about that extremely tentative great leap forward of neoliberal ideology, the market, and policies oriented toward capitalist economic restructuration; in some important respects it may represent a triumph of "modernism." And from an altogether different point of view, it is possible to view the triumph of modernism in an optimistic light. As Marshall Berman has written:

> 1989 was not only a great year, but a great *modernist* year. First, because millions of people learned that history was not over, that they had the capacity to make their own history—though not, alas, in circumstances chosen by themselves. Second, because in the midst of their motions,

> those men and women identified with each other: even in different languages and idioms, even thousands of miles apart, they saw how their stories were one story, how they were all trying to make the modern world their own. I fear that vision has faded from our public life.[8]

One thing demonstrated by Chiapas 1994 is that the vision to which Berman refers, almost nostalgically, has once again been drawn into focus by the appearance of neo-Zapatismo, the forthright clarity of the communiqués from the CCRI-CG (Clandestine Revolutionary Indigenous Committee-General Command), and the writings of Subcomandante Marcos. At the same time, and particularly in Chiapas, there still remain bipolar axes of difference—women and men, capital and labor, North and South, Indian and white—through which peoples' lives are organized, and disorganized, and made miserable. In a sense, then, the "'modern' bipolar world of the post-World War II era" is stronger—more vicious, more destructive, more retrenched—than ever. In any case, the most serious problem facing most national liberation movements—including the EZLN—may not be "ideological exhaustion" but rather the threat of physical extermination.

In any case, it is difficult to determine the ideological resources available to participants in such movements when their own voices are muted and their own practices obscured by the superimposed discourses of Northern academics. If such movements derive their meaning only from the terms of academic discourses, how different is the conservative claim that the EZLN is led by "outside agitators" from the supposedly radical claim that the EZLN is a "postmodern political movement?"

The EZLN and the state

Maybe what really identifies the EZLN as a postmodern movement for Burbach is this: "What distinguishes the EZLN from its predecessors is that it is not bent on taking power in Mexico City, nor is it calling for state socialism."

But in addition to being a curious reason for regarding the movement as postmodern, this is straightforwardly and simply wrong; wrong about the EZLN, and wrong about its predecessors. First, in their declaration of war in late 1993, the first order from the General Command of the EZLN to its military forces was to "Advance to the capital of the country, defeat the Mexican Federal Army ... and permit the liberated peoples to elect, freely and democratically, their own administrative authorities."[9] Second, from the time of the conquest and even before, Mexican history has been racked by large-scale popular uprisings and rebellions by peasants and Indians. A key feature of these mobilizations is that most were, precisely, *not* "bent on taking power in Mexico City." Perhaps that's why the peasants and Indians invariably lost, why each rural revolt has ended with the victory of the dominant class.

Whatever the extent of violence exercised during earlier popular uprisings, there has often been a strong antimilitaristic streak running through them, and an even stronger repudiation of the power of the state, whether colonial or neocolonial, patrimonial or capitalist. Two obvious examples that spring to mind are the popular armies led by Emiliano Zapata and Francisco Villa between 1911 and 1920. But neither Villismo and Zapatismo [Mark I] were "bent on taking power in Mexico City," nor were either of them calling for "state socialism." To try to forge a new basis for social life in a way that is grounded in the experience and responds to the demands—or the requirements for living—of *los de abajo*, of the misnamed *marginados* (who are in fact not the least bit "marginal" to the continuing reproduction of specific forms of exploitation) is hardly to call for state socialism. In any event, "state monopoly capitalism" is a more accurate term for the sort of social system Burbach correctly insists the neo-Zapatistas are repudiating.

At any rate, throughout the world, peasant movements have tended to regard the state as alien and distant, and typically their revolts have been directed not at the seizure of state power but at the replacement of an alien form of rule by a different social order. Hence it could be argued that the failure to aim for state power is rather more pre- than post-modern. If Burbach is right about the neo-Zapatistas' relation to the state, then the EZLN is typically premodern; but if he is wrong, than it is more modern than "postmodern."

The other side of this coin is Burbach's claim that the EZLN's objective "is to spark a broad-based movement of civil society in Chiapas and the rest of Mexico that will transform the country from the bottom up."

It is undeniable that the EZLN is distinguishable from other popular social movements in Mexico in the last sixty years in its success at not only precipitating "a broad-based political and ideological dialogue," but also in actively mobilizing large groups of people. It is no less certain that the current effort is not without precedents outside the conventional circuits of power that flow to and from the state and the ruling party, the PRI. Many Mexican activists and popular organizations—some more visible and predictable than others—share the objective of generating a broad-based movement to transform society from the bottom up. Alongside human rights organizations, peasant *coordinadoras,* and the popular organizations that sprang out of the rubble of the earthquakes in Mexico City in 1985, are the unofficial and independent trade unions, the millions of people who voted for Cuauhtemoc Cardenas in 1988, and movements such as the peasant mobilizations in the northern state of Chihuahua in the 1980s that linked up with peasant mobilizations in Chiapas, just as others had a century earlier. What distinguishes the EZ, then, is not its *objective,* but the genuinely unprecedented success with which its initiative has been embraced and taken seriously by many currents in Mexican society.

Yet however unprecedented the EZLN's apparent success has been up to now (in April 1995), it is still hard to see what this has to do with its postmodernity. Broad-based movements in Mexican society have both "modern" and "premodern" antecedents, and organization in "civil society" has long been a staple of popular mobilizations. When in his concluding section Burbach again insists that the EZLN's "postmodernist perspective" is demonstrated by "the demand for authentic democracy, and transforming society from the bottom up," one can't help wondering why good old Marxist socialism, with its commitment to securing human emancipation and a thorough democratization of society beginning with "freely associated direct producers" would not be the epitome of postmodernity.

The attempt to pin the postmodern label on the EZLN is shot through with contradictions, which are nicely summed up in the following observation:

> Another central factor facilitating this revolt's postmodernity is that it is not a rebellion against a typical autocrat or dictator like Batista or Somoza, but a movement that traces its lineage back to the early twentieth-century Mexican revolution.

To begin with, it is unclear exactly what Batista or Somoza are supposed to typify. But the main thing is that the rebels—communicating in languages understood only by themselves and a handful of anthropologists, linguists, missionaries, and former Maoists—yet again appear pretty premodern and the enemy they have identified, manifestly modern. What distinguishes the EZLN, even by this account, is not their postmodern redefinition of temporality, space, and experience itself, but, on the contrary, their sense of palpable connection with a tradition. Burbach's observation that "The struggle of the EZLN ... [is] over how to mobilize the population to recapture the country's revolutionary ideals" certainly captures something important about what the neo-Zapatistas are trying to accomplish and how they are self-consciously building upon past struggles of historical peasantries in Mexico. But that observation neatly and decisively subverts his claims for the EZLN as a "postmodern political movement."

So where does this leave us? The language of postmodernity has added nothing to our understanding of Chiapas. If anything, it has obscured and detracted from what is valuable in Burbach's account. It is especially depressing to observe this effect in an otherwise illuminating and politically sympathetic study, and it is a measure of the price we have to pay for this surrender to fashion. Instead of bringing us closer to an understanding of a complex social movement, it simply serves to underline the profound distance between postmodern intellectuals and the activists or supporters of the EZLN.

Why not interject some remarks of a Chihuahuan peasant, asked whether people in northern Mexico, followers of Francisco Villa, had joined the revolution in 1910 to recover control of their land. "Put it that we now have land," replied Cruz Chavez in 1986,

> but that was a fight. And justice? And freedom? When will we get that? Can you tell me? Look, we're gonna die of old age without seeing them, because the more time that passes, justice and freedom only get worse in our country.[10]

Now I can imagine at least two different ways of connecting these remarks to what is happening in Chiapas today. We could simply take Cruz Chavez's words with those of Subcomandante Marcos and measure them both against some abstract repertoire of signifiers to find out, for example, whether they are elements of pre- or post-modern discourses. Alternatively, we could consider these discourses historically, comparing the ways in which words like "freedom" and "justice" figure in their respective vocabularies, and how they relate to their concrete and changing historical referents, their material and social conditions, their political practices and struggles. We could consider as well how the labor process in Mexican agriculture has or has not changed since 1910, how political democracy has or has not advanced. And we could explore the ways in which the EZLN is trying in practice to answer the questions posed by Cruz Chavez in a different region of Mexico, under different historical conditions, and building differently on a long history—including the 1910 revolution—of political struggle.

In the first case, it is hard to see how our objective as intellectuals could be anything else than to appropriate those discourses, to claim them as our own. In the second, we would simply be trying to understand and explain. The latter objective is in some ways more modest. At least it is less likely to exaggerate the power of intellectuals, because it acknowledges that we are talking *about* social and political practices undertaken by specific people other than ourselves, instead of claiming that our own discourse is the only real practice, our academic discourse the only real politics.

Derek Sayer has suggested that "we might want to consider the possibility that the status of 'organic intellectual' of anything other than a ruling class might just be a contradiction in terms."[11] However difficult it may be to accept, this suggestion does have the virtue of acknowledging both the limits and the grounding of intellectual activity. Something approximating, however remotely, the determinative power that postmodernist intellectuals claim for their own discursive practices—the power to create reality itself—is, in the real world, possible only for servants of a ruling class, with the power of the state underwriting their discourses. The rest of us should be content to see our intellectual activity function as a critical instrument, as a challenge to ruling ideologies, maybe as a guide to political action when possible, but above all as a way of enhancing or broadcasting, but not replacing, the voices of those who oppose oppression.

NOTES

Versions of this paper were presented as talks in New Haven; Zamora, Michoacán; and Chicago in the autumn of 1994 and in Austin, Texas in March 1995. Thanks to Gil Joseph, Eduardo Zárate, José Lameiras, Alexandra Stern, Bryan Roberts, and Guillermo de la Peña for those invitations and their comments. I also learned a lot from the students in my seminar on state formation and popular culture in revolutionary Mexico in the autumn of 1994: Elea Aguirre, Maribel Alvarez, Guillermo Nuñez-Noriega, Mike Rolland, and Paola Sesia-Lewis. For the rest I relied as in the past on the support, insight, and criticism of my collaborators in Tucson, Arizona, Raquel Rubio Goldsmith and Eva Tessler.

1. Gayatri Chakravorty Spivak, to a seminar at the Pembroke Center for Teaching and Research on Women, Brown University, March 1988.
2. Aijaz Ahmad, "The politics of literary postcoloniality," *Race & Class* 36, no. 3 (1995): 5.
3. Thomas Friedman "New Mexico," *New York Times*, 15 March 1995, p. A17.

4. Deedee Halleck, “Zapatistas On-Line,” *NACLA Report on the Americas* 28, no. 2 (September/October 1994): 30.
5. Quotations from ibid.: 31-32.
6. Roger Burbach, “Roots of the Postmodern Rebellion in Chiapas,” *New Left Review* no. 205 (1994): 113-124.
7. See also Antonio Garcıa de León, “Paradoxes of modernization: The new agrarian question and the peasant movement in Mexico,” *Journal of Historical Sociology* 8, no. 4 (December 1995): 430-447.
8. Marshall Berman, “Why Modernism Still Matters,” in Scott Lash and Jonathan Friedman (eds.), *Modernity and Identity* (Oxford, Basil Blackwell, 1992), p. 55.
9. *Shadows of Tender Fury: The Letters and Communiques of Subcomandante Marcos and the Zapatista Army of National Liberation* (New York: Monthly Review Press, 1995), p. 53.
10. Interview with Cruz Chavez Gutierrez in El Tascate, Namiquipa, Chihuahua, July 1986. This man was the grandson of an earlier Cruz Chavez, who led the town of Tomochic, Chihuahua, in a briefly successful and still influential armed uprising against the Mexican state in the early 1890s.
11. Derek Sayer, “Some Dissident Remarks on ‘Hegemony’” in G. Joseph and D. Nugent (eds.), *Everyday Forms of State Formation* (Durham, NC: Duke University Press, 1994), p. 373.

Five theses on actually existing Marxism

FREDRIC JAMESON

First thesis

"Postmarxisms" regularly emerge at those moments in which capitalism itself undergoes a structural metamorphosis.

Marxism is the science of capitalism, or better still, in order to give depth at once to both terms, it is the science of the inherent contradictions of capitalism. This means on the one hand that it is incoherent to celebrate the "death of Marxism" in the same breath with which one announces the definitive triumph of capitalism and the market. The latter would rather seem to augur a secure future for the former, leaving aside the matter of how "definitive" its triumph could possibly be.[1] On the other hand, the "contradictions" of capitalism are not some formless internal dissolution, but relatively lawful and regular, and subject at least to theorization after the fact. For example, for any given moment of capitalism, the space it controls will eventually become oversaturated with the commodities it is technically capable of producing. This crisis is then systemic.

Capitalism is however not merely a system or mode of production, it is the most elastic and adaptable mode of production that has appeared thus far in human history, and has previously overcome such cyclic crises. It has achieved this by means of two basic strategies: the expansion of the system, and the production of radically new types of commodities.

The expansion of the system. Capitalism has always had a center, recently the hegemony of the United States and previously that of England.[2] Each new center is spatially larger and more inclusive than preceding centers, and thus opens up a wider territory for commodification in general, and for new markets and new products alike. According to a somewhat different version of the historical narrative, we can speak of a national moment of capitalism that emerged from the eighteenth century industrial revolution. This first moment is that which Marx himself experienced and theorized, albeit prophetically. It was followed at the end of the nineteenth century by the moment of imperialism, in which the limits of the national markets were burst and a kind of worldwide colonial system established. Finally, after the Second World War and in our own time, the older imperial system was dismantled and a new "world system" set in its place, dominated by the so-called multinational corporations. This current moment of a "multinational" capitalism is uneasily balanced (after the disappearance of the Soviet Union) between the three centers of Europe, the United States, and Japan, each with its immense hinterland of satellite states. This third moment, whose convulsive stages of emergence were not really complete until the end of the cold war (if then), is clearly far more "global" than the preceding age of imperialism. With the "deregulation" (so to speak) of the immense areas of India, Brazil, and Eastern Europe, there is a scope for the penetration of capital and the market qualitatively greater than in earlier stages of capitalism. Is this then to be considered the definitive achievement of what Marx prophesied as the world market, and thereby the final stage of capitalism—including among other things, "the universal commodification of labor power"? It is to be doubted. The inner class dynamics of the new moment have scarcely had time to work themselves out, in particular the emergence of new forms of labor organization and political struggle appropriate to the scale at which "globalization" has transformed the world of business.

The production of radically new types of commodities. There is a second requirement for overcoming systemic crises: that is, the recourse to innovations and even "revolutions" in technology. Ernest Mandel makes these changes coincident with the stages just described: steam technology for the moment of national capitalism; electricity and the combustion engine for the moment of imperialism; atomic energy and the cybernetic for our own moment of multinational capitalism and globalization, which has come to be labeled by some as postmodernity. These technologies are both productive of new types of commodities and instrumental in opening up new world spaces, thus "shrinking" the globe and reorganizing capitalism according to a new scale. This is the sense in which characterizations of late capitalism in terms of information or cybernetics are appropriate (and very revealing culturally), but need to be recoupled with the economic dynamics from which they tend rather easily to be severed, rhetorically, intellectually, and ideologically.

If the overall lines of this periodization of capital are accepted, it becomes at once clear that the various "post-Marxisms" of, in particular, Bernstein at the turn of the last century or of poststructuralism in the 1980s, along with their posited "crisis" or "death" of Marxism, have been simultaneous with precisely those moments in which capitalism is restructured and prodigiously enlarged. And these in turn have been followed by various theoretical projects of a more modern—or indeed in our time postmodern—Marxism attempting to theorize the new and unexpected dimensions taken on by its traditional object of study, capitalism as such.

Second thesis

Socialism as a vision of freedom—freedom from unwanted and avoidable economic and material constraints, freedom for collective praxis—is in our time threatened on two ideological levels at once: that of "discursive struggle" (in the words of Stuart Hall) in an argument with worldwide Thatcherism about the market system;[3] and that which plays on even deeper anti-utopian anxieties and fears of change. The two levels clearly imply one another, insofar as the market argument presupposes a set of views about human nature which the anti-utopian vision then rehearses in more apocalyptic and libidinal ways.

Discursive struggle (as opposed to outright ideological conflict) succeeds by way of discrediting its alternatives and rendering unmentionable a whole series of thematic topics. It appeals to trivialization, naiveté, material interest, "experience," political fear, and historical lessons, as the "grounds" for decisively delegitimizing such formerly serious possibilities as nationalization, regulation, deficit spending, Keynesianism, planning, protection of national industries, the security net, and ultimately the welfare state itself. Identifying this last with socialism then allows market rhetoric to win a double victory, over liberals (in the U.S. usage, as in "New Deal liberals") as well as the left. The left is thus today placed in the position of having to defend big government and the welfare state, something its elaborate and sophisticated traditions of the critique of social democracy make it embarrassing to do without a more dialectical understanding of history than much of the left possesses. In particular, it is desirable to regain some sense of the way historical situations change, and the appropriate political and strategic responses along with them. But this also demands an engagement with the so-called end of history, that is, the fundamental ahistoricality of the postmodern in general.

Meanwhile, the anxieties associated with utopia, which spring from the fear that everything that makes up our current identity and our current habits and forms of libidinal gratification would disappear under some new social dispensation, some radical change in the societal order, are now far more easily mobilizable than at other moments in the recent past. Evidently, at least in the richer half of the world and not only in the dominant strata, the hope for change of destitute people in the modern period has been replaced by the terror of loss. These anti-utopian anxieties need to be addressed head-on, in a kind of cultural diagnosis and therapy, and not evaded by way of consent to this or that feature of the general market argument and rhetoric.

All arguments about human nature—that it is basically good and cooperative, or that it is evil and aggressive and requires the taming of the market, if not Leviathan—are "humanistic" and ideological (as Althusser taught us), and should be replaced by the perspective of radical change and the collective project. In the meantime, the left needs aggressively to defend big government and the welfare state, and to continuously attack market rhetoric on the basis of the historical record of the destructiveness of the free market (as Polanyi theorized it and Eastern Europe demonstrates).

Third Thesis

But such arguments in their turn presuppose the taking of a position on what is surely the central concept in any Marxian "unity-of-theory-and-practice," namely Revolution itself. This is the case because it is the untenability of that concept that is the principal exhibit in the post- or anti-Marxian arsenal. The defense of this concept, however, requires a number of preliminary preparations: in particular, we need to abandon to iconology everything that suggests that revolution is a punctual moment rather than an elaborate and complex process. For example, many of our most cherished iconic images of the various historical revolutions, such as the taking of the Winter Palace and the Tennis Court Oath, need to be set aside.

Social revolution is not a moment in time, but it can be affirmed in terms of the necessity of change in what is a synchronic system, in which everything holds together and is interrelated with everything else. Such a system then demands a kind of absolute systemic change, rather than a piecemeal "reform," which turns out to be what is in the pejorative sense "utopian," that is, illusory, not feasible. That is to say that the system demands the ideological vision of a radical social alternative to the existing social order, something which can no longer be taken for granted or inherited, under the state of current discursive struggle, but which demands re-invention. Religious fundamentalism (whether Islamic, Christian, or Hindu), that claims to offer a radical alternative to consumerism and "the American way of life," only comes into significant being when the traditional left alternatives, and in particular the great revolutionary traditions of Marxism and communism, have suddenly seemed unavailable.

We must imagine revolution—as something which is both a process and the undoing of a synchronic system—as a set of demands which can be triggered by a punctual or political event such as a left victory in an electoral struggle or the dismantling of colonial authority, but which then takes the form of wider and wider popular diffusion and radicalization. These waves of new popular demands, which emerge from even deeper layers of the hitherto silenced and deprived population, then radicalize even an ostensibly left government and force ever more decisive transformations on the state. The nation (but in our time the world, as well) is then polarized in the classical dichotomous fashion in which everyone, however reluctantly, must take sides. The question of violence is then necessarily posed: if the process is not really a social revolution it does not necessarily have to be accompanied by violence. But if it is, then the previously dominant side of the dichotomy will of necessity have recourse to violent resistance, and in that sense alone, then, violence (however undesirable) is the outward sign or visible symptom that a genuinely social revolutionary process is in course.

The more basic issue raised here is thus not whether the concept of revolution is still viable, but rather that of national autonomy. We must ask whether, in the world system today, it is possible for any segment of integrated sections to uncouple and delink (to use Samir Amin's term) and then to pursue a different kind of social development and a radically different type of collective project.

Fourth thesis

The collapse of the Soviet Union was not due to the failure of communism but rather to the success of communism, provided one understands this last, as the West generally does, as a mere strategy of modernization. For it is by way of rapid modernization that the Soviet Union was thought, even fifteen years ago, virtually to have caught up with the West (an officially anxiety-provoking perspective we can scarcely remember any longer).

Three further propositions need to be affirmed in connection with the collapse of the Soviet Union. The first is that internal social and political disintegration is part of a larger worldwide pattern in the 1980s which has enveloped in a structural corruption both the West (Reaganism and Thatcherism, other parallel forms in Italy and France) and the Arab countries (what Hisham Sharabi calls "neopatriarchy"). It would be misleading to explain causally this structural corruption in moral terms as it springs from the quite material social process of the accumulation of wealth unproductively in the very top layers of these societies. It has become clear that this stagnation is intimately related to what has been known as finance capital as it distances itself and diverges from its origin in production. Giovanni Arrighi has shown that the various moments of capital all seem to know a final stage in which production passes over into speculation, in which value parts from its origin in production and is exchanged more abstractly (something not without its cultural consequences as well).

It must also be stressed that categories like those of efficiency, productivity, and fiscal solvency are comparative ones, that is to say, their consequences come into play only in a field in which several unequal phenomena are competing. More efficient and productive technique drives out older machinery and older plant only when the latter enters its force-field and thereby offers or is challenged to compete.

This leads us to the third point, namely that the Soviet Union "became" inefficient and collapsed when it attempted to integrate itself into a world system that was passing from its modernizing to its postmodern stage, a system that by its new rules of operation was therefore running at an incomparably higher rate of "productivity" than anything inside the Soviet sphere. Driven by cultural motives (consumerism, the newer information technologies, etc.), drawn in by calculated military-technological competition, by the bait of the debt, and intensifying forms of commercial coexistence, Soviet society entered an element in which it could not survive. It may be claimed that the Soviet Union and its satellites, hitherto isolated in their own specific pressure area as under some ideological and socioeconomic geodesic dome, now began imprudently to open the airlocks without spacesuits prepared and thus to allow themselves and their institutions to be subjected to the infinitely more intense pressures characteristic of the world outside. The result can be imagined as comparable to what the sheer blast pressures did to the flimsy structures in the immediate vicinity of the first atomic bomb; or to the grotesque and deforming weight of water pressure at the bottom of the sea on unprotected organisms evolved for the upper air. Indeed, this result confirms Wallerstein's prescient warning that the Soviet bloc, despite its importance, did not constitute an alternative system to that of capitalism, but merely an antisystemic space or zone within it, one now evidently blown away, with only a few surviving pockets in which various socialist experiments are still able to continue.

Fifth thesis

The Marxisms (the political movements as well as the forms of intellectual and theoretical resistance) that emerge from the present system of late capitalism, from postmodernity, from Mandel's third stage of informational or multinational capitalism, will necessarily be distinct from those that developed during the modern period, the second stage, the age of imperialism. They will have a radically different relationship to globalization and will also, by contrast to earlier Marxisms, appear to be more cultural in character, turning fundamentally on those phenomena hitherto known as commodity reification and consumerism.

The increasing significance of culture for both the political and the economic is not a consequence of the tendential separation or differentiation of these realms, but rather of the more universal saturation and penetration of commodification itself, which has now been able to colonize large zones of that cultural area hitherto sheltered from it and indeed for the most part hostile to and inconsistent with its logic. The fact that culture has today largely become business has a consequence that most of what used to be considered specifically economic and commercial has also become cultural, a characterization under which the various diagnoses of so-called image society or consumerism need to be subsumed.

And in a more general way Marxism enjoys a theoretical advantage in such analysis, namely that its conception of commodification is a structural and a non-moralizing one. Moral passion generates political action, but only of the most ephemeral kind, quickly reabsorbed and recontained and little inclined to share its specific issues and topics with other movements. But it is only by way of such amalgamation and construction that political movements can develop and grow more extensive. Indeed, I am tempted to make the point the other way around, that a moralizing politics tends to develop where a structural cognition and mapping of society is blocked. The influence of the religious and the ethnic today is to be grasped as a rage at the perception of the failure of socialism, and a desperate blind attempt to fill that vacuum with new motivations.

As for consumerism, it may well be hoped that it will turn out to have been as historically significant as it was necessary for human society to pass through the experience of consumerism as a way of life, if only in order more consciously to choose something radically different in its place. But for most of the world the addictions of consumerism will not be objectively available; it then seems possible that the prescient diagnosis of the radical theory of the 1960s—that capitalism was itself a revolutionary force in the same way in which it produced new needs and desires that the system could not satisfy—will now find its realization on the global scale of the new world system.

On a theoretical level, it may be suggested that the currently urgent issues of permanent structural unemployment, of financial speculation and ungovernable capital movements, of the image society, are all profoundly interrelated on the level of what might be called their lack of content, their abstraction (as opposed to what another age might have termed their "alienation"). The more paradoxical level of the dialectic is met when we rejoin issues of globalization and informatization. There is a seemingly intransigent dilemma when the political and ideological possibilities of the new world networks (on the left as well as in business or on the right) are then coupled with the loss of autonomy in the world system today and the impossibility for any national or regional area to achieve its own autonomy and subsistence or to delink or uncouple itself from the world market. Intellectuals cannot find a way through this passage by the mere taking of a thought. It is the ripening of structural contradictions in reality that produce the dawning anticipation of new possibilities: yet we can at least keep this dilemma alive by "cleaving to the negative" as Hegel might have said, by keeping alive that place from which the new can be expected, unexpectedly, to emerge.

Notes

Dedicated to the memory of William Pomerance.

1. The "critique of political economy" never wished to be a science in the sense in which "political economy" was itself conceived, let alone academic forms of "economics." That is, as "critique" it isolates the basis of the error it

identifies, rejecting a radical discontinuity between theory and practice, facts and values.

2. Following Giovanni Arrighi, *The Long Twentieth Century* (London: Verso, 1994), in sequence: the Spanish-Genoese moment, the Dutch supersession, the English empire, the U.S. hegemony, and beyond that the possibility of the prospect of the Japanese supremacy.

3. "Discursive struggle" in this usage is struggle for control of the terms and rules of the discourse.

4: AFTERWORD

In defense of history

JOHN BELLAMY FOSTER

> It is impossible at the present time to write history without using a whole range of concepts directly or indirectly linked to Marx's thought and situating oneself within a horizon of thought which has been defined and described by Marx. One might even wonder what difference there could ultimately be between being a historian and being a Marxist.
>
> —MICHEL FOUCAULT[1]

"Modern authoritarianism," sociologist Norman Birnbaum has observed, "is not subtle, but it is omnipresent. Its new form is not obeisance to human authority alone, but a reification of the present, a refusal to believe that human institutions could be different." It is not to be wondered at therefore that in the 1990s—in an age of capitalist triumphalism—the right has once again proclaimed the "end of history": the eternal triumph of capitalist institutions worldwide and the end of the class struggle, along with the "end of ideology."[2]

Such claims could be easily dismissed, if it weren't for the fact that they have also been advanced—in a much more intellectually compelling way—by critical thinkers with close ties to the left. Postmodernists too assert that there has been an ending of sorts, and that we live in a world that is in a certain sense post-historical, an eternal afterwards. But rather than presenting a grand narrative of capitalism's final triumph, they more commonly argue that we must liberate ourselves from all grand narratives, including those of progress and emancipation. In the words of Jean-François Lyotard, writing in *The Postmodern Condition:*

> I will use the term *modern* to designate any science that legitimates itself with reference to a metadiscourse ... making an explicit appeal to some grand narrative, such as the dialectics of Spirit, the hermeneutics of meaning, the emancipation of the rational or working subject, or the creation of wealth.... I define *postmodernism* as incredulity toward metanarratives.[3]

According to Lyotard, "the grand narrative has lost its credibility, regardless of what mode of unification it uses, regardless of whether it is a speculative narrative or a narrative of emancipation."[4]

This rejection of grand narratives, characteristic of postmodernism, is part of a deeper epistemological skepticism which pervades this form of thought. In the sympathetic account of cultural theorist Dick Hebdige, "postmodernism as a discourse (or rather compound of discourses) is rather like Saussure's paradigm of language, in that it is a system with no positive terms. In fact, we could say it's a system predicated, as Saussure's was, on the categorical denial of the possibility of positive entities *per se*." The meaning of "postmodernism" is therefore notoriously difficult to pin down, and can be defined in the end—beyond its emphasis on endless "language games" (Lyotard)—only by what it rejects. A certain "rudimentary coherence," Hebdige contends, arises from its reliance on three central negations: (1) "against totalization"; (2) "against teleology"; (3) "against utopianism."

Postmodernism, as a general form of thought, has an anti-totalizing, anti-generalizing bias with respect to society, rejecting not so much the narrative form per se, as any kind of grand narrative—such as the Marxist critique of capitalism, or even the more neutral proposition of the historical centrality of capitalism—opting instead for a decentered, even chaotic approach to society, which is viewed as inherently fragmented. Characteristic of postmodernism, as Hebdige observes, is "a marked antipathy to sociological abstractions" such as class, capitalism, or even society. This skepticism is carried over into a rejection of teleology, in which it is denied that history is purposive, or even that it is possible to have definite knowledge of the origins, causes, tendencies, and fundamental constitutive elements of history. Typical of postmodernist interpretations of society, according to Hebdige, is "the evacuation of any axis of power external to discourse." For example, postmodernist historian F.R. Ankersmit states, "Suppose we ask for the cause of ... 'the Industrial Revolution' or of 'the Cold War.' We now ought to remember that these terms do not refer to an historical reality outside the text but to narrative substances. This means such questions are not questions about the cause of a complex state of affairs at the end of the eighteenth century or after World War II, but a question about the cause of a notion or narrative substance." Lastly, postmodernism offers only skepticism regarding the possibility of a collective destiny for humankind. Depictions of any future beyond the endless present—particularly if based on concepts of reason or progress—are viewed as illusory and even dangerous (since giving rise to totalitarian tendencies).[5]

There can be little doubt that these negations are directed at Marxism first and foremost, and Enlightenment modernism in general only secondarily. All three of the founding negations, Hebdige argues, "involve ... an attack on marxism as a total explanatory system" that "can be traced back to two sources: on the one hand, historically to the blocked hopes and frustrated rhetoric of the late 1960s and the student revolts ... and, on the other, through the philosophical tradition to Nietzsche." At issue is an understanding of history as a narrative of human progress or emancipation. Denying notions of linear (or even nonlinear) progress, postmodernists alternately describe history as defeat (dystopia) or as chaos. "For postmodernists," Henry Kariel has noted in his postmodernist tract, *The Desperate Politics of Postmodernism,* "it is simply too late to oppose the momentum of industrial society. They merely resolve to stay alert and cool in its midst. Consciously complying and yet far from docile, they chronicle, amplify, augment it. They judge it as little as it judges itself. Determined to assail nothing, they are passionately impassive."[6]

Such passionate impassivity, verging on nihilism, has even affected the historical profession. A good example of this is provided by Ankersmit in an article on "Historiography and Postmodernism" written in 1989 for the journal *History and Theory.* "For the postmodernist," Ankersmit states, "the scientific certainties on which the modernists have always built are all as many variants on the paradox of the liar. That is, the paradox of the Cretan who says that all Cretans lie." Historians have always been searching for the essence of history, but this search is meaningless:

> Compare history to a tree. The essentialist tradition within Western historiography focused the attention of historians on the trunk of the tree. This was, of course, the case with the speculative systems; they defined, so to speak, the nature and form of this trunk. Historism and modernist scientific historiography, with their basically praiseworthy attention to what in fact happened in the past and their lack of receptiveness towards aprioristic schemes, were situated on the branches of the tree. However, from that position their attention did remain focused on the trunk. Just like their speculative predecessors, both the historists and the protagonists of a so-called scientific historiography still had the hope and the pretension of ultimately being able to say something about the trunk after all. The close ties between this so-called scientific social history and Marxism are significant in this context. Whether it was formulated in

ontological, epistemological, or methodological terminology, historiography since historism has always aimed at the reconstruction of the essentialist line running through the past or parts of it.

> With the postmodernist historiography found in particular in the history of mentalities, a break is made for the first time with this centuries-old essentialist tradition.... The choice no longer falls on the trunk or the branches, but on the leaves of the tree. Within the postmodernist view of history, the goal is no longer integration, synthesis, and totality, but it is those historical scraps which are the center of attention. Take, for example, *Montaillou* and other books written subsequently by Le Roy Ladurie, Ginzburg's *Microstorie*, Duby's *Sunday of Bouvines* or Natalie Zemon Davis's *Return of Martin Guerre*. Fifteen or twenty years ago we would have asked ourselves in amazement whatever the point could be of this kind of historical writing, what it is trying to prove. And this very obvious question would have been prompted then, as it always is, by our modernist desire to get to know how the machinery of history works. However, in the anti-essentialist, nominalistic view of postmodernism, this question has lost its meaning. If we want to adhere to essentialism anyway, we can say that the essence is not situated in the branches, nor in the trunk, but in the leaves of the historical tree.[7]

By the time we reach the present, Ankersmit contends, the leaves of the historical tree have finally "blown away." "What remains now for Western historiography is to gather the leaves ... and to study them independently of their origins.... [W]hat is important is no longer the place they had on the tree, but the pattern we can form from them now." For postmodern historiography "historical context has lost its traditional importance ... because one has 'let go of' the historical context. Everything now announces itself unannounced and in this lies the only hope we still have of being able to keep our heads above water in the future."[8]

Such skepticism toward not only grand historical narratives but also the very idea of meaning in history—though taken to extremes in postmodernist historiography—is not entirely new, and indeed has shaped much historiography in the period since World War II. Thus Sir George Clark felt it necessary to introduce the second *Cambridge Modern History* in 1957 with the remark that "some impatient scholars take refuge in skepticism, or at least in the doctrine that, since all historical judgements involve persons and points of view, one is as good as another and there is no 'objective' historical truth." Writing in the 1970s, U.S. historian Hayden White argued in his *Metahistory* that "when it is a matter of choosing among ... alternative visions of history, the only grounds for preferring one over another are *moral* or *aesthetic* ones."[9]

This growing twentieth-century aversion to any notion of "objective" history was in part a rational response to the nineteenth-century proclivity to see history in teleological terms as embodying definite and inexorable forms of human progress. Despite his focus on the *Decline and Fall of the Roman Empire,* Gibbon assured the readers of his famous study "that every age of the world has increased, and still increases, the real wealth, the happiness, the knowledge, and perhaps the virtue, of the human race." Such views, so characteristic of nineteenth century thinkers, were however anathema to post-World War II Western intellectuals emerging from the experience of the holocaust and immersed in the cold war.[10]

After World War II it became common for liberal historians and philosophers to insist that all speculative, a priori approaches to history—a sin they associated principally with the great systems of Hegel and Marx—be excluded from the realm of valid historical interpretation. For example, Sir Isaiah Berlin argued in 1954 in his influential essay *Historical Inevitability* that Hegel and Marx, along with thinkers as varied as Bacon, Condorcet, Saint Simon, Fourier, Owen, Comte, H.G. Wells, Bernard Shaw, and Toynbee, fell prey to forms of "determinism"—"whether they be teleological, metaphysical, mechanistic, religious, aesthetic, or scientific"—which had the "common conclusion" that the "individual's freedom of choice is ultimately an illusion." In conceiving an objective logic (or lawful character) to history, these thinkers, Berlin argued, had succumbed to a "determinism" which denied both free will and the role of accident in history.[11]

Yet, as E.H. Carr replied in his *What is History?,* such criticisms of Hegel and Marx (not to mention the bulk of the Enlightenment tradition) were erroneous. As Carr explained, philosophical determinism—the doctrine that all effects are traceable to either a single cause or a hierarchy of causes, and could not have happened differently unless the conditions had changed—in no way contradicts the postulate of human freedom, nor denies the role of contingency in human affairs, since both of these can be seen as part of a larger chain of causality. Such philosophical determinism (not to be confused with the fatalistic notion that history is in some way predetermined, or crude monocausal conceptions of the historical process) "is a condition of our capacity to understand what is going on around us. The nightmare of Kafka's novels lies in the fact that nothing that happens has any apparent cause, or any cause that can be ascertained: this leads to the total disintegration of the human personality." Although history has no single, definite, predetermined logic independent of human action and changing conditions, this is no reason to jettison the notion that everything ultimately has a cause(s); or the idea that the logic of historical inquiry involves precisely the search for those causal relationships, or determinate boundaries and framing of events, which we can ascertain.[12]

"That historical explanation cannot deal in absolutes and cannot adduce sufficient causes," E.P. Thompson has written,

> greatly irritates some simple and impatient souls. They suppose that, since historical explanation cannot be All, it is therefore Nothing: it is no more than a consecutive phenomenological narration. This is a silly mistake. For historical explanation discloses not how history must have eventuated but why it eventuated in this way and not in other ways; that process is not arbitrary but has its own regularity and rationality; that certain kinds of events (political, economic, cultural) have been related, not in any way one likes, but in particular ways and within determinate fields of possibility; that certain social formations are—not governed by "law" nor are they the "effects" of a static structural theorem—but are characterized by determinate relations and by a particular logic of process.... Our knowledge may not satisfy some philosophers, but it is enough to keep us occupied.[13]

Even in the present skeptical age, most historians and historically oriented social scientists have not altogether abandoned the search for causality in history, but are rather distinguished primarily by the peculiar hierarchy of causes that they attribute to historical events. "Every historical argument," as Carr states, "revolves around the question of the priority of causes." For Weber it was the evolution of rationality, for Marx the organization of productive relations. The main liberal objection to Marx has not been that he saw causality (one might even say a certain logic) underlying history, but rather that he saw a particular type of causality—i.e. the class struggle—as playing a central role in the determination of history; and that as a result Marx viewed the present itself as a transitory historical phase. Where Marx dealt with class conflict, liberals have tended to focus on the individual and the evolution of human rationality (as manifested in individuals), pointing to an end to ideology and history in the idealized and eternal present. According to contemporary possessive individualism there is no beyond—except in the technological sense.[14]

Postmodernists have walked away from this great debate, arguing that reason itself is open to question, and that all that is left is the irony of discourse: signs and signifiers without significance. The very concept of ideology is to be avoided, according to Foucault, because "like it or not, it always stands in virtual opposition to something else which is supposed to count as truth" and requires "drawing the line between that in a discourse which falls under the category of scientificity or truth and that which comes under some other category."[15]

At best postmodernist thought contends that there is no center to history, and that power is scattered—so attention should be given to the micro-aspects of history and to the mental margins, where power/knowledge relations can still be discerned, albeit in a disconnected fashion. Anything else, we are told, smacks of "foundationalism" or "essentialism." For Foucault "the true historical sense confirms our existence among countless lost events, without landmark or a point of reference." As opposed to "traditional history," inspired by attention to epoch-making events and to the "heights" of the historical process (thereby relying, Foucault argues, on "metaphysics"), "effective history" or "genealogy" "shortens its vision to those things nearest to it—the body, the nervous system, nutrition, digestion, and energies; it unearths the periods of decadence." "Genealogy," Foucault insists, echoing Nietzsche, "is history in the form of a concerted carnival."[16]

Foucault's standpoint here speaks to the strengths and weaknesses of postmodernist thought. Its rejection of grand historical narratives, of any central struggles that define history, indeed of any historical subject, coupled with its insistence on the constitution of our knowledge within diffused power relations, leads it to "genealogical" investigations of power "nearest to the body"—areas that social theory has been insufficiently attentive to in the past. Its concentration on discourse, as the sole constitutive element in social relations, has revealed much about the role of language in the ordering of power. Its researches have thus increased our critical understanding of many aspects of society previously neglected. In particular, it has had a deep influence on feminist analysis, racial formation theory, cultural theory, political conceptions of surveillance and control, etc. Its emphasis on what is most personal has struck a chord in a period in which the personal has become political. Its stress on difference has seemed to suggest a political and theoretical openness lacking in other theoretical perspectives—though this is illusory given postmodernism's own closures or negations. Its unending skepticism, even nihilism, and rejection of

Enlightenment modernity, has given it a radical cast, while at the same time keeping it free from any radical project.

But the only possibility that remains open to such a perspective in the end—as Foucault's work itself suggests—is a kind of "micro-politics: local struggles, around particular issues—anything more is suspected of leading to improper 'totalizations,' and thus to totalitarianism."[17]

The weaknesses of postmodernism—from an emancipatory perspective—thus far overshadow its strengths. Missing from Foucault's analysis, like that of postmodernism generally, is any conception of a counter-order to the disciplinary orders described. In the more extreme case of "textual postmodernists"—those postmodernist thinkers like Derrida, as distinct from Foucault, who deny any reality outside the text—the political and historical weaknesses from a left perspective are even more glaring. By undermining the very concept of history—in any meaningful sense beyond mere story-telling—such theorists have robbed critical analysis of what has always been its most indispensable tool.[18]

The denial within postmodernist theory of the validity of historical critique covers up what is really at issue: the denial of the historical critique of capitalism, leading to a convergence between left thought infected by Nietzsche and the dominant liberal "end of history" conception. The danger of such ahistorical or anti-historical views, as E.P. Thompson observed, is that one loses sight not of "reason in history" in some abstract sense, but rather of "the reasons of power and the reasons of money."[19]

Historical materialism at its best provides a way out of this dilemma. This is not to ignore the fact that Marxism—which has sometimes given rise to its own crude interpretations and historical travesties, as in the case of Stalinism—has frequently been identified with the kind of "totalizations" and "essentialisms" that postmodernist theorists have singled out. As Thompson pointed out in a 1977 essay on Christopher Caudwell, Marxism has sometimes relied on " 'essentialist' tricks of mind," the "tendency to intellectualize the social process"—"the rapid delineation of the deep process of a whole epoch." These are things that the historian (and social scientists in general) should guard against. But to abandon theory and historical explanation entirely in order to avoid "essentialism" and "foundationalism" is a bit like throwing out the baby in order to keep the bathwater clean. Marx himself provided another model, actively opposing theory (even "Marxist" theory) that purported to be "suprahistorical." In his *Theses on Feuerbach,* he presented what still ranks as the most thoroughgoing critique of what he called the "essentialist" conception of human beings and nature. Indeed, historical materialism has long engaged in its own self-critique, precisely in order to expel the kinds of "essentialisms," "positivisms," and "structuralisms" that have intruded on the philosophy of praxis itself—a self-critique that has produced the insights of theorists like Gramsci, Sartre, Thompson, and Raymond Williams.[20]

These thinkers distanced themselves from the positivistic "official Marxism" that grew out of the Second International and later turned into a caricature of itself in the form of Stalinism. Yet they held firm to the critique of capitalism and their commitment to the struggles of the oppressed. Moreover, these particular examples tell us that if what has sometimes been called "the postmodern agenda"—consisting of issues like identity, culture, and language—is to be addressed at all, this can only be accomplished within a historical context. And here one might openly wonder with Foucault "what difference there could ultimately be between being a historian and being a Marxist."

When placed within a more holistic historical materialist context—animated by the concept of praxis—the problems raised by postmodernism look entirely different. As David McNally says, "Language is not a prison-house, but a site of struggle." What the contributions in this volume have in common is the insistence that issues like language, culture, nationality, race, gender, the environment, revolution, and history itself are only effectively analyzed within a context that is simultaneously historical in character, materialist (in the sense of focusing on concrete practices), and revolutionary.

Such analyses do not abandon the hope of transcending capitalism, nor of the notion of human progress as a possible outcome of historical struggles. It is said that Nicholas I, Czar of Russia, issued an order banning the word "progress." Today we no longer believe, in a nineteenth century sense, in automatic human progress, embodying some definite content—the idea that the Czar found so threatening. But this does not mean, as the philosopher Michael Oakeshott contended with respect to political activity in the 1950s, that we "sail a boundless and bottomless sea" that has "neither starting-point nor appointed direction" and that our only task is "to keep afloat on an even keel." History—as centuries of struggle and indeed progress suggest—is more meaningful than that. To abandon altogether the concept of progress, in the more general sense of the possibility of progressive human emancipation, would only be to submit to the wishes of the powers that be. Such political disengagement by intellectuals on the left in the present epoch could only mean one thing: the total obeisance to capital.[21]

The irony of post-*modernism* is that while purporting to have transcended *modernity,* it abandons from the start all hope of transcending capitalism itself and entering a post-*capitalist* era. Postmodernist theory is therefore easily absorbed within the dominant cultural frame and has even given rise recently to texts such as *Postmodern Marketing,* which attempts to utilize the insights of thinkers like Foucault, Derrida, Lyotard, and Baudillard to market goods within a capitalist economy. Perhaps this will be the final destiny of postmodernist theory—its absorption by the vast marketing apparatus of the capitalist economy, adding irony and color to a commercial order that must constantly find new ways to insinuate itself into the everyday lives of the population. Meanwhile, historical materialism will remain the necessary intellectual ground for all those who seek, not to revel in the "carnival" of capitalist productive and market relations, but to transcend them.[22]

Notes

1. Foucault, *Power/Knowledge* (New York: Pantheon Books, 1977), p. 53.
2. Norman Birnbaum, *Radical Renewal* (New York: Pantheon Books, 1988), pp. 194-95; Harvey J. Kaye, *The Powers of the Past* (Minneapolis: University of Minnesota Press, 1991), pp. 146-47.
3. Jean-François Lyotard, *The Postmodern Condition* (Minneapolis: University of Minnesota Press, 1984), pp. xxiii-xxiv.
4. Ibid., p. 37.
5. F.R. Ankersmit, "Reply to Professor Zagorin," *History and Theory* 29, no. 3 (1990): 285.
6. Dick Hebdige, *Hiding in the Light* (New York: Routledge, 1988), pp. 185-99; Henry S. Kariel, *The Desperate Politics of Postmodernism* (Amherst: University of Massachusetts Press, 1989), p. ix.
7. Ankersmit, "Historiography and Postmodernism," *History and Theory* 28, no. 2 (1989): 142, 148-149.
8. Ibid.: 149-152.
9. Sir George Clark, "General Introduction," *The New Cambridge Modern History,* vol. I (Cambridge: Cambridge University Press, 1957), p. xxv; Hayden White, *Metahistory* (Baltimore: Johns Hopkins University Press, 1973), pp. 433; Peter Novick, *That Noble Dream: The "Objectivity Question" and the*

American Historical Profession (New York: Cambridge University Press, 1988), pp. 598-603. The discussion of the philosophy of history in this and subsequent paragraphs is heavily indebted to E.H. Carr's *What is History?* (New York: Vintage, 1961).

10. Edward Gibbon, *The Decline and Fall of the Roman Empire,* vol. IV (London: Methuen, 1897), p. 169.
11. Isaiah Berlin, *Historical Inevitability* (London: Oxford University Press, 1954), pp. 19-25.
12. Carr, *What is History?,* pp. 119-22; see also Howard Sherman, *Reinventing Marxism* (Baltimore: Johns Hopkins University Press, 1995), pp. 270-85.
13. E.P. Thompson, *The Poverty of Theory* (New York: Monthly Review Press, 1978), p. 50.
14. Carr, *What is History?,* p. 117.
15. Foucault, *Power/Knowledge,* p. 118.
16. Foucault, *The Foucault Reader* (New York: Pantheon, 1984), pp. 89-95.
17. David Morley, "Postmodernism: The Rough Guide," in James Curran, David Morley, and Valerie Walkerdone (eds.), *Cultural Studies and Communication* (New York: Arnold, 1985), p. 59.
18. Bryan Palmer, *Descent into Discourse* (Philadelphia: Temple University Press, 1990), p. 27.
19. E.P. Thompson, *Making History* (New York: The New Press, 1994), p. 363.
20. Ibid., pp. 117, 123; Marx, Letter to "Otechestvennye Zapiski," in Teodor Shanin (ed.), *Late Marx and the Russian Road* (New York: Monthly Review Press, 1983), p. 136.
21. Michael Oakeshott, *Political Education* (Cambridge: Bowes & Bowes, 1951), p. 22; Carr, *What is History?,* p. 148, 205-8.
22. See Stephen Brown, *Postmodern Marketing* (New York: Routledge, 1995).

CONTRIBUTORS

Aijaz Ahmad is senior fellow at the Centre for Contemporary Studies, Nehru Memorial Museum and Library, New Delhi, and author of *In Theory: Classes, Nations, Literatures* (1992).

Terry Eagleton is Warton Professor of English Literature at Oxford.

John Bellamy Foster teaches sociology at the University of Oregon and is a member of the board of directors of Monthly Review Foundation. He is the author of *The Theory of Monopoly Capital* (1986) and *The Vulnerable Planet* (1994), both published by Monthly Review Press.

Fredric Jameson is head of the Literature Program at Duke University. He is the author of *Postmodernism, or the Cultural Logic of Late Capitalism* (1991), among other books.

David McNally teaches political science at York University, Toronto, and is author of *Against the Market: Political Economy, Market Socialism and the Marxist Critique* (1993) and a forthcoming book on language.

Kenan Malik is a London-based writer, researcher, and broadcaster, and author of *The Meaning of Race: Race, History and Culture in Western Society* (1996).

Francis Mulhern is a professor in the School of English, Cultural, and Communications Studies at Middlesex University, London.

Meera Nanda, a science writer for the mainstream and progressive media in India and the United States, is associated with the department of science and technology studies at Rensselaer Polytechnic Institute, Troy, NY.

Daniel Nugent teaches anthropology and Latin American history and is author of *Spent Cartridges of Revolution: An Anthropological History of Namiquipa, Chihuahua* (1993). He recently collaborated on a play, *13 Dias/13 Days: How the Zapatistas Shook the World,* performed on tour by the San Francisco Mime Troupe in 1996-97.

Bryan D. Palmer teaches in the history department at Queen's University, Kingston, Ontario. His books include *Goodyear Invades the Backcountry* (Monthly Review Press, 1994) and *Descent into Discourse: The Reification of Language and the Writing of Social History* (1990). He is writing a biography of James P. Cannon, the founder of the U.S. Trotskyist movement.

CAROL A. STABILE teaches media criticism at the University of Pittsbur and is the author of *Feminism and the Technological Fix* (1994).

ELLEN MEIKSINS WOOD is the author of *The Pristine Culture of Capitalism* (1991), *Democracy Against Capitalism* (1995), and, with Neal Wood, *A Trumpet of Sedition: Political Theory and the Rise of Capitalism* (forthcoming), and is an editor of *Monthly Review*.

INDEX

i

j

k

l